The Dawn of the Dhamma

THE DAWN OF THE DHAMMA

Illuminations from the Buddha's First Discourse

By

Sucitto Bhikkhu

Foreword by Venerable Ajahn Sumedho

BUDDHADHAMMA FOUNDATION

Bangkok, THAILAND

The Dawn of the Dhamma,
Illuminations from the Buddha's First Discourse
by Sucitto Bhikkhu
© 1995 : BUDDHADHAMMA FOUNDATION
2nd. Edition: June, 1996

ISBN 974-7890-13-5

Published by:

Buddhadhamma Foundation,
87/126 Tesabahl Songkroh Rd.,
Lad Yao, Chatuchak, BANGKOK,
THAILAND, 10900
Tel : (66) (2) 589-9012, 580-2719 ; Fax : (66) (2) 954-4791

For:
Amaravati Buddhist Monastery,
Great Gaddesden,
Hemel Hempstead,
Hertfordshire, HP1 3BZ, ENGLAND

Printed by:

AMARIN PRINTING AND PUBLISHING PUBLIC COMPANY LIMITED
65/16 Moo 4 Soi Wat Chaiyapurk, Taling Chan, Bangkok 10170
Tel. 424-2800-1, 424-1176, 424-8396, 424-8893, 424-9723
FAX. (662) 433-2742

Cover Illustration: George Sharp

DEDICATION

The second printing of this book for free distribution has been made possible through the generosity of Mrs. Sujitpan Lamsam and Mrs. Vanee Lamsam in memory of Mr. Kasem Lamsam and Vachareevan Lamsam.

May all beings live happily, free from fear, and may all share in the blessings springing from the good that has been done.

Contents

FOREWORD

Many years ago, Venerable Sucitto began to write out in calligraphy the first sermon of the Buddha, the "Dhamma-cakkappavattana Sutta" or the "Discourse on Setting in Motion the Wheel of Dhamma." His original intention was to present me with an esthetically pleasing gift as a gesture of his gratitude and appreciation.

The Sutta is one that most monks and nuns have memorized and chant regularly, as we used to do and as is still done regularly in monasteries in Thailand. In this discourse, the Buddha offers the teaching of the Four Noble Truths: the Truth of *Dukkha,* Suffering or Unsatisfactoriness; the Truth of *Samudaya,* the Cause of Suffering; the Truth of *Nirodha,* the Cessation of Suffering; and the Truth of *Magga,* the Path leading to the Cessation of Suffering.

This is the essential teaching of the Buddha which leads his followers to liberation from ignorance and it is the ground of our practice. We reflect on the Four Noble Truths until we have insight and profound understanding, and the realization of these Truths for ourselves is the aim of Buddhist meditation. All Buddhists agree that this is the fundamental teaching, and, at inter-Buddhist meetings, we can avoid emphasizing the differences between the Mahayana and Theravada traditions through references to the Noble Truths.

In spite of this, or maybe because of it, the teachings seem to be taken for granted or treated as basic material for beginners. In Thailand, the Four Noble Truths are frequently recited and pronounced in perfunctory references in which they are reduced to the seemingly insignificant words of *Duk-Samuday-Nirodh-Mag* (Thai derivations of the Pali). Then a more advanced teaching is announced or other aspects of Buddhism are described, commented upon and debated at length. So the essential teaching is given cursory acknowledgment but is not properly understood. This seems to happen to many religions: the heart becomes hidden under many added layers; the original jewel is smothered under filigree.

And yet the marvel of this essential teaching is that it stands alone and really needs no other comments or additions. As a tool for practice, it is perfect. If one reflects and investigates one's own experience of life in the context of these Truths, then delusion disappears and profound insight into the Truth is realized.

Art can be a means to point to Ultimate Truth, the way to that Truth and the myriad obstacles that cover and hide it; highly personal images can take us to the impersonal Truth. In this way, Venerable Sucitto's work began to take on various unique elaborations which illuminate the text. Over the years, he developed a style that reflects his own deep understanding and his ability to manifest ideas in forms that arouse our own interest in studying and investigating the Four Noble Truths. The images range from minute squiggles, Celtic knots, dots, stars, flowers and knotted roots; to empty landscapes, sun rays and light; to the countless forms of beings from hell to heaven. All the images and his stylized calligraphy are spontaneous creations from his mind.

Venerable Sucitto's series of paintings starts with the statement: *Evam me sutam* ("Thus have I heard") placed at the centre of the *Dhammacakka*, the Wheel of Dhamma, that was set rolling through the recitation of this sermon. The Wheel, which is the main feature of this painting, is covered in traditionally auspicious symbols. From the bottom border which is filled with tortured hell beings ascend coarse, twisted, serpent-shaped roots. These change as they rise up the sides into leaf and flower designs, which in turn give way to more angelic shapes on the top border. The cosmos with its infinite variety of permutations and convolutions is now to be reflected upon in terms of the liberating Dhamma rather than grasped and rejected according to humanity's desires and fears. All conditions are impermanent: the abstract concepts of nothingness or "neither-perception-nor-non-perception," the coarse, perverted insanities of hell, and all of the possibilities in between these extremes. "All conditions are impermanent" is a reflective statement that encourages us to look at the conditioned realm as an object, no longer blindly becoming hypnotized by or absorbed in it. Enlightenment is in the Right Knowing.

One of my favorite frames is found in the chapter entitled, "Light in the World." It portrays the scene after the Buddha's sermon was delivered: "And a great measureless radiance surpassing the very nature of the devas was displayed in the world." The painting is of two *bhikkhus* receiving alms at sunrise. Indeed, there is a measureless radiance in the freshness of the sunrise and purity and generosity of both the monks and the lay people making the offering—a timelessness and humility in the goodness of human life in ordinary daily activity.

The last painting, *"Dhammacakkappavattana suttam nitthitam,"* mirrors the Wheel with the footprints of the Buddha. The *Dhammacakka* that was set rolling is still rolling. The Sangha is still listening, contemplating, reflecting and practicing accordingly.

I have encouraged Venerable Sucitto to write a commentary on the Dhammacakkappavattana Sutta to accompany his fine paintings as an expression of an individual human being who has contemplated this Sutta in his own practice. Venerable Sucitto's ability to describe his insights in words is equally impressive. The formed and formless realms are explained in words as well as in pictures, and, of course, it is the mind of Venerable Sucitto that is being exposed for our interest and inspiration, or our bewilderment. They are all there, from *"Evam"* to *"Nitthitam,"* in vibrant color: the six realms of existence—celestial Brahmas to hideous hell beings—all arising and ceasing in the mind.

I wish to express my gratitude to Venerable Sucitto for making the offering and to Khun Vanee Lamsam, a longtime and dedicated supporter, for sponsoring the printing of a special edition of this marvellous work for free distribution so that many beings may benefit from it.

The *Dhammacakka* is still rolling on.

Venerable Sumedho Bhikkhu
Amaravati Buddhist Monastery

AUTHOR'S PREFACE

I began this series of illustrations in January 1980 at Chithurst Monastery. At that time I did not conceive of there being a series and Chithurst was hardly a monastery. What sustains the spiritual life is that it becomes independent of one's own volition; it has a life of its own that one comes to recognize and serve. So taking things as they came and adapting accordingly, after four and a half years, Chithurst was a firmly established monastery, and there was a series of paintings. I was able to present them with gratitude to my teacher, Venerable Ajahn Sumedho, on the occasion of his 50th birthday.

In the winter of 1979-80, we had just started on the work at Chithurst. A lot of it was manual labor—the reconstruction of a near-derelict house. Partly in response to the amount of physical and outgoing energy that was needed, some of the monks expressed an interest in developing our limited range of devotional and reflective chants. The Dhammacakkappavattana Sutta was a natural choice—a medium-length, steadily-intoned chant that expounds the heart of the Buddha's teaching. It was ideal for both tranquillity and reflection, and could help to bring the whole community together in a devotional form. A few of us began to learn it from the Royal Thai Chanting Book, but it occurred to me that the Sutta could be written out in a way that would make it easier to read (!) and this would be a way of expressing gratitude to the traditions and to Ajahn Sumedho, my teacher. My penchant for graphic and verbal images had drawn a certain amount of artist's material my way — notably, a calligraphy pen with which I proceeded to write out the Sutta. With some memories of Celtic Gospels (such as the Lindisfarne Gospels and the Book of Kells), I used a variation on half uncial script and added a few illuminations to the capitals. People were pleased and wanted to print copies of the work so I thought I'd better do it again, but more properly this time, with perhaps a full-page illumination of the opening paragraph....

I had a draftsman's pen then, and a few colored inks. I found some paper in a drawer in the office. After I had completed the first paragraph, an idea for a design for the second popped up. This went on for four and a half years, punctuated by monastic retreats, long work projects and sojourns in two branch monasteries. At times, the work would rest for a month or two. At best, I could only pursue it in whatever spare time arose — at night or on Observance Day.* It felt right that way: just to use what time became available rather than to seek out time and make an obsession out of creation. This space gave my eyes and hands time to learn and my mind time to digest ideas and allow images to gather and merge. Most helpful of all for the creative act, I could contemplate the perception of "having to get this finished," and the dispassion to let each painting be unsatisfactory without making a problem out of it.

Every one of these paintings gave me an example of the Buddha's teaching in practice. "Birth is suffering" — the anxious moments with a blank sheet of paper, making pencil marks, trying to get an image to settle into the space and find balance thematically and graphically with the text. "Aging is suffering" — the struggle and concern to make it turn out right, coupled with the awareness that it was obeying unseen laws of its own. "Death is suffering" — the finished product, lettering uneven, coloring dull, forms murky and distorted ... Well ... let it be. I don't remember really finishing any of them; rather, I just came to realize that there was no point in tinkering any more with each one. Misshapen as they were, they were good enough. Those that stand now were mostly first drafts. There were two retakes and one abortion. Most of them earned the right to live, through sheer persistence. I wanted to be able to present them on a suitable occasion; furthermore, I knew I would be going to help establish Amaravati Buddhist Monastery which would require all my energies. I finished the last one the night before Ajahn Sumedho's birthday. That was the right time to finish.

---

* Buddhist Sabbath days occurring every couple of weeks, during which the community often practices meditation through the night.

Every one of these paintings is a manifestation of the joy of the Dhamma—for myself anyway. This is why they are good enough. All of these images arose—I created none of them. Some came in meditation, some from memories, some from art works, mandalas and *thangkas* in the monastery. In the earlier pen and ink drawings, it was mainly images that arose—lines and shapes and quasi-caricatures. The later illustrations are paintings in which the color or a combination of colors arose first— particularly in the section on the *deva loka*. This change of emphasis reflects a change over the years in my attitude towards spirituality. Things seemed to have definite existence in my early years as a bhikkhu; and my attitudes were more hard and fast, with clear-cut edges. Time and experience seem to have worn out that conceptual certainty; my mind came to feel out experiences and things rather than define them. And a subtle sense of joy and wonder at the mystery of things and their indefinable essence permeated my perception. The borders to the paintings opened up and disappeared, only to reappear as linear movements that support and attend to space rather than restrict it. Sometimes I would just paint a swash of color on the paper and enjoy it—or the feeling of the brush, the magic of the perception then changing as a color suffused a space.

The co-operation and interest of other people were important aspects of the value of these paintings to me. I used what people chose to give me freely. Each painting embodies this virtue of generosity (*dana*). George Sharp, the Chairman of the monastery's Trust, himself a professional illustrator, gave me a set of colored inks. So I used those. Some poster paint came my way, so I used that; a Thai classical artist gave me some tempera; my mother gave me some acrylics; a bhikkhu friend, some oils; another Dhamma friend not only gave me numerous fine sable brushes, but also made photographic reproductions of the series and a set of color transparencies for exhibition purposes. Another Dhamma friend gave me some watercolor paper, while another mounted and heat-sealed the completed works. Seeking nothing can make one's life immensely rich. That people should take part in this way, and actually appreciate the paintings, is for me an honor; the joy of the spirit that sustained the work overshadows the imperfections of the craft.

Being asked to write a commentary on the illuminations, however, presented its own problems owing to the responsibilities of establishing and maintaining Amaravati Buddhist Monastery. A year after the first request (1985), I wrote the above remarks. Then six years fluttered by, with the illustrations hanging on the wall of Amaravati's meeting hall. As the hall was redecorated at the beginning of 1991, the series was removed and put in store. This movement into retreat seems to have caused a stir in the realm of those who delight in creation. Within three months, a letter came from the Sanghapala group in California, who were looking to set up a small Buddhist monastery there as a branch of Amaravati. They were interested in having the illustrations published with a commentary for when the monastery was projected to open.

I asked Ajahn Sumedho for a month's "sabbatical" to write the commentary, incarcerated myself in a room with a shrine and a word-processor, and eventually emerged somewhat dazed with a manuscript. A few interested monks and nuns got down to reading and tidying up the draft, pinning some of my drifting thought processes into literary form and doing what they could to polish the style without making the work appear as an abstract and authoritative statement on the Dhamma. There is enough of that conceit in religious teaching and in human pronouncements in general. Rather than a proclamation of enlightened wisdom, this is a record of some thoughts I have had through years of practice. May it encourage others to develop their own insights, and thus be for the welfare of many.

Sucitto Bhikkhu,
Chithurst Buddhist Monastery,
December 1992.

INTRODUCTION

The Dhammacakkappavattana Sutta is the first sermon of the Buddha. In the Theravada recension of the Buddha's teaching, presented in the ancient Pali language of India, there are three main divisions: the Discourses (*Sutta Pitaka*), the Books of the Discipline (*Vinaya Pitaka*) and the Books of Metaphysics (*Abhidhamma Pitaka*). The Sutta appears twice in this body of work known as the Pali Canon: namely in the *Vinaya Pitaka* (*Mahavagga:* [I], 6, 17-31) and in the *Sutta Pitaka* (*Samyutta Nikaya:* [V], Truths; II, 1).

Scholars generally agree that the material in these works was collected over a period of time which extended beyond the Buddha's passing away (*Parinibbana*). It is traditionally held that the main body of the *Sutta Pitaka* was recited by the Venerable Ananda at a Sangha Council held soon after the *Parinibbana,* and, at that same meeting, the Venerable Upali recited the texts of the *Vinaya*. Even though these are enormous texts, it is not impossible for clear-minded beings to remember them and learn them by heart—in fact, there are a few bhikkhus in this present day and age who can do just that. However, it is generally agreed that these early recitations were later polished and augmented into the texts that we have today. In fact, some of the suttas are set in a time that postdates the Buddha's life, while chapters of the Vinaya relate the affairs of the First and Second Sangha Councils (held about 100 years apart). So, subsequent additions and commentaries are an accepted part of the Canon. It is generally agreed that the text of the Abhidhamma is of a later date than that of the other two Pitakas; which does not mean that the ideas expressed in the Abhidhamma are necessarily of a later date — only that its casting into a fixed form is.

As these texts became established, a high degree of uniformity and agreement prevailed. The Sangha was obviously most concerned to preserve the teaching of the Buddha, and if groups of monks learned and recited sections of it by heart, any spurious additions would immediately be noticed by others who had learned that text. Much the same practice prevails today with the monks' regular recitation of the *Patimokkha* (the Monastic Rule). Since it is always recited in a group, mistakes become quite apparent. With this method of preserving the teachings, any subsequent additions would only be made with the consent of a council of elders.

The process of oral transmission affects the style of the text — formulae and stock passages abound. These may be irritating to a modern reader, but are helpful to a reciter and supportive to a listener. Rather like a mantra, or an often-repeated story, familiar phrases have a calming effect. They establish certain themes in the memory of the listener, change the mental mode from discursive rational processes to those of reflection, and create a feeling of belonging. Thereby the listener, the reciter and the text itself come together. The listener and the reciter are taken into the timelessness of a tradition. This is an experience that lifts us out of the particular concerns of the day or of our personal identity. Chanting itself, done in a monotone, has a tranquilizing effect on the mind, whatever the content, both for those who listen and those who chant. The reciters have to learn, when chanting in a group, to enunciate simultaneously and at the same rhythm and pitch; this requires the attention that is supportive of contemplation.

After a few hundred years, the material of the Pali Canon was written down. This occurred at the beginning of the Christian Era in what is now Sri Lanka. After that, no further addition to the Canon took place. There are several extant manuscripts, which differ slightly, owing to copyists' errors and the ravages of time. The first text using the Roman alphabet was composed in Thailand under the direction of King Chulalongkorn in the latter years of the 19th century. Somewhat after that, the Pali Text Society was founded in Britain by T.W. Rhys Davids. This Society has taken upon itself the task of producing a Roman alphabet edition of the Pali texts as well as a translation into English. The text that I have used as a basis for the illuminations is actually the version written in the Royal Thai Chanting Book, and is chanted by contemporary Thai bhikkhus. It differs from the Pali Text Society edition on a few minor points.

The accepted status of the Dhammacakkappavattana Sutta as the first of the Buddha's discourses gives it a particular appeal. It also elucidates the Four Noble Truths, the teaching that he calls "particular to Buddhas," and which is considered to be the heart of his dispensation. Nowadays the Sutta is especially chanted on Asalha Puja which, in the Buddhist calendar, usually falls on the full-moon day of July. This is traditionally held to be the day when the Sutta was first taught by the Buddha, and it also immediately precedes the beginning of the three month monastic Rains Retreat (*Vassa*).

In Thailand today, many men will take ordination as Buddhist monks for the period of the *Vassa*. The *Vassa* is recognized as a time for more detailed and thorough practice when the bhikkhus refrain from traveling, and determine to abide together in their monasteries. This gives the teacher an excellent chance to supervise his disciples, as well as allowing the Sangha the opportunity to clarify the observances and principles of training together. So for many monks, the Dhammacakkappavattana Sutta signifies a time when they can attend to their meditation practice and training with vigor and in a supportive environment of stability and instruction.

Part of that practice may well be to learn the recitation of several suttas, including the Dhammacakkappavattana Sutta, both for their own reflection and to support the practice of the laity, who will congregate at such recitations. A group recitation followed by a period of meditation and a *desana* (talk on Dhamma) on the theme of the Sutta would form an intrinsic part of the monks' and laity's observance of Asalha Puja. Because this happens every year throughout the Buddhist world, the occasion has a value that extends beyond the meaning of the Sutta itself. It establishes a community in the Dhamma, and a sense of kinship with Buddhists near and far, from bygone ages up to the present.

All of these considerations may help to explain the approach that I have taken in this current work. My intention is not to present a scholarly exegesis of the meaning of the Sutta; such interpretations as I offer should be understood as reflections from my own practice of the Dhamma rather than absolute statements about the meaning of the words. However, I have tried to consult the extensive compilations of the suttas and to follow a pattern of reviewing the Sutta phrase by phrase, if not always word by word.

SOME NOTES ON THE TEXT

The quotations of translations from the Pali scriptures are from various sources, all of which I would recommend reading. The comprehensive edition is that presented by the Pali Text Society, which has been working on authoritative editions of the texts in Pali, with translations into English, for most of this century. Some of the earlier translations have aged a little, especially when seen in the fuller light of understanding of the nature of the teachings and the practice. There is a recent translation of the *Digha Nikaya* (The Long Discourses) by Maurice Walshe, entitled "Thus Have I Heard," and published by Wisdom Publications. Wisdom are also currently in the process of publishing a new translation of the *Majjhima Nikaya* (Middle-Length Discourses) by Venerable Ñanamoli Thera. Ven. Ñanamoli also made some other fine translations of suttas and produced a book called "The Life of the Buddha" (published by the Buddhist Publication Society), which is made up, for the most part, of extracts of suttas compiled into a narrative framework. Its excellence is not only in the quality of translation, but in the breadth and interest of the numerous extracts, which avoid the repetition of the complete texts. The Buddhist Publication Society produces many good books, commentaries on suttas and writings of contemporary Buddhists at very low cost.

I have quoted from the Pali scriptures many times in the course of this book. Generally I have used the Pali Text Society translation, or Ven. Ñanamoli's; occasionally I have used a translation of my own. Quotations from the *Sutta Nipata* are generally from the translations of Ven. Dr. H. Saddhatissa, published by Curzon Press. I have retained the Pali titles for the Nikayas to avoid the confusion of differing English translations. *Digha Nikaya*, for example, is literally "The Collection of Long (Suttas)," although the PTS translation is titled "Dialogues of the Buddha" and Maurice Walshe's is titled "Thus Have I Heard." *Majjhima Nikaya* has up to now been known as "Middle Length Sayings," and *Anguttara Nikaya* as "Gradual Sayings." What new translators make of these titles is yet to be seen.

I have referred to the suttas of the *Digha* and *Majjhima Nikaya* by their Pali name and their number in the Nikaya: for example, Sabbasava Sutta is the second sutta in the *Majjhima Nikaya*. The *Samyutta* and *Anguttara Nikayas* have always had more complex references, owing to their construction — small suttas collected into chapters in books based on a particular theme within the Nikaya as a whole. In the *Samyutta*, the theme is a topic such as "Cause;" in the *Anguttara*, the theme is a number — "Nines," for example, brings together suttas in which nine-fold topics are referred to. In the case of these Nikayas, my reference begins with a Roman numeral in square brackets. This refers to the volume of the PTS English translation. The subsequent word refers to the "book" within that volume, and any other word to the chapter within that book. A subsequent Roman number refers to any other subsection, with the Arabic numeral referring to the number of the actual Sutta.

USE OF PALI

I have used Pali in the commentary when that Pali word covers a range of meanings that the English can't. If one tries to translate every word into English, one frequently has to use different English words in different contexts. The ideal solution is for the English language to take in these words as its own—as it has embraced "igloo" and "khaki" for example. When such incorporation seems possible, as in the familiar, almost untranslatable "dukkha," I have used ordinary Roman type; otherwise, the Pali appears in italics.

"Kamma"—the Pali version of Sanskrit "karma"—is used not just to be consistent with the use of Pali throughout, but also to avoid confusion with the Vedic view of "karma." The Vedic use, or at least the modern rendition of that term, signifies a process of cause and effect that pertains above and beyond the individual will. As such, it brings in notions of fate and destiny. The Buddha recognized that the kamma of the body, for example, was beyond our will—it is born, ages and dies according to bodily kamma. However, he stressed that the most significant kamma was the activity produced by intention, whose results are experienced by the mind. Because of the significance of intentional activity of body, speech or mind in the *present,* liberation is possible in this lifetime—we don't have to exhaust the results of all past kamma.

Another problematic word is *sankhara.* Often, and most broadly, the word is translated as "condition," which doesn't immediately mean very much to a modern reader, although conditionality (and therefore, the Unconditioned) is the understanding of existence that is the foundation for the Buddha's transcendence.

> *The Tathagata has taught the root of all that grows into existence; and he has explained what brings around its cessation.* (Vinaya Mahavagga: [1])

A "condition" is something that affects the existence of something else: a necessary condition for fire may be wood, for example. Note that a condition is more than a cause: wood doesn't cause fire. And one might add many other conditions that are necessary for fire: the intention to create a fire, the application of heat, the non-appearance of water, etc.

The understanding of the Buddha was that what the ordinary person perceives as reality are conditions, and all conditions are ephemeral and impermanent (as the intention to create fire, the wood and the rest in the above example). Also, all conditions depend on other conditions: wood on trees, trees on earth, rain and air (and the non-manifestation of herbivores), and so on. But where does it all begin? Where is the root condition of them all? Here the Buddha concerned himself only with the conditions of the human body and mind, most particularly with the mind. Hence *sankhara* is often translated as "mental formations."

One of the most significant conditions that arises through the activity of the mind is volition (or intention, or will). The mind not only receives impressions from the other senses, it determines what to attend to, what to ignore, and what to do with what it attends to. This determining is intention (*cetana*). Intention is the basis of *kamma*—actions that have a result which sustains a mode of personality. When thoughts are kamma-productive, they stimulate activity and the results of the activity are acquired by the agent of the thought. If you think of stealing something and are moved by that thought, then what is immediately created is the impression of being the owner of that thought. One may then dismiss the thought (good kamma, kammically wholesome) or act upon it. If it is acted upon, this is bodily *sankhara*, and kammically unwholesome, which again sets up conditions of identity. By one's actions, good or bad, is one known and defined; for one's actions, one is responsible. Therefore kamma-formations is another important condition of *sankhara*.

When thoughts and actions are not identified with, then they are called *dhamma*, meaning "things" in a more universal, impersonal way. An important Buddhist reflection is that "all *sankhara* are impermanent; all *dhamma* is not-self." The conditions that we identify with are of a transient nature; and things which we do not take as ours do not belong to some higher, other self either. Hence God — or the Universal Whole, or Ultimate Truth — is not a super-person either, or an identity. It is the whole, not a fragment that can be defined into an identity separate from anything. The Buddhist reference to this whole is "the Dhamma," a term also reserved for the presentation of Truth that we call the Buddha's "teachings."

THE BACKGROUND

"Buddha" means "The One Who Knows," "The Awakened One." It is, of course, a title that can be applied to a rare kind of human being — one who has realized Ultimate Truth through his own personal efforts (unlike "*Arahants*," who realize enlightenment through following the teaching of a Buddha). The title Buddha is sometimes expanded to "*Sammasambuddha*," meaning "completely self-enlightened." There are also *Paccekabuddhas* (Lone Buddhas), who have accomplished an enlightenment in like fashion, but who have no ability to teach others. The Buddha of this age spoke occasionally of Buddhas of past ages. They are listed as 28 in number in a way that is suggestive of mythical truth rather than historical record. There is also mention of a future Buddha, Metteyya (or Maitreya in Sanskrit), who will arise in the world of humans when the teachings of the Buddha Gotama have died out.

Before his enlightenment, the Buddha was known as Siddhattha Gotama, born the son and heir to Suddhodana, an elected chief of the Sakyan Republic. This republic, occupying a fragment of modern Nepal, was a vassal state of the larger kingdom of Kosala. Kosala occupied the northeast corner of modern Uttar Pradesh, and now includes Gorakhpur, Ayodhya and Varanasi. Throughout his adult life he gave ethical and contemplative teachings, acquired a considerable reputation and a number of followers, and passed away at a ripe old age, near the present town of Kasla in Uttar Pradesh. Nothing more definite than that is certain concerning the biography of the Buddha. Scholars even question the dates of his birth and death, mostly plumping for 563 – 483 B.C.

The Buddha regarded his teaching, rather than his past life, as the thing of importance; he only alluded occasionally to his life before enlightenment. Therefore, much of what passes for his biography has been pieced together from allusions in the scriptures and commentarial and apocryphal accounts—which were, no doubt, affected by devotees of later centuries trying to assemble a human image of the Master for devotional purposes. A notable modern effort, which also provides interesting descriptions of the Buddha's country at that time, is "The Historical Buddha" (H.W. Schumann; trans. M.O'C. Walshe; Penguin London 1989).

By his own later accounts, Siddhattha, as a young man, reflected on the human lot of aging, sickness and death. The futility of living in a way that provided no means of dealing with these issues motivated him to leave home and wander as a religious ascetic (equivalent to a modern sadhu) at the age of 29. At that time, it was not unusual for older men to leave the family life when they were advanced in years and had fulfilled their family responsibilities. A strong family structure and inter-dependency however, made it more unusual for younger men, and even rarer for women.

The Indian spiritual culture, into which Siddhattha was born, had two main branches: that of the brahmins, who were priests learned in the lore of the Vedas, and the only ones legitimately entitled to interpret the scriptures and perform rites and sacrifices to the Vedic gods on behalf of other folk; and the *samanas* (literally "strivers"), who stepped outside of the brahmin framework, and were seeking religious truth by themselves in any number of heterodox ways. The Buddha frequently referred to his disciples as *samanas*, just as those who were not his disciples would refer to him in terms of no greater respect than "the samana Gotama."

Among the *samanas* were the wanderers, called *paribbajikas*, apparently from brahmin caste. They had no particular doctrine in common, but were all independent seekers who might adopt a wide range of views and practices, staying with one teacher for a while and forming a group, then wandering off to another teacher and practice—rather in the fashion of modern spiritual seekers. The only commonly held ascetic practice seems to have been that of celibacy, while some would take up extreme forms of self-mortification. In the suttas, there is mention of six famous teachers: Purana Kassapa, Makkhali Gosala, Ajita Kesakambali, Pakudha Kaccayana, Nigantha Nataputta (another name for Mahavira, the founder of the Jains) and Senjaya Belatthaputta. The teaching of Nigantha Nataputta prescribed a rigorous purification by asceticism and sense restraint, whereas the other teachings, though not fully presented, ascribe no importance to the actions of the individual in determining their future destiny.

Tradition has it that, after leaving his father's home, Siddhattha spent six years as a wandering ascetic. He practiced for some time with Alara Kalama, a yogi who taught him how to attain the meditative absorption called the Sphere of Nothingness. Having mastered this, Siddhattha still felt dissatisfied, as it seemed to be a temporary evasion of the problems of life. He then sought out another teacher, Uddaka Ramaputta, who taught him a deeper absorption called the Sphere of Neither-Perception-nor-

THE LAND OF THE BUDDHA

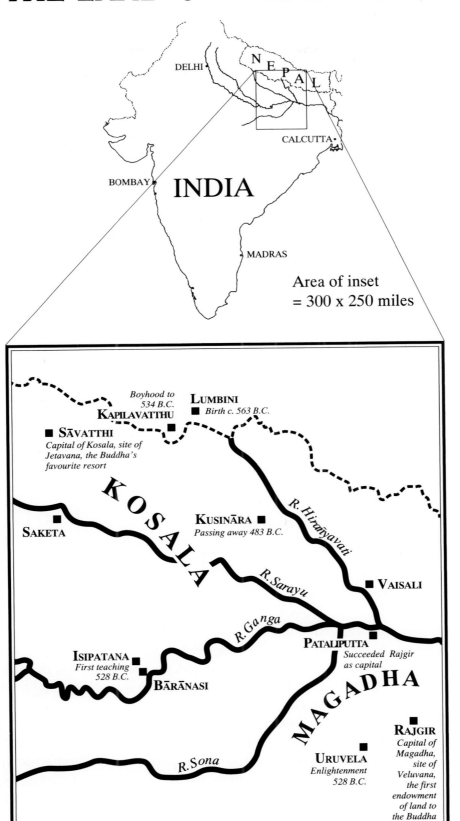

DELHI

N E P A L

CALCUTTA

BOMBAY

INDIA

MADRAS

Area of inset
= 300 x 250 miles

Boyhood to
534 B.C.
KAPILAVATTHU

LUMBINI
Birth c. 563 B.C.

■ **SĀVATTHI**
Capital of Kosala, site of
Jetavana, the Buddha's
favourite resort

KOSALA

SAKETA

KUSINĀRA ■
Passing away 483 B.C.

R. Hiraññavati

R. Sarayu

VAISALI

R. Ganga

ISIPATANA
First teaching
528 B.C.

BĀRĀNASI

PATALIPUTTA
Succeeded Rajgir
as capital

MAGADHA

R. Sona

URUVELA
Enlightenment
528 B.C.

RAJGIR
Capital of
Magadha,
site of
Veluvana,
the first
endowment
of land to
the Buddha

Non-Perception. Siddhattha also perfected this state but rejected it on the same grounds. During this time, perhaps periodically, the Buddha-to-be lived with a group of five fellow ascetics, who all looked to him as an example. They, however, lost faith in him when, after six years of extreme asceticism, he decided to abandon that path and adopt a more moderate (though by modern standards austere) style of practice. He wandered off on his own, and came at last to a place in the kingdom of Magadha called Uruvela—now known as Bodh-Gaya. Here he practiced a form of meditation which was endowed with the reflective faculties of the mind, rather than being merely a temporary trance-like transfiguration of consciousness. This led to the insights that undermined the foundations of the unawakened state. What was left was clarity, liberation and profound understanding of how the mind works.

The Buddha had realized that it was not going to be easy to convey his insights to others in a way that they could follow. By all accounts, he even doubted whether it was worth the effort—given the power that attachment has over people's minds. Fortunately, compassion prevailed and he felt that there were those with "but little dust in their eyes" who would be able to see what he was pointing at. He considered locating his former teachers, but ascertained that they were both dead. Then he thought of his five former companions who were at that time some 130 miles away in the Deer Park near the ancient holy city of Varanasi (also called Baranasi). Accordingly, he set off on foot in that direction.

This was only seven weeks after his own unique enlightenment, so at that time he probably had not formulated a teaching. Certainly, his first dialog, with a naked ascetic called Upaka, whom he met on the way, bore no fruit. The Buddha coolly but confidently proclaimed to him his own realization in personal terms:

> *"Victorious over all, omniscient am I*
> *Among all things undefiled,*
> *Leaving all, through death of craving freed...."*
> To this, Upaka replied: "May it be so, friend," and went off taking a different road. (Mahavagga: [I])

So the approach of giving a direct, personal testimonial to enlightenment was not well understood. Upaka responded with the equivalent of "So what?" The teaching was too subjective, and ultimately, it didn't relate to the listener's experience. The Buddha must have learned from that uninterested response; in the future, he rarely made proclamations about Ultimate Truth. Instead, he taught conventional truths which, if used skillfully, would lead to the experience of Ultimate Reality. The most constantly reiterated theme of this teaching is, of course, the exposition in terms of the Four Noble Truths.

When the Buddha arrived at the Deer Park, the Group of Five at first did not want to receive him. However, being moved by his radiant presence, they found themselves offering him a place to sit, although they

THE SUTTA

Thus have I heard. Once the Blessed One was staying in the Deer Park at Isipatana, near Varanasi. There he addressed the bhikkhus of the Group of Five thus: "There are two extremes which should not be followed, bhikkhus, by someone who has gone forth. Devotion to pursuing sense pleasure, which is low, vulgar, worldly, ignoble and produces no useful result; and devotion to self-denial, which is painful, ignoble and produces no useful result. Avoiding both these extremes, bhikkhus, the Middle Way that a Tathagata has Awakened to gives vision and insight knowledge, and leads to peace, profound understanding, full realization and to Nibbana. And what is the Middle Way that a Tathagata has Awakened to, which gives vision and insight knowledge, and leads to peace, profound understanding, full realization and to Nibbana? It is the Noble Eightfold Path—that is to say: Right View, Right Intention, Right Speech, Right Action, Right Livelihood, Right Effort, Right Mindfulness and Right Collectedness. This is the Middle Way that a Tathagata has Awakened to.

"Bhikkhus, there is this Noble Truth about dissatisfaction. Birth is problematic; aging is hard; dying is also hard to bear. Sorrow, lamentation, pain, grief and despair are all painful. Association with what you dislike is unpleasant; being apart from what you like still did not want to hear what he had to say. But the Buddha touched upon a theme that would have had immediate relevance to those seekers: "Give ear ... the Deathless has been found; I instruct, I teach Dhamma. If you practice as I teach you, you will gain realization in terms of your own experience here and now. And you will come upon and abide in the supreme goal of the spiritual life. ... " Though they were still reluctant, they were impressed by the clarity and the confidence with which the Buddha spoke. So they listened and opened their hearts. ...

is unpleasant; not getting what you want is unpleasant. In brief, the five grasped aggregates are unsatisfactory.

"Bhikkhus, there is the Noble Truth of the Origin of Suffering. It is desire, which gives rise to fresh birth, bound up with relish and passion, running here and there, delighting in this and in that; in other words, sense desire, desire for existing and desire for extinction.

"Bhikkhus, there is the Noble Truth of the Cessation of Suffering. It is the complete fading away and cessation of this desire; its abandonment and relinquishment; the freedom from, and discarding of it.

"Bhikkhus, there is the Noble Truth of the Way leading to the Cessation of Suffering. It is the Noble Eightfold Path: namely, Right View, Right Intention, Right Speech, Right Action, Right Livelihood, Right Effort, Right Mindfulness and Right Collectedness.

"There is this Noble Truth of Suffering: such was the vision, insight, wisdom, knowing and light that arose in me about things not heard before. This Noble Truth must be penetrated to by fully understanding Suffering: such was the vision, insight, wisdom, knowing and light that arose in me about things not heard before. This Noble Truth has been penetrated to by fully understanding Suffering: such was the vision, insight, wisdom, knowing and light that arose in me about things not heard before.

"There is this Noble Truth of the Origin of Suffering: such was the vision, insight, wisdom, knowing and light that arose in me about things not heard before. This Noble Truth must be penetrated to by abandoning the Origin of Suffering … This Noble Truth has been penetrated to by abandoning the Origin of Suffering: such was the vision, insight, wisdom, knowing and light that arose in me about things not heard before.

"There is this Noble Truth of the Cessation of Suffering: such was the vision, insight, wisdom, knowing and light that arose in me about things not heard before. This Noble Truth must be penetrated to by realizing the Cessation of Suffering … This Noble Truth has been penetrated to by realizing the Cessation of Suffering: such was the vision, insight, wisdom, knowing and light that arose in me about things not heard before.

"There is this Noble Truth of the Path leading to the Cessation of Suffering: such was the vision, insight, wisdom, knowing and light that arose in me about things not heard before. This Noble Truth must be penetrated to by cultivating the Path … This Noble Truth has been penetrated to by cultivating the Path: such was the vision, insight, wisdom, knowing and light that arose in me about things not heard before.

"As long, bhikkhus, as these Four Noble Truths in their twelve aspects were not seen clearly as they are, I did not declare to the world—with its devas, maras and brahmas, with its samanas and brahmins, its monarchs and ordinary folk—that I had realized the complete and perfect Awakening. But as soon as these Four Noble Truths in their twelve aspects were seen clearly as they are, then I taught the world—with its devas, maras and brahmas, its samanas and brahmins, its monarchs and ordinary folk—that

I had realized the complete and perfect Awakening. The knowledge and the vision arose in me: 'Unshakeable is my deliverance. This is the last birth. There is no further becoming.'"

Thus spoke the Blessed One, and the Group of Five bhikkhus were gladdened and they approved of his words. Now while this discourse was being delivered, the untarnished and clear insight into Dhamma arose in Venerable Kondañña thus: "Whatever has the nature to arise, has the nature to cease."

When the Wheel of Dhamma had been set rolling by the Blessed One, the devas of the earth raised the cry: "At Varanasi, in the Deer Park at Isipatana, the matchless Wheel of Dhamma has been set rolling by the Blessed One, not to be stopped by any samana, or brahmin, or deva, or mara, or brahma, or anyone in the world." When they heard what the Earth devas had said, the devas of the realm of the Four Great Kings cried out with one voice: "At Varanasi. … " When they heard the cry of the devas of the realm of the Four Great Kings, then the devas of the realm of the Thirty-Three cried out with one voice … When they heard the cry of the Thirty-Three devas, the Yama devas cried out with one voice … When they heard the cry of the Yama devas, the Tusita devas cried out with one voice … When they heard the cry of the Tusita devas, the Nimmanarati devas cried out with one voice … When they heard the cry of the Nimmanarati devas, the Paranimmitavasavatti devas cried out with one voice … When they heard the cry of the Paranimmitavasavatti devas, the devas of the retinue of the Brahma deities took up the cry: "At Varanasi, in the Deer Park at Isipatana, the matchless Wheel of Dhamma has been set rolling by the Blessed One, not to be stopped by any samana, or brahmin, or deva, or mara, or brahma, or anyone in the world." So indeed in that hour, at that moment, the word travelled up to the realm of the highest divinities. And this ten-thousandfold world-system shook and rocked and quaked. And a great measureless radiance, surpassing the very nature of the devas, was displayed in the world.

Then the Blessed One uttered the great exclamation: "Truly, it is the good Kondañña who has understood, it is the good Kondañña who has understood." Thus it was that the name of Venerable Kondañña became: Añña-Kondañña — "Kondañña who understands."

This concludes the Discourse on the Setting in Motion of the Wheel of Truth.

1

THE GREAT WHEEL OF THE LAW

The title Dhammacakkappavattana Sutta has been translated as "The Sutta that Set in Motion the Wheel of the Truth," and, rather oddly, as "The Sutta on the Foundation of the Kingdom of the Norm." "Sutta" literally means "a thread" and is the usual way that a discourse of the Buddha is titled. It is a metaphor that suggests that what follows is an account of the gist of what may have been a longer or more loosely structured talk that the Buddha gave to a religious seeker. As I have previously commented, these are oral recitations that have been compiled in formulaic style for easier memorization. They may also have been categorized and summarized for more succinct appreciation.

At any rate, this "thread" is what the word suggests—the main strand of a teaching, given to a group of religious seekers over a period of time. In the Vinaya account of this discourse, the Sutta is followed by a comment that the Buddha then exhorted the four disciples who had not realized Truth with further instruction. One can only surmise, as the talk is not recorded, that it was a talk of similar nature, of which the Dhammacakkap-pavattana Sutta conveys the core meaning.

The word "Dhamma" (Dharma in Sanskrit) has a number of meanings that all imply a universal rather than a personal viewpoint. In one sense, it just means things, as part of a universal structure—all things from bicycles to thoughts are *dhammas.* Generally, when used in this context, a lower case "d" is used. When thoughts are referred to in the purely *personal* context, identified with as *my* thoughts, they are called *sankhara.* This gives a useful reflection on the way that terms are designated: often what appears to be the same thing will be referred to by different words. It depends on our way of looking at it.

Another meaning of *dhamma* is the proper order of things. This is a central concept in the Vedas. It is the duty of each person to live in accordance with *dhamma,* which may mean his or her profession, religious observance, or the social mores of that particular society, village or family. This is close to the meaning of *dhamma* as a teaching. When encountering one of these wandering teachers, people might very well inquire, "What is your dhamma?" i.e., "What are your principles?"—Be they doctrine or observance. In the Buddhist sense, the teaching of the Buddha is a *dhamma,* but it is elevated as it is seen to be not just a conventional system, but a universal teaching that relates to principles which abide in the makeup and the activities of human beings and celestial beings too. Hence in our linguistic conventions, we give it a capital letter.

Ultimate Truth, realized through liberation from every form of attachment, is also called "Dhamma:" the Universal Truth, the Law, The Way It Is. In such contexts, it's probably best just to adopt the word Dhamma into the English language.

The Dhamma of the Buddha has a "conventional" application that creates order and harmony on the plane of everyday social life, and a "transcendent" teaching that focuses on individual liberation from attachment. In the Buddha's teaching, the conventional and the transcendent do not conflict; the transcendent realization of Ultimate Truth relies upon the conventional observance of morality and conduct. One result of this is that the Buddha's teaching transformed the tradition of independent, almost anarchic, truth-seekers into an Order—the Sangha. The Sangha exists within a high degree of uniformity, discipline and an infrastructure based upon dependence and unanimous agreement.

Furthermore, the Buddha presented a teaching that illuminated a way of experiencing Ultimate Truth which householders could realize for themselves without relying on the interpretations of brahmins. In the full practicing system of Dhamma, the "gone-forth" religious seekers and those living the family life support and encourage each other. No wonder that this teaching can be applied anywhere at any time. The Buddha called it: "The Elephant's Footprint:" every other religious teaching fits inside it.

The next element of the title is the word *cakka.* This word also has several meanings. Its root meaning is that which is always turning. So it can mean

All followers of the Buddha, no matter what their denomination or beliefs or style of practice, can relate to this Sutta.

a wheel, or a cycle; it can also mean a vehicle, or, in another sense, a sphere — hence a region or realm (a sphere of influence). When used in the formulaic epithet of the *raja cakkavattin* — the Wheel-bearing Monarch — it implies one who rules over a vast territory, the known world, the universe, or the continent. So *"Dhammacakka"* can either be the vehicle of the Truth, or the Realm where the Norm of the Universal Truth holds sway. This realm is, to most of us, not a place in space and time, but a sense of community with all practitioners of the Dhamma.

This sermon is also called *"-ppavattana,"* which means it starts the Wheel turning. All followers of the Buddha, no matter what their denomination or beliefs or style of practice, can relate to this Sutta. And one never really outgrows it; it always remains a touchstone for practice because it reflects on the spiritual path in such fundamental terms. It is that which establishes the main theme of the Dhamma, and the community of Sangha — those who practice the Way.

As this Realm is vast in letter and spirit, this will be an ant's meanderings along its main street, sometimes drifting a little this way and that, but at least indicating that the Realm is worth visiting. I hope the reader is more amenable than the original Group of Five …

evam me sutaṃ

ekaṃ samayaṃ Bhagavā bārānas-
iyaṃ viharati isipatane migadāye
tatra kho bhagavā pañcavaggiye
bhikkhū āmantesi

2

THUS HAVE I HEARD

Evam me sutaṁ.
Thus have I heard.

Following an ancient tradition, all the suttas begin with these first three words: "Evam me sutam." It is a reference to the oral tradition which says that the person who first heard this discourse was the Buddha's disciple Ananda. Venerable Ananda, however, was not present when this teaching was given. It is believed that when he became the Buddha's attendant after twenty years in the Order, Venerable Ananda asked if he could be present whenever the Buddha gave a talk on Dhamma, and if the Buddha could give him the essence of all his earlier discourses or sermons. Thus when reading this text, the reader must bear in mind that it is by no means a strictly literal account of what the Buddha said, but something which has been recorded. The reciter is making it clear that what he is transmitting is devoid of any personal additions or interpretations. This is the way this particular teaching came to him, and he is simply reciting it as faithfully as possible.

Ekaṁ samayaṁ bhagavā Bārāṇasiyaṁ viharati Isipatane migadāye tatra kho bhagavā pañcavaggiye bhikkhū āmantesi …

> Once the Blessed One was staying in the Deer Park at Isipatana, near Varanasi. There he addressed the bhikkhus of the Group of Five thus …

All the suttas begin with a brief description of the place where the sermon was delivered. The setting here is the Deer Park at Isipatana, known in modern times as Sarnath. Highly regarded as the place where the Buddha gave the First Sermon, it has been a Buddhist pilgrimage site for many years. A column built by Emperor Asoka, an Indian ruler (third century B.C.) who converted to Buddhism, and did much to propagate it throughout his empire, marks the spot where the First Sermon is believed to have been given. Sarnath is located near Varanasi, or Baranasi as it is sometimes called. Varanasi was a holy city long before the time of the Buddha, and over the centuries, many thousands of people have gone there to die. It is considered very auspicious to die and be cremated at Varanasi, and to have one's ashes thrown into the river Ganges. Being a holy place at that time, Varanasi also became the natural resort of seers, sages and mendicants as well as people from all over the surrounding area who would gather to exchange views on matters of religious doctrine and practice. This is where Gotama and his ascetic companions had been dwelling until he had decided to abandon the extreme of self-mortification and to withdraw from the others in order to practice in solitude. And it was to this place that, as an Awakened One, Gotama returned to begin teaching his five companions.

The Sutta addresses these five as the *pañcavaggiye bhikkhu,* the Group of Five bhikkhus. Nowadays, "bhikkhu" just means a Buddhist monk. Etymologically, "bhikkhu" comes from the word used for alms and is still used within that context in countries such as India, Afghanistan or Pakistan where it survives as *baksheesh,* meaning a tip, a gift made as a special favor. If you go to those places nowadays, you will meet more *"baksheesh!"* than bhikkhus.

Anyway, these five were named Kondañña, Vappa, Bhaddiya, Mahanama and Assaji. Kondañña was the eldest. Many years previously, as a novice brahmin, he had been invited to Suddhodana Raja's palace along with seven of his peers to see the baby Siddhattha and give predictions as to his destiny. They all agreed that this babe would be either a great emperor or a Buddha; although it was Kondañña alone who reckoned that Siddhattha was destined for Buddhahood. Four of the brahmins that had been present at the Raja's palace later told their sons to keep their eyes on Siddhattha, as he was destined for greatness. These sons grew up to become the other four of the Group of Five.

The Buddha here is addressed as "Bhagava" which means "The One who has Great Fortune" or "The Blessed One," sometimes translated as "The Lord." The term is always used in a spiritual context by his disciples, and implies someone who has both a great deal to offer and the capacity to make it accessible to the manyfolk. The Buddha, however, generally referred to himself as the "Tathagata," or "Thus Gone"—someone who has completed the round (of birth), finished, gone beyond—not as "Bhagava." This is because a Buddha does not identify with any of the qualities he manifests, that is, he regards all these as less important than the fact that he has gone beyond. As a source of inspiration and encouragement for the unawakened disciple, the power of such a living presence of Truth in human form as a Buddha cannot be overestimated. However, the Buddha repeatedly emphasized holding to the Dhamma, his teaching, as something that would have a greater and clearer long-term value than devotion to him as "The Blessed One." Adoration of the Buddha seems to have been a cause for the long delay in Venerable Ananda's own enlightenment.

Around the frame of the painting are some of the beings who revere the Buddha. At the top appears a line of devas (heavenly beings), who are all exclaiming their delight that a Blessed One has come into the world to turn the Wheel of the Law. Down at the bottom are the beings in the hell realms, in states of misery. It is said that in the lowest hells, it is pitch-black and there are only a few times when it is possible to see. These are, when a Tathagata is born, when he attains Awakening, when he begins the teaching of the Dhamma, and when he leaves the mortal realm. I think that in my most deluded teenage years, just seeing a picture of the Buddha with that inexplicable but evocative gentle smile and stillness sent some light into my mind. Not much, but enough of a glimmer to consider that it might be worth finding out what he had to say ... one day. Maybe it's like that in hell. Hell is depicted in my painting by three animals—the pig symbolizes delusion; the rooster is greed; and the snake represents hatred. The overwhelming presence of these is what hell is.

The Great Wheel of the Law here is represented by a wheel with eight spokes. This symbol has come down to us from the early centuries of Buddhist India, there being no iconography in the Buddha's time. The earliest symbols used by Buddhists were—the Bodhi Tree with an empty space underneath it; the Bodhi leaf (here decorating the rim of the Wheel); the Parasol (a symbol of elevated status) poised over an empty space or a throne; the special and highly decorated Footprints; the Stupa (ceremonial tomb containing the ashes of a cremated saint); and the Wheel, which may have been a transformed sun symbol or simply that which is conducive to going places.

In my painting, there is a large *naga,* or serpent-figure coiled around part of the wheel. *Nagas* are different from ordinary snakes. They are often mentioned in the scriptures as possessing special powers. They are giant hooded snakes who live in the water, but can take on human form and give birth to their young on the flat plains. They then go back to the sea when the land floods. *Nagas* appear in the celestial realms as well as part of the retinue of Virupakkha, a celestial World Guardian, who is mentioned later in this Sutta. There also seem to be a few ranging round free-lance, generally harmless if you don't annoy them but occasionally needing to be tamed by an Arahant.

Snakes can slough their skins and seemingly transform themselves, so

7

the serpent is a figure of transformation; in sundry early religions, it acts as the intermediary between the earthly plane and the heavenly plane. The Buddha himself is sometimes referred to as the "Great Naga"—someone undergoing a journey of transformation from the worldly to the spiritual plane.

Here the serpent is used as a symbol of the practice of Dhamma, the transformation of the human mind as it applies itself to the realization of Ultimate Truth. Such an Awakening deserves auspicious signs, so here the *naga* has the figures of the sun and moon on its hood and wears a lotus as a crown. The sun and moon represent the polarities of rationality and mystical intuition or gnosis; the lotus is the crown of their union—enlightened wisdom that has the depth and sensitivity of gnosis and the analytical precision of rationality. Such is the fruition of the practice that is intimately related to the teaching. As it comes alive, the Dhamma sloughs off the old skin of habit and attachment that we have taken ourselves to be. Shedding one's skin can be alarming, but for those who are prepared for such an experience, the Buddha gave the following words …

Dve me bhikkhave
antā pabbājitena
na sevitabbā yo cāyam
kāmesu kāmasukhallikānuyogo
hīno gammo pothujjaniko
anariyo anatthasaṁhito
yo cāyam
attakilamathānuyogo
dukkho anariyo anatthasaṁ-
-hito ete te bhikkhave
ubho ante anupagamma
majjhima paṭipadā tathāgatena
abhisambuddhā cakkhukaraṇī
ñāṇakaraṇī upasamāya
abhiññāya sambodhāya
nibbānāya saṁvattati

3

THE TWO EXTREMES

Dve me bhikkhave ... na sevitabbā
There are two extremes which should not be followed, bhikkhus,
by someone who has gone forth.

The manner in which the Buddha gave his teaching is indicative of his realization of Dhamma as: here and now, not delayed in time, inviting one to investigate, leading inwards, to be realized by the wise within their own experience. Therefore the Buddha tried to make his teaching relevant to the experience of the people he was addressing. Sometimes he would respond with silence to people who were just tangled up in confused ways of thinking—it was a way of indicating that Truth went beyond speculation. Sometimes he would answer a question with a counter-question to encourage the person to examine his or her own views and beliefs. Sometimes he would highlight an incident that had just occurred or a particular experience that a person was going through. In this Sutta, addressed to a group who must have heard a whole range of ideas about the nature of existence and Truth, the Buddha concerned himself with talk on the means of their practice.

In this way, his approach differed from that of the other *samana* teachers who seemed to have taught doctrinally: that there is no consequence to deeds in this life, that the world is an illusion in which nothing has any reality, or that one can achieve liberation only through severe asceticism (see *Background* in the *Introduction*). Here the Buddha focuses on the experience of the Way rather than its notional goal. Right now, liberation and salvation after death are only ideas and views in the mind; what can be directly known is how things are at this time and place. Focusing on the means, the here and now of how one lives, brings one into the present moment, and into a state of mind where there is no view to defend or uphold. Then, direct reason has the possibility to operate. This epitomizes the Buddha's teaching method.

For example, one time the villagers of Kesaputta* asked the Buddha what they should believe in because so many different people were giving them different ideas. His response was firstly to affirm their right to have doubts when given conflicting views. Then he appealed to their own understanding: "If you act in ways that are cruel or mean, does that seem good to you or not?" "No, they replied, we don't think that's a very good thing to do."

"Then it's best not to do it, isn't it?" commented the Buddha. "And what about being calm and kind, is that valued by you or not?" And they replied, "Well, we think it's very good."

In this way, he helped them to realize the value of concentrating on means rather than doctrines. Otherwise one is liable to get caught in "the tangle of views" and come no nearer to Truth. The Buddha's teaching asks one to reflect on what one already knows or on one's principles, and to proceed from that intuitive sense of certainty.

But in the case of the Group of Five, the Buddha was addressing "those who had gone forth," *samanas* — "strivers" — who had made a one-pointed commitment to personal realization. They needed no recommendation that Truth was worth seeking or that one had to apply oneself to it; they just needed to have the means clarified. So the Buddha gave some advice on the cultivation of right means as an expression and experience of enlightenment itself.

The Sutta proceeds with:

> *Yo cāyaṁ kāmesu ... anariyo anatthasañhito*
> Devotion to pursuing sense pleasure, which is low, vulgar, worldly, ignoble and produces no useful result; and devotion to self-denial, which is painful, ignoble and produces no useful result.

These are the two extreme positions that a *samana* might take if following the advice of teachers who taught in terms of a goal rather than a Way. At first glance, it seems obvious that anyone with a serious spiritual commitment would avoid such positions. However, the very notion of transcendence to a sphere beyond the conventional reality allows the possibility of discarding, sometimes deliberately, the normal conventions of life. This applies just as much to 20th century *"samanas"* — as anyone familiar with

---

* Here follows the gist of the "Kalama Sutta." (*Anguttara Nikaya:* [1], Threes, 65)

the present-day spiritual network will know. Under the guise of liberated wisdom, people will justify the most crazy and harmful sexual indulgences, or the use of drugs and liquor—"to release ego-bound conditioning." Sometimes, even quite sincere disciples will condone or experiment with such practices. What adds substance to this way of thinking is that there *are* many harmful repressive tendencies in modern life.

The other extreme of self-denial, or self-mortification, is rarer nowadays. Although asceticism does have a certain appeal, it is usually in the religious life of traditional monastic orders that some degree of self-mortification, deprivation or asceticism is practiced. Rigorous discipline and asceticism (including self-flagellation in a few Christian monastic orders) is not unusual; an almost military discipline and life of hardship is a major part of the traditional Zen life; and certainly, in the continuing *samana* life of India, long periods of fasting and other kinds of physical mortification are observed with the aim of transcending worldly life and reaching higher states of consciousness. In this regard, the Jains stand out. Their tradition is of an even longer duration than the Buddhist Sangha, and still attracts spiritual aspirants today.

The relevance of a reflection on self-denial to an average follower of the Buddha, who is not interested in hair shirts and prolonged standing on one leg, may seem slight. This reflection is more subtle, and often is one aspect of an oscillation of the mind between two positions. If one overindulges in food and drink for example, then the natural reaction (unless you're told that this extreme is good for you) is to feel a sense of regret, and then to veer towards complete abstinence. One feels annoyed with one's "weakness," and decides to be firm and cut it out. However, abstinence without wise reflection and insight doesn't solve the need syndrome that made one indulge in the first place, so after a period of abstinence one feels rather wretched, and decides to have just a *little* drink … which leads to another ….

In meditation, one can observe the mind following similar tendencies: periods of hard concentration, followed by periods of daydreaming and laxity; moments of really applying oneself—back straight, jaw tight and fierce one-pointedness on the meditation object … then, strained from the effort, or feeling that one has achieved something through that, one thinks that it's now time to relax and integrate into "normal life," get a few beers or just go to the movies. On a meditation retreat, one can adopt the view that one should not even think or talk. Then, at the end of the retreat, one returns to the world of daily life having gained little or no understanding about one's relationship to the sensory world. By itself, refraining from thinking and talking doesn't lead to a liberation that is Ultimate—not bound to time and place, here and now. We have to get beyond this very predicament of being bound to extremes that continually block out a careful investigation of our sensory experience. Having seen its ultimate pointlessness, it is from this very situation that one should be "going forth."

In this second picture, some of the highly evolved, yet ultimately

On a meditation retreat, one can adopt the view that one should not even think or talk. Then, at the end of the retreat, one returns to the world of daily life having gained little or no understanding about one's relationship to the sensory world.

endless, goings-on of the two extremes are suggested by the border of Celtic knot-work. The snakes (no *nagas*, these) coil around the heads of the characters typifying the two extremes, and face the words relating to them. On the left, the rather corpulent character is *kamasukhallikanuyogo*, sensual indulgence, gorging itself on a chicken drumstick, and featured with a made-up, decorative face. The other portrait is of a tortured ascetic, complete with thorns and anguish coming out of every pore. Above them is the *mudra* or hand gesture that signifies the turning of the Wheel of the Law, the *Dhammacakkappavattana mudra*. At the bottom is a conch which is used in Tibetan religious art as a symbol for the sending forth of the Dhamma.

The Buddha's proclamation of the Way that goes Beyond is at first indicated:

> *Ete te bhikkhave … nibbānāya saṁvattati.*
> Avoiding both these extremes, bhikkhus, the Middle Way that a Tathagata has Awakened to gives vision and insight knowledge, and leads to peace, profound understanding, full realization and to Nibbana.

Here, we should understand that the Buddha describes this not as *his* Way, but as an ancient Path that had become overgrown and lost. It is a Way that he Awakened to and discovered rather than created. Here, he refers to himself as one of the Tathagatas, a word that defies adequate translation. "Thus Gone" has to be stretched to include: Gone into the Thus-ness of Things—one who has seen things as they really are. Another of its implications is explained by the Buddha in a subsequent discourse:

> *Bhikkhus, as a Tathagata speaks, so he acts; as he acts, so he speaks. Therefore he is called a Tathagata.* (Anguttara Nikaya: [II], Four, 23)

So Tathagatas are those who say what is known through direct experience. Their teaching is an explanation of their own practice. And what are the characteristics of such a practice? They are referred to in a very broad scope which includes: "vision, insight knowledge, leading to peace, profound understanding, full realization and Nibbana." The Path encompasses all of these. The "middleness" of the Way implies a kind of balance. It offers the encouragement to see clearly in analytical and gnostic terms rather than reject or adhere to experience. And the results? Peacefulness and true understanding; Nibbana—the cooling of the fire, the calming of the wind, the settled quality and sensitivity of still water.

4

THE PATH BEYOND

Katamā ca sā ... sambodhāya nibbānāya saṃvattati.
And what is the Middle Way that a Tathagata has Awakened to, which gives vision ...
and leads to ... Nibbana? It is the Noble Eightfold Path—that is to say:
Right View, Right Intention, Right Speech, Right Action, Right Livelihood, Right Effort,
Right Mindfulness and Right Collectedness.
This is the Middle Way that a Tathagata has Awakened to.

The frames of the illuminations often come in a pair or triad that form a set, relating to each other in certain ways. The contents of this frame follow from the previous panel; this is what the "Middle Way" is about and how it can be defined in conventional terms. It also continues to approach human life broadly. Here, the Buddha is not formulating a particular set of beliefs or assumptions that you have to take on board before you can understand the teachings; he teaches in a way that is accessible to any religious Path. Coincidentally, at the time of creating these particular paintings, I was in the habit of visiting a small, rarely-used church near the monastery where I was living. The monastery was very busy with renovation work, and in my free time I would go to the nearby church to practice my chanting and meditate. I developed a great appreciation of the calm atmosphere, the simplicity and the sense of dedication within that tiny old church. Such things go beyond the beliefs of any one religion. Remembering this, I have framed the broad outlines of the Buddha's teaching with the window of the church.

The lotus is often used in Buddhist art as a symbol of purity, for the Path is one of purity—the purity of selflessness. The lotus arises from the mud of the ordinary earthbound mind and always turns towards the sun—to that which is higher than low or selfish feelings. In this way, it conveys the mood of the word *"ariyo"* meaning "noble," for nobility is the quality in us that rises above pettiness, selfishness and narrow-mindedness.

The different aspects of the Path are all characterized as *"samma,"* meaning "Right," "Perfect" or "Consummate." The Buddha is talking about following the principles of being "noble" in different aspects of life. The first factor, Right View (*sammaditthi*), is concerned with having a proper perspective on life. Right View places wisdom on an experiential, rather than abstract, foundation and is, in turn, the basis for Right Thought or Right Intention. The list continues with "Right"-ness in one's speech and action. It can be called "virtue." The last three factors relate to the direct practice of mind cultivation: *"vayamo"* (effort); *"sati"* (mindfulness) and *"samadhi"* (collectedness, concentration). These are most often cultivated through formal meditation exercises.

Wisdom, virtue and meditation can be reference points for anyone on the spiritual path. Together they present a complete and integrated approach. Various religions or different ways of cultivating the mind may emphasize one aspect or another. For example, some religions place a great stress on morality and conventions with promises of heavenly rewards for those who obey, and punishment for those who don't. Such attitudes often omit and may even reject the possibility for personal reflection. Unguided by wisdom, moral commandments lead to fundamentalism with the intolerance, repression and blinkered conceit that it brings about.

A subtler attachment to virtue is the belief that if you just keep performing good actions, such as ritual offerings to gods, then this in itself will get you somewhere without any further work on the mind. This affects Buddhism too. In Buddhist countries, there's a very strong feeling about accumulating "merit" by making offerings to monks or temples. This has a certain truth in it, and was even acknowledged by the Buddha: generosity is a sign of a selfless heart—a great blessing to the world. Unfortunately, the idea of "gaining merit" can substitute for true selflessness, and make one feel that no further cultivation is necessary. So the Buddha always pointed out that the highest kind of merit, even greater than giving alms to a Buddha, was to cultivate meditation properly.

> *Fruitful as the act of giving is … yet it is still more fruitful to go with confident heart for Refuge to the Buddha, the Dhamma and the Sangha and determine the five moral precepts. … Fruitful though that is, yet it is still more fruitful to maintain loving-kindness for the period of time that it takes to milk a cow. … Fruitful though that is, it is still more fruitful to maintain awareness of impermanence for only as long as a finger-snap.* (Anguttara Nikaya: [V], Nines, 20)

At the other extreme are those who don't bother with any morality or conventions, and think that they can become enlightened just through sitting in meditation. This is more common in the West. People can get really obsessive about having the right conditions to SIT in, and yet pay no attention to selfless actions, kindness or sense restraint. Meditation becomes motivated by the need for self-affirmation, a drive to attain *samadhi,* experience bliss or remodel oneself. That's the meditation fanatic's attitude! However, a steady and sensitive mind leads to proper understanding and right conduct in daily life. So the Buddha always related meditation, not to ecstatic trances or complex abstractions, but to good sense that would manifest in mundane, as well as transcendent, terms.

Then again, wisdom itself can be developed to the point where it loses contact with reality, as in the case of metaphysics. Philosophy and theology rely heavily upon intellectual understanding yet fall short in the development of wisdom through attention to actual experience. So having a mind full of ideas does not necessarily grant one any clearer perspective on how to live one's life. Even with proper wisdom and virtue, without the assiduous practice of inner contemplation that meditation exercises make possible, one is sowing good seeds but is not tasting the fruit.

If, individually, no single aspect of the spiritual path is conducive to "peace, profound understanding and full realization," where is the Way? It is broader and yet more exacting than any of these possibilities:

> *I do not say that you can attain purity by views, traditions, insight, morality or conventions; nor will you attain purity without these. But by using them for abandonment, rather than as positions to hold onto, you will come to be at peace without the need to be anything.* (Sutta Nipata: [V], 848)

The Middle Way, that is, the Eightfold Path, is the balance and counterbalance of all the spiritual fundamentals. It summarizes the ways in which one cultivates a spiritual path and then qualifies that with the reminder that the Path is to be cultivated in ways that are "Right." Consider that bland prefix, "Right." *"Samma"* means "whole" or "complete." It means ways that are not partial, biased or self-oriented, but ways that are of benefit to others as well as to oneself. *"Samma"* conveys a whole, balanced feeling. This is the "rightness" that is noble rather than perfectionist; and—to consider another meaning of noble—it is also an indication of something rare. If we practice meditation with wrong view, we will always remain obsessed with ourselves—trying to cultivate something for ourselves or simply be mesmerized by a particular problem, vice or virtue. Meditation is not an answer in itself; we need the guidance to ward off the obsessiveness that accumulates around anything that is seen in personal terms. To abandon self-conscious drives and ambitions without abandoning the practice requires skill. How can I, an unawakened worldling with a head full of noise, acquire that skill?

How to find that right balance is explained in the subsequent teaching—a teaching that the Buddha said was peculiar to fully enlightened beings. And it's based upon something that *everybody* knows about.

Meditation is not an answer in itself; we need the guidance to ward off the obsessiveness that accumulates around anything that is seen in personal terms.

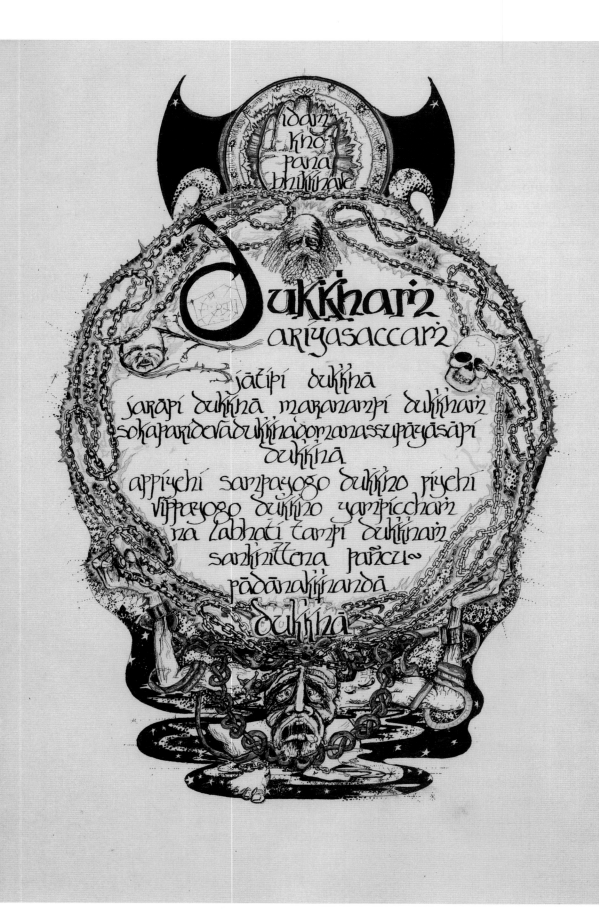

5

THE FIRST NOBLE TRUTH:
Having To Hold On Is Suffering

The Buddha then goes on to expound the Four Noble Truths, the centre-piece of his teaching. They are central because they point to a universal human experience: a feeling of lack in our lives. At times, we feel a sense of need, or lack, or dissatisfaction that can vary from mild weariness to utter despair. This can be triggered off by physical feelings, or by mental impressions concerning ourselves or other beings. It is characterized by feeling there is not enough. Even if we are physically well and mentally skilled, we can feel disappointed that life isn't offering us enough, or we are not making enough of it or doing enough; or that there's not enough time, space and freedom. We can feel anxiety over the state of the planet and the environment; our perceptions of the present and the future are not secure and problem-free. Even "too much" means not having enough space, future and ease. The list is endless. Just reflect upon your activities and pursuits: notice that there is a constant effort to change or cope with what is disagreeable, or to stimulate well-being. This is universal.

It is worthwhile considering that, however altruistic one's actions are, the *feeling* of unsatisfactoriness is the same. This feeling is what the Buddha called *dukkha* — and fittingly, there just isn't a satisfactory English word to cover its meaning. Dukkha is not an objective physical reality such as disease and famine. Sometimes having little is fine or even peaceful; at other times, we can feel devastated that there's a stain on the dining-room tablecloth. Just to get in touch with that feeling is an entrance to the spiritual realm, because it provides a reference point to where and how the experiences of life are actually affecting us. We may assume that we are beings guided by rational principles, but we only choose to be rational when that cool and objective mode suits us. What drives us, what we find pleasing, inspiring, worthwhile (and the reverse) is calibrated in a different zone of the psyche. To get in touch with that other zone is essential if one wants to live in an undeluded way.

By pointing at dukkha, the Buddha highlights a fundamental that we may have only glimpsed or seen as related to a particular set of circumstances. He is not implying that life is miserable; most things have a mixture of pleasure and pain and neutrality in them. However, there is a constant restless quality of disquiet. With happiness, there is an undertone of wanting more of it, holding onto it or even continuing to stimulate it; because by itself, it changes. And when the source of happiness passes, we begin to feel bored or dissatisfied, and seek out something else. If we don't find it, we feel much worse.

Life does have its dark side, it can be painful at times; but we can make it more painful for ourselves, psychologically and emotionally, by wanting the happiness to last, or the painful aspects never to manifest. But even the most acute pain and fear can be borne. We can actually practice with pain; we can work with it; we can become serene through it. What is really painful is the mental perception that you can't bear it for another moment. You can see this without having acute pain. Just with life being the way it is, things go wrong and the mind will feel, "Why should this happen to me?" When you feel sick, thoughts may arise saying, "Why should I have to put up with this? I wanted to do something, and this has spoiled it all." Or: "The weather's not very good, and it's ruined my day." Or: "Why do you have to say things like that, you know how that hurts me!" This kind of suffering goes on and on. We never seem to be able to get rid of it in normal activities, regardless of where we go, and no matter what we do. Trying to avoid being blamed, losing one's job or disappointing others can lead people to states of extreme stress and nervous breakdown. Then, even if our personal situation is not causing us any anxiety, we are still aware of the suffering of others.

For many of us, the urge to take on spiritual practice arises through recognizing that whatever we do, wherever we go, this mood prevails; and it even follows us into spiritual practice! I've seen this myself: being in a quiet place and living as a meditating monk not having to worry about anything, I could feel irritated at a frog croaking: "Why do there have to

Dukkha is not an objective physical reality such as disease and famine. Sometimes having little is fine or even peaceful; at other times, we can feel devastated that there's a stain on the dining-room tablecloth.

be frogs croaking, why don't they shut up—and stop disturbing me!" It's not a deliberate intended response—it's an instinctive reaction. So we feel that that's the way we are, and the possibility for change, even if we wish to change, seems remote. Habits and instincts define our identity, and that's where dukkha gnaws more deeply into our hearts.

It's important to understand that the Buddha's teaching separates the dukkha that we experience because of the way life apparently is from the dukkha that is created emotionally from not wanting things to be that way, or from assuming that life is wretched. As is pointed out in this Sutta, things change, and change can be effected without the naivete that assumes that solutions are going to be permanently satisfactory or the pessimism that assumes that it's all hopeless. The Buddha taught dukkha *and* the cessation of dukkha. The particulars of unpleasant circumstances can come to an end or be brought to an end, even if problems then surface in other areas. Accepting that life has its dark, problematic side needn't be depressing. Most fruitfully, the kind of suffering that is the mental reaction to a situation, even on an instinctive plane, can be completely abolished. With the ending of that kind of suffering, the mind is clearer and wiser, and more capable of effecting positive change in the world of ever-changing circumstances.

The Buddha talked about dukkha in a succession of examples that begin with the way life appears, and then take us into the heart of the matter—firstly with how we respond, and then with what we take ourselves to be:

> *Idaṁ kho pana bhikkhave ... yampicchaṁ na labhati tampi dukkhaṁ*
> Bhikkhus, there is this Noble Truth about dissatisfaction. Birth is problematic; aging is hard; dying is also hard to bear. Sorrow, lamentation, pain, grief and despair are all painful. Association with what you dislike is unpleasant; being apart from what you like is unpleasant; not getting what you want is unpleasant.

To illustrate this, I have drawn the picture of the Buddha's hand raised in the *mudra* or gesture of teaching. Underneath it, an anguished person is carrying a mass of blazing chains. These are looped in a repetitive pattern that forms a circle linking up a baby, an old man and a skull. To add to his suffering, two snakes wind themselves around the arms and neck of the struggling being.

How is birth problematic or suffering? Well, giving birth is physically painful; and also birth is appearance into an uncertain realm. Notice how babies suffer: coming into the world must be a desperate and frightening experience. For the majority of beings, including people in the world today, it means the end of guaranteed nourishment, and the beginning of the struggle to survive. Even for the small percentage of privileged humans in affluent societies, with birth begins a life of physical discomfort and the need to sustain or defend what has been born. Yet the obvious long- or short-term consequence of birth is death. It leads not to an eventual high, but to an unavoidable decline. So whatever the joy, there is an element of suffering or stress arising sooner or later because of birth.

... the obvious long- or short-term consequence of birth is death. It leads not to an eventual high, but to an unavoidable decline.

23

Then there is what we can make of birth: birth is the unfulfilled; and it seeks fulfillment. So birth is the beginning of need, a mood that accompanies anything that arises which we attach to.

When something new arises in one's life, if it's pleasant and wished for, there is happiness—and the need to sustain it, or the wish not to be parted from it. When something beautiful to behold arises, how long can you continue to be thrilled by it? A few minutes? Can you make it through an hour before it starts to pall? How about a day, let alone a year? Of course, we live with many options. If we get bored with looking at the painting, read something; when that becomes boring, go for a walk, visit a friend, go out for dinner together, watch a movie; if this routine gets tedious, regress into your past life, astral travel; then write a book about it … and so on. All these are more births, or as the Buddha put it, *birth*—the same habit taking different forms. But that new birth is suffering too, because sooner or later we meet with another obstacle, another disappointment, or we tire of the whole merry-go-round. High-option cultures just give you a few more spins on the wheel.

The sheer momentum of birth after birth has its disquieting aspects too: you can only be born into one thing at a time—are you sure you're doing the right thing? Maybe you're missing out on a really great opportunity somewhere else. Then these multiple options become a strain. Can you develop shamanism, play classical guitar, study ecology and cybernetics, have a successful fulfilling relationship with your partner, your parents and relatives, and your children, come to a mature understanding of the political arena, grow your own organic food and hold down a suitable job working with the right kinds of people for the right ends, all at the same time? It's a lot to keep going, isn't it? But if any of these go wrong or if you miss out on a really fulfilling experience, you're likely to feel disappointed or personally to blame, so cram it in and hold on tight!

Jara is the aging process, this means maturing—not only just getting old. Growing up is unsatisfactory because you start to get affected by all the stuff of a confused world. There's a lot said nowadays about having been emotionally, let alone physically, damaged as a child. Is there anybody who

> **Birth is the unfulfilled; and it seeks fulfillment. So birth is the beginning of need.**

hasn't been damaged—by their parents, their uncle, their school or their dog? Then what about falling under the influence of social prejudice, competitive behavior patterning, sexism, racism ... whatever happened to our childhood innocence? Scarred and stained by something sooner or later, isn't it? Psychologically one starts to develop instincts and habits, and even good habits blunt the joyful wonder of childhood consciousness.

Our habits prescribe the way we relate to others, and of course model our own future. This habitual activity is what is called kamma.* Its key feature is that its effects don't die away when the action is completed; it actually changes how we will perceive things and act—it moulds our identity. Through the workings of kamma, our own good and bad actions of body and speech affect ourselves and others. Life offers many opportunities to create good kamma, through actions of kindness for example; however, even good kamma creates an identity which can become moralizing, or is constantly needing to do something, and hasn't transcended the experience of pain, separation from the loved, and death.

We are born into a kammic predicament in which everything affects everything else. So our own traumas and problems get perpetuated in others. As we recognize what effect others may have on us, our relationships become guarded, or take on the form of manipulating or being manipulated by fellow humans. Many people would cherish a totally trustworthy harmonious relationship, but that's not going to be possible until each individual finds harmony within. So people like to hold onto a few safeguards, and have a few alternatives in mind in case this one doesn't work out.

But having to live with feelings of insecurity, and an inability to commit oneself, is also far from blissful. So you see a therapist who might tell you that, yes, you do have some problems. Because of this, you decide to have a course of counselling—which can be a pretty painful experience and hard on the pocket. And meanwhile, as you grow up, you are saturated with the woes and horrors of the media, disillusioned by humanity, depressed by global warming. No-one can take too much despair, so you seek out some place or someone or some habit to absorb into, just to limit the amount of stuff you have to be sensitive to. It's a shame that, even then, the body, with its needs and illnesses, doesn't leave you alone ... then there are the medical bills ... so you bluff your way into a meaningless job, and get some insurance (if you are in a society where such things exist); anyway, hold on ... because here comes *maranam*, death.

Death and dying generally involve a certain amount of pain and degradation; and grieving. We imagine that death only happens to older people, but that's not true—human beings are always surrounded by forces of destruction that can terminate their lives at any moment. Life involves a lot of stressful holding on, even for ducks and squirrels, let alone for human beings who have surrounded themselves with, or invented, fire,

---

* The Sanskrit form of the word—"karma"—is more common, but can be confused with the Vedic view on karma which has a "predestined" slant to it.

electricity, cars, and *lots* of weapons. These are all created to make our lives more secure. The fear of death, or even of discomfort, actually fills our lives with potentially deadly things.

According to the Buddha's usage, death may also refer to the disappearance of any mental or physical experience. When something pleasant ends, we can feel sad; or, if it wasn't too important, we can remember it and form some kind of view or opinion about it. When it's something you've done, like these paintings, you can feel critical of them; or, maybe if you have no criticisms, then it sets up a pattern of expectation for the next painting, or for someone else's painting. This can happen with anything that you've done; you think back on it and always see its flaws. Alternatively, if it was something you enjoyed doing and now it is finished—that also brings an unhappy feeling, a feeling of longing or nostalgia. Death is the ending of the known and the familiar. So when we come to the end of something, we reach out for something new to hold onto. For example, after the meal, we can go for a walk, or maybe have a rest, or there's conversation in which we can bring back the pleasant past, or plan for a pleasant future, or create and sustain a pleasant present. All that is the movement towards birth. And birth is the opportunity to go through this whole dukkha one more time …

… because each birth is about getting what is pleasing, getting away from what we don't like and fulfilling our desires. This involves a lot of stressful reaching out, holding, jealousy, possessiveness and defensiveness. We could try to get away from it all, become a hermit say … or maybe meditation would be the way to stop these desires and possessiveness … only to find out that that is another wish to get away from what is no longer pleasant. So after the trip to India, the three month retreat, we've had enough of that, what is wanted now is the "integration into daily life," "sharing with another being" or becoming a teacher. And those same old instincts crop up again in different forms. Birth is pretty deluding: it always looks like a fresh thing until we've learned to look at that feeling in the heart—the same old compulsive drives, needs, holding on … suffering. Frustrating, isn't it?

A few important words finish this section of the Sutta:

> *Saṅkhittena pañcupādānakkhandhā dukkhā.*
> In brief, the five grasped aggregates are unsatisfactory.

This sums up what has been said before about dukkha, but it does so in a significant way. The five khandhas represent the classification by which the Buddha, perhaps following the terminology of the time, analyzed the *experience* of life. The word khandha is translated as "aggregate" (meaning a "heap"), because the khandhas are categories or groups of phenomena heaped together for the sake of reference. It should be remembered that they have only conventional reality. The khandhas are: form (*rupa*), feeling (*vedana*), perception (*sañña*), mind formations (*sankhara*) and sense consciousness (*viññana*). I'll explain those terms in more detail later; what the list implies is—everything.

Death is the ending of the known and the familiar. So when we come to the end of something, we reach out for something new to hold onto.

The principle at work here is not one of physical science. Rational science has dominated Western ways of perception and activity, and, despite its technical brilliance, has created a gap between the observer and a universe from which he or she feels separate. The intuitive sense of connection with the universe (which is the root meaning of the word "religion") is thereby lost. This has led to all kinds of disorders of the repressed intuitive faculties. The analysis of the five khandhas begins with the understanding (as of science after Einstein) that we are only observing our *experience* of the universe. There is no separation; our perceptions and state of consciousness are aspects of the raw material of the experienced universe.

Things are experienced in terms of their form (*rupa*)—this khandha is made up of four ways in which matter "behaves." Matter is experienced in terms of its ability to extend and have size (symbolized as earth), to stick together and have shape (symbolized as water), to have the possibility of movement (symbolized as air) and to be measured in terms of temperature (symbolized as fire). What things *are* we don't know: thousands of years of more refined and complex definitions in terms of elements, atoms, particles, subatomic particles and quarks has created a richer classification, but is no nearer to Absolute Truth. And for most people, these scientific definitions are mind-boggling; they are not accessible in terms of direct experience. Earth, water, air and fire *are*, and for the sake of proper relationships within the Universe, they are adequate. As always, the Buddha used systems and conceptual truth only for the purpose of directing the mind towards Ultimate Truth—the experience of Nibbana, enlightenment. And in terms of the practice of liberation, most of the work we need to do is on the forces that bind us. For this reason, coming to some manageable definitions of the Universe is all that is necessary.

Things are experienced in terms of mental or physical feeling (*vedana*) which may be painful, pleasant or neutral. *Vedana* is no more specific than this. As with form, there are many further ways in which one can describe feeling, but this classification gives you a simple way of understanding how things affect you. In the process of cognition, first of all there is a feeling, which attracts attention, and then a perception arises. Perception (*sañña*) means the way in which you recognize something: as dark or light, hostile, familiar, human, emotional … whatever. The analysis points out that things are *interpreted* swiftly, and it is on this interpretation that mental impulses and attitudes (*sankhara*) are founded. Fashion, cosmetics, advertisements and propaganda are notable examples of how perceptions are created; *sañña* is the image-maker. And examples of *sañña* in operation are: we mistrust some people because of the way they move, detest "creepy" spiders, adore "cuddly" furry creatures like cats, and buy a soft drink because of the shape of the bottle or because we saw a commercial with some good-looking people drinking it on a beach.

Consciousness (*viññana*) is that which makes phenomena present for us. It is sixfold, that is, eye-consciousness, ear-consciousness, olfactory-, taste-, touch- and mind-consciousness. The phenomena

The analysis of the five khandhas begins with the understanding (as of science after Einstein) that we are only observing our experience of the universe.

27

that arise dependent on mind-consciousness (i.e., thoughts, emotions, perceptions) we call "mental," the "inner" world; things arising because of the other five aspects of sense-consciousness, we call "physical," the "external" world. However, in the analysis of the Buddha, this division is not so absolute. In fact, in his teaching, he often makes a point of overriding this apparent division by referring to "any feeling, mental or physical" or "contemplating things internally and externally." This is because the teaching does not discriminate between what appears as mind and what appears as matter; it comes from understanding the experience of all things—and that occurs within the matrix of the sixfold sense consciousness and its designations:

> *That by which one is conscious of the world, by which one has conceit of the world— that is called 'world' ... And through what is one conscious of the world? Through what has one conceit of the world? Through the eye, the ear, the nose, the tongue, the body and the mind....* (Samyutta Nikaya: [IV], Sense, Worldly Sense, 3)

These five khandhas are described as "grasped aggregates" or "categories" and not as causing suffering, but as suffering itself. They are also seen as equivalent to birth, aging, death and desire. Grasping is a vivid metaphor for what we otherwise term "attachment;" it means that something is held as permanent or absolute which is actually not that way. When one is attached to cigarettes for example, they become an absolute necessity in life. You always have to have a pack with you. However, in reality, cigarettes are not necessary. So what, then, is the attachment involved with these aggregates that makes them unsatisfactory?

For a lifetime, at least, we are endowed with aspects of sense-consciousness, perceptions and mind stuff. They certainly appear to be a real foundation for what we are. Is the Buddha implying that we shouldn't experience these, that as long as these aggregates are manifesting, we will suffer? Well, no. The Buddha points out that *holding* onto these is suffering; in other words, grasping and believing in the thoughts of the mind, and the perceptions that arise; or grasping and believing that the sensory appearance of the world is Ultimate Reality—will always take you to dissatisfaction, and even to despair. Thoughts and perceptions are notoriously unreliable; people can believe in the craziest ideas and assumptions about the nature of the world, life after death, men, women, and God; not to mention their continually biased perceptions about ordinary daily life.

Moreover, even the most innocuous thoughts and perceptions, when attached to, give rise to the experience of being separate from the world; an "inner being" is inferred who thinks and feels and perceives. Why are our opinions and attitudes so important to us? How about form? Have you ever felt self-conscious about the form of your body, or winced when somebody called you fat or thin? And yet is form really what you are?

Is that almost incessant babble of thoughts or the ups and downs of the emotions your true nature? Yet we worry about them, defend them and will motivate our lives around them. Why? Because our whole sense of personal existence is based upon clinging to these five aggregates as our inner being, our self. Although this "inner being" can never be located, and is really just a mood created by attachment to the khandhas, it is held to be the author of thoughts and feelings, the owner and senior incumbent within the body, the director and controller of the senses. Once an identity gets created around the khandhas, we expect fulfillment from them. We instinctively assume that we will find fulfillment in our own bodily form or in someone else's; or in feelings that are pleasing, stimulating or soothing; or in great views and ideas; or out of some combination of all these as they manifest in sense consciousness. And although we always fail to do so, we feel that this is just a temporary fault in the system, just an unlucky break — or that it is our fault. In the West, guilt and shame are more common aspects of self-view than pride. We feel there is something wrong with us if we are not able to be fulfilled in the sensory world because we believe that we should be.

We may feel that somehow we have to get ourselves out of this predicament, but when we are the predicament, how to get out?

Thereby, we can fall into the two extremes of, on the one hand, naive optimism (things will work out all right in the end) or, on the other, despairing pessimism (I'm getting a bad deal, or, I'm a loser). In between those two we drift — blaming others and asserting ourselves, blaming the society and defending ourselves, or blaming ourselves and worshipping others. We may feel that somehow we have to get ourselves out of this predicament, but when we *are* the predicament, how to get out? This endless going-on, this *samsara*, is called grasping at the five aggregates as self. It is suffering; check it out for yourself.

Then consider when you see a newborn baby, who is born? Is it a man, a woman, a kind sensitive soul, a burden on the earth's resources, an element of the divine, another mouth to feed or what? And when someone dies? Who is that? And in between that, is it your friend, your peer, someone you yearn for, someone who disgusts you, or nobody special? Something is there, but all that we designate as the being (whether it is ourselves or someone else) is the arising and ceasing of these five aggregates affected by birth, aging and death, and by the attitudes of the society (which hasn't got past suffering and grasping either).

As with the man at the bottom of the picture, the twin experiences of suffering and grasping coil like serpents around our arms (symbolizing activities) and head (which represents views and perceptions). What we hold onto, what the mind perceives as self and the "apparent" real world to be protected from, are the very positions and habits that make up the experience of suffering. What if we didn't hold onto those chains — would they still burn and bind? There is the possibility, as the Buddha realized and tried to exemplify and explain, to live with this process of the five aggregates without attachment — without seeing self in the processes of birth, aging and death. And with that clarity there is the end of all sorrow and a realization of an Ultimate Truth beyond grasping. Whoever understands where and what dukkha really is, is on the Path to that realization.

6

THE SECOND NOBLE TRUTH:
Getting Burned

Circles can be peaceful, but they can also be vicious when they represent, as these do, the regenerative aspect of the suffering that they describe. In the last frame, the man holds onto his chains which are symbolic of the world of the five aggregates. The more he feels burdened by it, the harder he holds on, imagining all the while that, by this effort, he is preventing himself from being overwhelmed. The circle in this picture is fire, and its repetitive cycle is caused by the three forms of desire rooted in self (*tanha*). These three desires chase each other in circles and are preoccupied with trying to eliminate each other. This is represented by the three violent creatures emanating from the central fire. The monkey at the bottom symbolizes the untrained mind that always darts hither and thither, and the hand at the top, as in the last painting, is the hand of the Buddha held in the symbolic teaching gesture (*mudra*). The little vignettes in the loops of fire I'll explain later.

If you felt dismayed by the First Noble Truth but were determined to get to the heart of the matter, as was the case with those five bhikkhus, you're probably ready to go through the fire of the Second Noble Truth, which is about the origin of suffering and, by inference, of grasping. The Buddha points out:

> *Idaṁ kho pana bhikkhave ... kāmataṇhā, bhavataṇhā, vibhavataṇhā.*
> Bhikkhus, there is the Noble Truth of the Origin of Suffering. It is desire, which gives rise to fresh birth, bound up with relish and passion, running here and there, delighting in this and in that: in other words, sense desire, desire for existing and desire for extinction.

First of all, I'm going to say something about *tanha,* generally translated as "desire." These translations are difficult, because the words don't exactly correspond to the same meaning in the two languages. Dukkha is almost impossible to catch in a single word, khandha doesn't mean much as an aggregate, and *tanha* as desire gives rise to some misinterpretations. What about the desire to realize Truth, is that suffering? Actually *tanha* means "thirst," and, as the context explains, is purely the kind of desire that wants something for *me.* At another time, the Buddha defined *tanha* simply as:

> *Desire for sights, sounds, for fragrance, for tastes, for things to touch, for ideas.*
> (Samyutta Nikaya: [II], Cause, Buddha, 2)

Tanha, then, is the desire that pulls things inwards, not the desire that radiates out—like aspiration or compassion. These are all aspects of spiritual Truth; it is a Truth that cannot be grasped selfishly. In fact, you could summarize spiritual training as the transformation of selfish desire into selfless desire, zest and aspiration. The desire that acts as a motivation to know how things really are, beyond the grasp of the gratification instinct, is the needed vigor to carry one through the rough patches. So it's important that, in abandoning the fantasized and deluded objects of desire, one doesn't sink into an apathetic fatalism; or into believing that the putting forth of energy in spiritual practice is another form of craving. Then consider the following reflection: isn't the desire to extinguish desire an aspect of the desire for extinction? Sometimes you wish you didn't have any desires, and feel really depressed by the inability to get rid of them— that's suffering, isn't it? When it comes down to it, a lot of the gratification instinct is about *getting rid* of itchy, hankering feelings.

Simply to recognize that suffering arises is the beginning of opening the mind to a deeper understanding.

The First Noble Truth seems to say that life is suffering; but more accurately, it states that there is a range of feelings that we have to bear with through the experiences of birth, aging and death. This is experienced as suffering as long as the way things *appear* to us is taken as an absolute truth. The heart of the matter is that life is not a flawed experience; rather it is made that way by an unconscious activity of the mind. We don't realize that we're doing it: we're simply not aware at the level of the mind where the activity is born. These two Truths (and a good deal of Buddhist mind training) help to focus our attention deeper in our heart so that we can stop the seeds of suffering from being planted.

Suffering arises, it has an origin. We can recognize that the feeling of emotional dissatisfaction begins; we were feeling pretty good, and then—we got offended, or the good time came to an end. In a little while, we feel upset or we hanker after some new way of enjoying ourselves. The fact that the arising of suffering can be noticed means that it arises from something other than suffering, and that there is something other than suffering that notices it. Whatever arises has a cause, is created. Simply to recognize that suffering arises is the beginning of opening the mind to a deeper understanding.

If we neither contemplate suffering nor wish to understand it, suffering is not so noticeable. Instead of looking at it, we keep shifting away from it to absorb into something else. This is the birth habit I mentioned earlier. But what that causes is an underlying sense of dis-ease, denial, and even cynicism in the psyche—the "get it while you can!" syndrome. A natural state of joy or contentment is considered impossible, and happiness arises only when we have our security, our creature comforts, our best friends. Then we say, "I don't suffer, life is great!" At such times—which we assume to be the norm—we easily forget our frequent disappointments and irritations, or try to ease the chafing of life with some balm of comfort or bluff heartiness. Also we unconsciously assume that calamities won't occur—that our partner won't get run down by a truck or that our child won't be crippled by disease. Most incredible of all, something in us is shocked by death: we still feel that sickness, death, betrayals, breakdowns and failures are an outrageous deviation from the smooth flow of life. This is what the Buddha called "unknowing" or *avijja*—the mind's contraction to a level where the full range of birth's potential is not accepted. Although this *avijja* is a buffer that the psyche uses to protect itself from suffering, it actually drives the dukkha deeper into our hearts, affecting our ability to be open and easeful with life.

For example, what happens when we try to recover from suffering? We often find something else to distract our minds; or perhaps we repress the pain. During a lifetime of many small disappointments, betrayals, threats and the rest, we develop a tough skin over our sensitivity, and a feeling that happiness is something we have to seek out. Eventually, there is so much hide protecting the heart that the innate joy of being alive becomes inaccessible. Many people would not even guess that happiness is an innate state of being, independent of circumstances. The Buddha found that happiness in the purity of his heart, and called that innate purity of being the Unconditioned. It is unconditioned because it is not dependent on conditions and one who realizes that experiences Nibbana, the highest happiness.

But for the average person, happiness is dependent on circumstances. They don't see suffering—because they have created the circumstances to avoid it. But the avoidance of suffering is not the cessation of suffering. Suffering remains a distinct possibility, and we take every step to prevent it. We tend to settle for guarded security. However, that too is suffering—the defensiveness and anxiety that someone might rob or attack us; or that

If we neither contemplate suffering nor wish to understand it, suffering is not so noticeable. Instead of looking at it, we keep shifting away from it to absorb into something else. This is the birth habit …

some insidious virus might be gnawing its way through our immune system. The average comfortable Westerner living with material adequacy is still always prone to anxiety: the possibility of losing one's partner, one's job, one's health, one's standing in the community, one's dignity or sense of well-being. When our happiness is dependent on a fragile tissue of circumstance, no-one can afford to relax and be at ease. Societies where people have a lot of opportunities and possibilities for pleasure are generally frantic, anxious or neurotic. And people who depend on fortunate conditions for their happiness become quite selfish and deluded, refusing to accept that there might have to be some constraint on how they use the planet, their bodies or other people. The right to pursue one's own happiness easily gets distorted into the right to do whatever turns you on, no matter what the effects might be on others; the right to use as much of the earth's resources as one likes, to have whatever one wants immediately and live a life of ever-renewing pleasure and vitality. Just as for an alcoholic, the gratification of desire only leads to more and more thirst, not to its quenching. That's the circle of fire, and it often begins with a pleasant, warm glow.

By our inability to relate and respond wisely to the down side of life, or even to accept that it might exist, we have taken dukkha deep into ourselves and buried it there—where it is difficult to extract. From not living in accordance with the changing rhythm of life, from expecting it always to be bright and positive, we create a spectre that haunts the heart, and affects the ways we view and live our lives. We make dukkha an ultimate truth that we run away from for as long as we can, by absorbing ourselves into the up side of the sensory world. But we can't commit ourselves for too long to any one thing because, like the waves of the sea, the sensory world has its down side. And remember the sensory world is a lot more than beer and parties: now we have all kinds of refined things to watch or taste, and the mind especially offers a vast potential for sensory enjoyment. There are so many things one can study, though this is hardly considered a sensory activity. But in the Buddhist analysis it is; we delight in intriguing ideas or in being aroused by tales of stirring adventure. Then again, one can alter one's consciousness completely with drugs. So the sensory world allows us to get absorbed into many states—into each of which we are propelled by kamma or volition, and each is experienced as the arising of the five khandhas. They are *births*—we experience "being born" into the sensory realm. And since we do it over and over again, no birth satisfies us for very long.

We try to become something in order to feel that we are making progress. This is another kind of thirst: it is the desire for existing or "becoming" as it is also translated. This means the desire for some "position" in the temporal or spatial world that consciousness projects. We "feel" ourselves to be immaterial things regarding experience, affected by it, even imperilled by it. And we seek to become in control of, or able to understand and direct, the life experience. "Becoming" is very powerful:

we do things now so that we can "be" in a better situation in the future. We study in order to qualify for a good job, to have a stable family life, or to have love and security and an adequate supply of sensory happiness. This is reasonable enough; but it often entails overriding the experience of the present. People work themselves hard and become very stressed chasing the dream of ease in the future. And the amount of stress that one undergoes in order to achieve one's goals makes it necessary to raise the expectations of what the future will provide.

People do certainly lie and cheat to get ahead, and after years of cheating and manipulating others, may feel disappointed that life doesn't live up to their expectations. How can it? There are the laws of cause and effect (*kamma-vipaka*) at work, and they operate according to the state of your intentions and actions. The way you act in the present determines how you're going to feel and the kind of situations you'll tend to find yourself with in the future. If you are an aggressive unscrupulous go-getter, you'll associate with the kind of people who fit into that way of operating. Naturally enough, such companionship will reinforce the drive to get something in the future. And the stress. The aggressiveness comes back to your own mind and body — until you find yourself "born" into an untrustworthy circle of associates, an ulcer or a coronary. This is how becoming leads to birth.

The process of becoming operates on a subtler level than big business competitiveness or desire for fame. The "inner self" that is the experience of becoming projects values and wishes onto everything. Notice when doing a mundane chore that the attitude is frequently one of wanting to get it done, wanting to have finished it in order to be peaceful, to relax or to enjoy oneself … That, too, is dukkha. Rushing along to get to the next moment, we fail to open and appreciate this moment. The laws of kamma are that if you operate in that way in this moment, the same momentum takes you through the next moment, coloring your awareness of the present with its moods and perceptions. You want to go to a show, so you hastily take a shower, change your clothes, abruptly cut off a friend who just phoned, leap into the car, find out that you left the keys in your other jacket, rush back to the house, trip over the dog in the hallway … the scenario proceeds to the traffic jam, the lost temper, the minor accident, and then finding out that the show has been cancelled anyway — which was what your friend was phoning you up to tell you. Just notice, a mind filled with desire does not appreciate *anything.* And most people hardly investigate the quality of the present moment, because as a sensory experience, it may be nothing special. However, to one who cultivates attention to the present, in whatever form the present moment takes, the mind begins to reveal its treasures: sensitivity, joy, confidence and serenity.

When we get tired of running around and sensory stimulation, then the third kind of desire operates: the desire for extinction. These terms are not to be taken as absolutes. They apply to mind movements that may be momentary or only vaguely perceived. *Vibhavatanha* is the desire to get rid

Notice when doing a mundane chore that the attitude is frequently one of wanting to get it done, wanting to have finished it in order to be peaceful, to relax or to enjoy oneself … That, too, is dukkha.

of something, to get out of it all. This is often a repressive influence, or simply an attitude of not wanting to be bothered: "I don't want to see this." It is also that force in us that denies our pain and sorrow, or makes us want to annihilate ourselves in sleep, drugs or with suicide. It often results from the other two forms of desire: if they are followed blindly, they leave us in states of mind that we dislike and therefore avoid being aware of. So we try to annihilate that awareness, even if it means destroying ourselves. What people don't realize is that *vibhavatanha* leads to birth too; birth in a negative state of repression or self-denial in this world—or in another life.

These three motivating influences of desire continue to operate on subtler levels of activity too. Even with a spiritual inclination, the mind can be motivated by the desire to get out of it all—*vibhavatanha*. The desire for spiritual attainment can be a form of *bhavatanha*—desire to become—when it is to enhance one's self-image, even just in one's own eyes. This can actually hinder and bar progress towards purification of the mind by making one unwilling to fully understand the various unenlightened habits that one has to work through.

Sense desire (*kamatanha*) in terms of spiritual aims, is the desire for refined and blissful states of mind to absorb into: sit padded up with an elaborate system of cushions (so that you won't have to be aware of bodily feeling) in a retreat centre where nobody bothers you and there's no untoward sensory impingement. Then … use a meditation technique that gets you into a state of absorption and cruise on refined mind states for a while. This doesn't always work for Westerners who have such overstimulated minds that to get them to quieten down through withdrawal often requires such manipulation and stressful effort that it is self-defeating. Being thwarted in this way, they then have the chance to develop insight into the Four Noble Truths by investigating suffering and realizing the wisdom that goes beyond desire.

The mind moves extremely fast, and desire creates so much movement that it is difficult to see what is really going on. Sometimes desires augment each other: you want to become something so that you will have more happiness on the sensory plane; you want to get rid of your habits so that you will become a more productive human being; you would like to have a really comfortable meditation cushion so that you can become a wiser, more compassionate being. Sometimes they fight with each other: I want to get rid of my disgusting sensual appetites, or maybe I should get into beer and T.V. to get rid of my attachment to purity, and show that I'm not obsessed with becoming enlightened. And so on … *I want*. This is the way it is. Such is the promotion of suffering.

Notice that the Buddha makes no moral judgement here. He does not tell you not to be this way or to cut it out; in fact, he doesn't say you are that way. He just says that there are these energies at work. Remember, the First Noble Truth points to the suffering which arises from grasping existence in terms of self. As soon as you start saying you are this way, and you should be another way, self-desire has slipped into the mind. So the

… the language of the Buddha's teachings is deliberately impersonal. This way, we don't get ashamed or defensive, and have the encouragement to investigate the way things are in a more open and objective light.

language of the Buddha's teachings is deliberately impersonal. This way, we don't get ashamed or defensive, and have the encouragement to investigate the way things are in a more open and objective light.

THE RING OF FIRE—DEPENDENT ORIGINATION

The outer rim of this picture contains various figures bound up in loops of fire, mapping out the compounding of dukkha. These emblems represent twelve linking factors of an analysis called Dependent Origination (or *Paticcasamuppada* in Pali). Just as studying the cause of suffering is helpful as it will lead to understanding what we have to do or not do, Dependent Origination provides many insights into the origin and cessation of suffering.

It is a profound analysis whose terms and connections may seem baffling at first sight. Accordingly, I have drawn up a table for reference, and recommend reviewing and reflecting on it while looking at the illustration.

In the picture, the interlinking motif represents another example of these vicious circles. With the First Noble Truth, the previous circle, the grasped aggregates reinforce and support each other; the experience of grasping and suffering (really two ways of looking at the same thing) are

Pali	English	Explanation	Image
Avijjā	ignorance, unknowing	not understanding the full meaning and implication of the Four Noble Truths	person holding hand over eyes
Saṅkhāra	Kamma-productive tendencies, "activities"	activities of mind which are aligned to self view	hand wielding hammer at forge
Viññāṇa	discriminative consciousness	the activity of the six senses, i.e., acting in a dualistic way defining the subject as distinct from the object	monkey
Nāma-rūpa	name-and-form	feeling, perception, contact, intention, attention and their objects	human body
Saḷāyatana	the six senses	eye, ear, nose, tongue, touch and mind	five arrows pointing to a central space
Phassa	contact, impression	(dependent on feeling and perception)	electrical contact between two fingers
Vedanā	feeling	painful, pleasant, neutral—bodily or mental	arrow in eye
Taṇhā	craving, desire	desire in terms of self—to have, to attain, to get away from	thirst-crazed face
Upādāna	grasping, clinging	clinging to sense objects, views, etc.	fraying rope
Bhava	becoming	being something—better or worse—and being nothing	Sisyphus
Jāti	birth	the experience of being a separate entity in a temporal context	baby
Jarāmaraṇa-soka-parideva-dukkha-domanassa-	aging, death, sorrow, lamentation, pain, grief and despair	the sense of ego-loss, through physical death or the breaking up of the psychological foundations of self	skull with rat

The inclination to not notice — to ignore — arises dependent on dukkha. We don't want to know about things not fitting in with our wishes, although there's no reason to assume that life should or could ever be the way we'd like it to be.

the force of torsion that creates those doubled loops. In this Second Truth, there is also a double-sided force — ignorance and desire. The interconnectedness of the loops points to the fact that, in Dependent Origination, each factor supports every other factor. Nor is the connection one of a simple causal sequence. Each factor that is described is present in every subsequently described factor, and the analysis is one of conditionality rather than causality. Just as water is a condition for ice, the absence of clouds a condition for a sunny day, having ears a condition for enjoying Bach fugues, so the conditionality of Dependent Origination is the structure of the potential for dukkha or its cessation. The essential point in this is that *conditions* arise in the present and can therefore be changed. *Causes*, on the other hand, are historical.

Right at the top is **ignorance** (*avijja*), the man with his hand in front of his eyes. People tend to take "ignorance" as pejorative; however, it refers to a lack of gnosis or insightful seeing as well as to foolishness and unknowing. It is summarized as "not understanding the Four Noble Truths" — or, perhaps more accurately, not understanding their implications. That is, as long as there is ignorance, the mind still expects to find an experience that is completely satisfying, and feels disappointed when things "go wrong." There is a parable of a man eating a bag of chilli peppers one by one, weeping at their fiery taste as he does so. When asked why he continues to eat the peppers, he replies: "I'm looking for the sweet one." This is ignorance.

The Buddha said that it is impossible to find the origins of ignorance. However, with experience, one can see that it is increased by wilfully ignoring the way life is, and substituting wishful fantasies, based on the viewpoint of a self imagined to exist within the five khandhas. Dependent Origination teaches that this view, its origins, purposes and results can be seen as dependent on many factors — all with ignorance as their foundation. The cycle of Dependent Origination works both ways: with the arising of ignorance and the acting on that, suffering follows; with the ending of ignorance is the ending of every kind of inner pain, shadow or stress. The uplifting aspect of Dependent Origination is that it brings the ending of dukkha down to one practice — that of replacing ignorance with wise attention.

Ignorance is a mental *inclination* of ignoring; it's not just a passive quality, although it may occur through a programmed impulse rather than a clearly conscious choice. If it were not something that was inclined towards, there would be no way of stopping it. However, a lot of the time one is not *conscious* of ignorance (one thing about ignorance is that one is often ignorant of it!) Reactions appear to happen automatically, without the awareness of where the motivation lies. When awareness is not developed to the point of knowing the mind, the "automatic" and "reflex" operations of our mind create the reality of our world.

The inclination to not notice — to ignore — arises dependent on dukkha. We don't want to know about things not fitting in with our wishes, although there's no reason to assume that life should or could ever be the way we'd like it to be. So ignorance affects our perceptions—the way we "see" things. If we're honest, we may notice prejudices, errors of judgement, definite biases towards seeing things "my way." Also ignorance distracts; what one doesn't want to know about is ignored. One's mind filters out flaws in a loved one's behavior, for example. Sometimes it is more conscious. They say the captain of the ocean liner, the *Titanic,* was informed of icebergs floating in the sea in front of his ship, yet chose to ignore the warning and went straight into them with the resultant death of almost everybody on board. Notice that there was an element of choice in the matter. Many accidents are caused by people not being attentive, thinking about something else with a chain saw in their hand, doing things automatically; and that inattention is due to our minds wanting to be somewhere else. Sometimes ignorance is deliberate and wilful; sometimes it could be prevented by being more attentive; sometimes it's ingrained in the ways we perceive things, and requires insight and the courage to undergo personal change to remedy. However, ignorance is always activated by some element of conscious or unconscious desire. Therefore ignorance and desire are the axis which allows this wheel of fire to spin.

As long as there is ignorance, actions tend to become automatic, compulsive, idiosyncratic, related to "my way of seeing things" rather than to the needs of a situation. Ignorance, therefore, is linked to **volitional "kamma-productive" tendencies** (*sankhara* *)—which include activities of body, speech or mind. Sankhara are symbolized here by the hand brandishing the hammer at the forge of creation. We're always creating. When we speak, we create ourselves in another person's mind; and so it is with our actions. Ignorance conditions actions and makes them into "activities" of a self. When there is ignorance we act, consciously or unconsciously, in order to prove ourselves or enhance ourselves. We also measure actions and speech in terms of self—we expect results, progress for ourselves or others we have identified with. We defend and justify our actions or assign to them a significance that they may not have. Alternatively, we may be highly self-critical. This "self-view" of *sankhara* means that we fail to measure the true worth or effect of actions and thoughts. Thereby it strengthens the habit of acting in unreflective ways. We do not clearly notice the motivation behind action, or the impersonal and changing nature of the energies and perceptions that feed them. Action becomes habitual activity and starts to form our identity.

Do you find that your life has repeating patterns in it, similar scenarios with different people involved? We seem to go through the same emotional cycles around different events, and have recurring patterns of thought—the same memories, the same habits—so we think, "That's the way I am." Habitual activities, even thoughts in the mind, are elements which forge the kamma—the self-defining and binding activities that shape our lives.

Many accidents are caused by people not being attentive, thinking about something else with a chain saw in their hand, doing things automatically; and that inattention is due to our minds wanting to be somewhere else.

---

* For some further discussion of the implications of this word, see Use of Pali in the Introduction.

Any identity, good or bad, is subject to stress, frustration, sorrow and death; if the kamma is unskillful, there are a lot more problems on the way, such as guilt, fear and the hostility of others. Then we act in ways to cover up or redress previous actions, again acting from self-view. Thus more kamma is established, strengthening the sense of identity, good or bad. This is the proliferating effect of *sankhara.* It is only when we understand motivation as coming from energies such as greed or love, rather than an existing self, that we find the still point of reflection and pull out of the spin. That freedom gives us the opportunity to act and speak in unbiased ways — in the way of Dhamma rather than *sankhara.*

The sixfold **sense consciousness** (*viññana*) is the agent through which sankhara manifest. This is the next link, symbolized by the monkey in the third loop. Dependent upon habits, reflexes and viewpoints that have been created, the monkey jumps: seeing, hearing, thinking, tasting, smelling and touching are sent running around this way or that. Consciousness is based upon the six sense organs and described as eye-consciousness, ear-consciousness and so on. It can also be defined in terms of how it is propelled. Interest and attraction towards a sense object is consciousness rooted in "greed." Generosity is consciousness rooted in non-greed. Aversion to a sense object is consciousness rooted in "hatred;" love is the opposite. Mind-consciousness may experience a lot of confused, wavering activities around its sense objects of thought and emotion. This is consciousness rooted in "delusion." Consciousness may be refined to varying degrees, from just above coma, to sleep, to wakefulness, caffeinated highs, alcoholic wooziness, ecstasy or the refined absorptive states arising through concentration. For liberation from suffering and enlightenment, the Buddha stipulated that the mental consciousness should be unclouded and attentive; and that the quality of intention should be known and trained. It is intention that directs the monkey.

> *Bhikkhus, whatever we determine, whatever we intend to do and whatever we are occupied with: this is the base for consciousness to be maintained on.* (Samyutta Nikaya: [II], Cause, Kalara, 38)

Intention (*cetana*) and sustained attention (*manasikara*), produce the experience of conscious motivation. Motivation in terms of greed, or hatred or confusion will send consciousness deeper into those realms. Motivation in terms of giving and love and intelligence will incline consciousness towards more positive states. This is how kammic tendencies are strengthened. However, good or bad motivation in terms of self will always heighten that sense of self and the inevitable dukkha which that entails.

Consciousness always works in terms of **name-and-form** (*namarupa*). Something only has presence (i.e., enters consciousness) because there is the sense of contact, and contact depends on something contacted (form). From that contact, designations, feelings and perception (name) arise. "Nama" is defined as: feeling, perception, contact, intention and attention — the neutral factors that pick up, define, locate and react to the data of consciousness. Even "formlessness" is a designation of a kind of indefinite form. So the world of form only has presence for us because of consciousness, and how we perceive it is very much affected by the mind states, attitudes and feelings that we have. There is a saying that when a pickpocket meets a saint, all he notices are the saint's pockets (if he has any of course). When an architect or a builder sees a house, a different set of perceptions arises than when a homeless person sees it, or a burglar, or an animal. In a way, we build our own world, and our world builds us. What we are conscious of moulds and determines the perceptions and attitudes we have. If you were attacked by a dog when you were a child, you probably will have some difficulty in perceiving dogs as loyal friends.

The thing that most profoundly affects consciousness, with whose rhythms and energies we are very much engaged, is the body. To be present in the sensory realm requires a physical body which has its needs, pleasant and painful feelings, its sickness and death. So consciousness depends upon and directs physical form, and is infused with attitudes and perceptions about it. Hence the fourth vignette, the body, is the connecting point for consciousness in the human world. The fifth vignette symbolizes the five "external senses" that relay information to the mind. The sixth vignette is of contact, the connection that is necessary for consciousness and its images to arise.

In the human birth, consciousness is programmed by bodily life. It constantly registers the pain that is a warning of injury to the body, and pleasure that is a signal for the preservation and development of the body. But the body inevitably experiences degeneration and death, making pain unavoidable, and pleasure ultimately futile. When there's ignorance, consciousness remains fettered to this sensory realm, because the dependent link is not seen as biological or purely a matter of how the system works—it is felt as "me." "I" appear to be a mental consciousness within a physical form, trying to seek solutions or remedies to it, or get as much agreeable experience as possible. Even if "I" am trying to get out of the physical form into some deathless or ethereal realm, "I" am always designated in terms of bodily presence or absence because of consciousness affected by self-view being attuned to bodily life. Consciousness is dependent upon the body for a lifetime, so no matter how ethereal the mind state, you still have to attend to the coarse functions of the body and be with its pains, its insatiable needs and its demise. The "I am" view associated with the body is always one of need, anxiety or pain. However, when one key log—the sense of "I"—is removed from this pile of dukkha, bodily life becomes an opportunity for bringing wisdom and compassion into the world.

In the vignette of **the six senses** (*salayatana*) depicted by the arrows and the central question, I've tried to illustrate what is the one direction of Buddhist mind-training. Sense consciousness normally takes us out—towards objects, or to thinking about what we can contact through the physical senses. However, in developing mindfulness, attention can be

The simple equation is that Truth has no personal identity, and personal identity has no Truth.

trained to look back into the mind, to focus on the intentions and reactions that govern conscious thought, speech and action. When you see something, you are aware of the seeing, and you reflect: "How am I seeing that?" If you're thinking or feeling something, rather than just acting upon it impulsively, you reflect: "Hmm, how do I react to that?" This is a way you can learn about what is skillful or harmful, what the attachments and compulsions are and where the sense of identity is being created. It's a way to investigate who we are, beyond our fluctuating and unsatisfactory identity. Who is the one who can freely contemplate the sensory world? There is always awareness of something in the domain of consciousness, even if it's the feeling of confusion, suffering or desire. But awareness has no personal identity. The simple equation is that Truth has no personal identity, and personal identity has no Truth.

We can continue this chain through **contact** (*phassa*) — that's the way that the senses operate. Apart from the physical needs and use of having contact, the inferred self needs contact to maintain its presence — self always exists in contrast to otherness. We get bored with the same old tastes, sounds, sights, people; but then sometimes it's nice to have the familiar. "Can't live with you, can't live without you" — sounds familiar? If you really want to contact the forms of your psyche, you could try floating in a sensory deprivation tank, or, more simply, sit where it's quiet and close your eyes: the natural inclination of the senses to make contact will bring up mental phenomena. For unenlightened beings, these will all be taken as aspects of themselves, and therefore unsatisfactory. However, the practice of sitting quietly with the eyes closed in meditation is useful in that, with steady attention, one realizes that all this stuff is something that can be watched, and is therefore a series of objects — not the subject, not self. We only experience contact because of feeling and perceiving something. And as what is felt or perceived must always be an object, how can we ever contact our true self? Hence contact affected by ignorance is the launching-pad for need or disappointment. From this contact arise the futile attempts to find ourselves or connect with our true feelings. Yet contact itself does not have to be dukkha. When there's no ignorance or self-view, contact provides opportunities for attention, insight and sharing.

Contact links up to **feeling** (*vedana*), the arrow in the eye. Something strikes visual consciousness and a feeling arises which is either painful, pleasant or neutral. It is said that the body only experiences painful and pleasant feeling, the eye, ear, nose and tongue only experience neutral feeling and the mind experiences all three. However, as the mind will *interpret* neutrality as pleasant (calm) at some times and painful (tedious, dull) at other times, in normal consciousness, one is dealing with mental feelings based on perceptions. For instance, people can derive pleasure from doing extremely stressful things to their bodies! It's a real problem: the mind's values (*sañña*) can get so distorted that we actually derive pleasure from bragging, abusing and fighting — even though these are abrasive and violent feelings in mind-consciousness. Powerful emotional pleasure may arise out of being attractive, even though attractiveness can be stressful in terms of cost, artifice and competition — and quite dangerous if you attract the wrong kind of person. ... Then there are the feelings associated with winning, being excited and so on. ... The pleasure of these feelings is not due to the mind as a sense organ (which may even crack up under the strain) but to confused perceptions. The most consistent determinant for feeling is whatever sensation or perception makes "me" feel important, sensitive or powerful.

When there is ignorance or un-knowing, we don't really know what we are feeling. As I have suggested above, much of the time we are in contact with our perceptions, because they can create images in accordance with desire. Such is the next loop of fire, **craving** — which is *tanha* in its fully conscious form. Here, it is represented by the thirsting mouth and the hand always reaching out to get water from a perceived mirage. Feeling links to desire. If what is felt through the senses is not desirable, or brings up aversion, the unawakened instinct creates a fantasy that is attractive. One of the bitterest aspects of the unawakened life is that when you have enough physically, your mind creates fantasies to crave. Nowadays in Western culture, our normal reality is composed of fantasies vividly portrayed on television, in movies, novels, shows and advertisements. They seem harmless enough, but the contact with them and the feelings they induce unconsciously affect our values. People end up voting for a fantasy, being governed by a fantasy, using fantasy money, having fantasy enemies and chasing fantasy goals. The only real element left is suffering, but that is repressed or not acknowledged because it doesn't fit into the fantasy. In the Brave New World, everybody's happy; ignore the rest.

Without ignorance, desire is not suffering. We can understand desire; it is something that we can watch in order to know its ethical quality. We can act on skillful desires with dispassion; we can respond to the signals of bodily need; and we can let go of desires that are born from greed, hatred or delusion. Then we are not acting in ignorance, and we can use the energy of desire to investigate the mind and bring goodness into the world.

Craving to have — or to annihilate — links up to **grasping** or **clinging** (*upadana*). Like desire, clinging is a function of natural bodily life — babies do it with good reason — but the un-knowing recreates that as a compulsive mental activity. And clinging to the wrong things is a frustrating, stressful and dangerous experience: clinging to sensory experience with ignorance is always going to let you down because there's no having enough, and all sensory experience is unreliable. It changes and ends. If you hang your life expectations on the sensory world, it will take you to despair; it's like climbing a mountain clinging to a fraying rope. Maybe we shouldn't have *any* clinging ... but those who wish to awaken hold onto the teachings and the practices that lead to liberation, so again the problem really is ignorance, clinging blindly. When there is no ignorance, we can hold onto things as physical necessities or mentally as workable conventions, responsibilities or commitments. The blanket "no clinging" statement is some-

Like desire, clinging is a function of natural bodily life — babies do it with good reason — but the un-knowing recreates that as a compulsive mental activity. And clinging to the wrong things is a frustrating, stressful and dangerous experience ...

thing which can be used to authorize opportunist shifts of loyalties and the dismissal of rules and precepts. The ultimate clinging is, of course, to the self-view.

When there's ignorance, clinging acts as a base for **becoming** (*bhava*) which I've already talked about. Out of craving, one attaches to some object, and then sees it as a way of personal development or fulfillment. In the traditional paintings on this theme, *bhava* is symbolized by a pregnant woman; it is that sense of an inner separate being which leads to birth. But here, I've related it more to the weariness of having to sustain the sense of personal development. Do you know the myth of Sisyphus, who was the person whose punishment in a Greek hell was that he had to roll a huge boulder up to the top of a mountain? It took him a long time to get this vast boulder up the slope, and whenever he got close to the top, it would break loose and roll down to the bottom and he'd have to go down and roll it back up. That's becoming. It leads to **birth** (*jati*). And such a birth is not the promised birth of fulfillment, but the experience of oneself as someone who's not quite there yet. So these two (the tenth and eleventh) vignettes link up, and with ignorance continuing, support dukkha.

One of the problems on the spiritual path, which we walk on as unawakened aspirants, is the sense of trying to *become* something. It's normal, because we have been doing that all the time with every pursuit that we have taken up. And the pursuit of ultimate well-being, of wisdom, enlightenment or whatever, really engages our becoming instincts. We always feel that we are not yet right. If only we try a *little* harder, we might get the boulder to the top of the mountain. Try a little harder, and we'll get there.

Where?

Who?

Wise instruction teaches us about humility, patience and the need to be with the present moment. Don't seek personal development. Practice developing beyond personal need; practice generosity, service, selflessness. Wise "becoming" is called *bhavana*, cultivation of the Path, not of self-view. If cultivation is always coming from self-views, you get caught up in the sense of failure, or the other kind of becoming—wanting not to become (*vibhava*), wanting to annihilate your desires and weaknesses. Thus you get "born" as a fanatic, a starry-eyed devotee or a tight-lipped zealot.

And whatever you get born into deepens the kammic, self-producing tendencies, so that when that birth ends, when you've given up on Buddhism and become a Sufi, or you've given up Sufism and taken to gestalt, you're even more preoccupied with yourself and your problems and your importance. So death in ignorance—that is, not waking up when your current "world," relationships, occupation or body end—takes you into the possibility for more dukkha. The twelfth factor of Dependent Origination is **aging-death-sorrow-lamentation-pain-grief-and-despair** (*jaramaranam sokaparideva dukkha domanassupayasa*), a comprehensive, if stark, summary of the consequences of attachment to birth. How many trips and games are we going to buy into and get infatuated with and disillusioned by, before we recognize the dukkha of attachment? Plenty, it seems, because dukkha is ignored. And so the habitual reactions to dukkha take you deeper into the cycle of ignorance … and round we go again. …

Not that becoming, birth and death are suffering on their own; when there's wisdom, as in the case of the Buddha, the identity of being an Enlightened One, a teacher, the head of an Order was not taken personally. He even referred to himself in the third person. This role is just something that happens out of the compassionate desire to offer the teachings to those who wish to hear. He never sought disciples; he even encouraged people to stay with their old religions, but to use them wisely. Even at his own death, he had no concern that his teaching might die out; he realized that he had offered what was necessary. So death can be freed from anxiety with the ending of the self-view.

The ending of things offers a peek into the Truth of Cessation, not dukkha.

We can even use death as a meditation object: with the ending of an experience, there's a moment when there's "not knowing"—a moment of space or emptiness. Normally the ignoring habit immediately starts up again and sends a mad monkey racing round and back to the beginning. The whole thing flashes by very quickly. But to let the mind notice and give its full due to the ending of a sound, a thought, a mood … is an opportunity to recognize a state of being which is empty, and yet vibrantly present. The ending of things offers a peek into the Truth of Cessation, not dukkha.

We can see that the origin of this suffering process is compounded out of craving and not seeing. The remedy that the Buddha points out is actually right here, in the *knowing*. In the context of the Second Noble Truth, we are knowing desire—not desiring to know. Cessation is not destruction or annihilation; it is the "arrest" of an activity so that it is seen clearly and ignorance does not condition the "activities" and so on. Thoughts, feelings, desires, attachments, suffering—these are to be held by attention until they are:

> *Dominated by mindfulness, surmounted by wisdom, yield deliverance as essence, merge in the Deathless and terminate in Nibbana.* (Anguttara Nikaya: [V], Tens, 107)

This requires bringing forth faith and wisdom so that there is the ending of un-knowing and, with that, the ending of all these possibilities for suffering.

idaṁ
kho
pana
bhikkhave

dukkhanirodho ariyasaccaṁ

yo tassa yeva
taṇhāya
asesavirāganirodho
cāgo paṭinissaggo mutti anālayo

7

THE THIRD NOBLE TRUTH:
Letting It All Go

Idaṁ kho pana bhikkhave ... cāgo paṭinissaggo mutti anālayo.
Bhikkhus, there is the Noble Truth of the Cessation of Suffering.
It is the complete fading away and cessation of this desire;
its abandonment and relinquishment; the freedom from and discarding of it.

Having highlighted the origin of suffering, the Buddha goes on to speak about its cessation. The way that the Buddha presented his teaching was to describe how to do it; his description of the results was much more sparing, at least in the Theravadin recension of his words. This teaching is like a tool-box that is offered to someone who wants to do the job and considers it worthwhile. It's not a teaching one finds immediately inspirational. One result, and perhaps even the purpose of such an approach, is that it doesn't arouse a lot of desire—you are not promised something in the future that is painted in such rosy terms that you get greedy and ambitious for it. In some ways, the presentation is rather daunting—plenty of talk about suffering and hindrances, not much about joy and bliss. But you have to want to practice from a very realistic perspective, and be prepared to go through some hard work and to develop some skills; it needs more than an immediate inspirational high to take you across. This is a fair approach—it identifies the root of the obstruction, and how to remove it. If you need to hold onto

If you need to hold onto something, maybe this isn't the way for you; if you want to follow it, be prepared to give up a lot and to bring forth your own energy.

something, maybe this isn't the way for you; if you want to follow it, be prepared to give up a lot and to bring forth your own energy.

One aim of these paintings is to enhance the meaning, rather than to dilute the message. Here the frame has become a smooth circle, the symbol of wholeness and fullness. The color within it is blue—the cool, spacious color. Within the circle sits a cross-legged bloated but radiant being. Cessation does not come about through wanting to become more joyous and wise or more attractive and popular. It is an expansive realization that is itself joyous and wise. It comes into being through giving up the mind-held images that we feel we need to be. The personal image portrayed here doesn't arouse a desire to become like that, but it may arouse in the heart a certain recognition of letting go.

This is a traditional Thai image, called "Phra Sankaccayana," which is a symbol of good fortune and benevolence in the Universe that comes about through personal relinquishment. The story goes that Phra (Thai for "Venerable") Sankaccayana was a bhikkhu at the time of the Buddha who was very handsome and had acquired a lot of magnetism through mind-cultivation. He was an *Arahant,* an enlightened being, but his personal attractiveness was stimulating some rather unenlightened interest in the hearts of many of the ladies of the area. This monk felt embarrassed that he should be receiving such attention, and he didn't think it was very helpful to the womenfolk either, so he decided to bloat himself up in order to look like a slob. And here he is in this painting, demonstrating letting go, and helping to induce it in others. There's a message there for those of us who feel we need to have charisma, a good image, and hordes of devotees to confirm our enlightenment.

Sometimes you meet teachers and sages who have a lot of personal charm. Sometimes they are wise and trustworthy, sometimes they are not. People make a lot out of the personal magnetism that a teacher may have. This has led to several disastrous incidents when some famous sage or another has been discovered salting away unaccounted millions in a Swiss bank account or seducing fourteen-year-old girls. My experience of sages is very limited, but I have met monks in Thailand who said little, looked small and insignificant, or were homely and garrulous, and yet exemplified a life of great purity, kindness and insight, even if they couldn't give rousing talks. Incidentally, in Theravada, monks and nuns are not supposed to talk about their attainments. Some people say it's because we don't have any, but it's really to prevent the arising of a cult based upon a personality. That would be detrimental to their practice. Even if the monk or nun is a very wise being, statements about their attainments would draw more attention to the personality than to the practice, and there is a natural inclination in that direction anyway. Most disciples at some time want to emulate their teacher, but this need not be encouraged. It's a process everyone has to go through (suffering a lot on the way), until there is the realization that there are no real role models. You have to work with *your* mind and habits, and the way Truth expresses itself through *you.*

Cessation does not come about through wanting to become more joyous and wise or more attractive and popular. It is an expansive realization that is itself joyous and wise.

In Buddhist monasticism, it is the *Vinaya* (the Code of Conduct) that provides the standard for personal behavior, not the teacher's personality or wishes. This creates a communally-held level of modesty, trustworthiness and community consciousness, in which no-one is out to prove they are or aren't anything. You learn to give up the desire to become somebody, and also the desire to drop out of it all and become nobody. Ideas about oneself or one's position are checked by this way of life. Rather than conceiving oneself as a teacher or as incapable of giving talks, there is the encouragement to explain the teachings of the Buddha in the best and most authentic way that you can, if asked to do so.

We'll talk more about the practice in the next phase of the Sutta; I'd just like to point out here how easy it is to mistake "abandonment" for "getting rid of." Maybe the words are nearly the same in English; but having been told about *vibhavatanha*, desire for nonexistence, as a powerful originator of suffering, one should be careful about the desire that wants desire not to exist. In the reality of spiritual practice, there is a great difference between abandonment as a state of not holding onto desire, and aversion to the existence of desires. Desire will always be experienced as a constriction of the mind around some object, to either have it or to repress it, whilst abandonment of desire is an equanimous, malleable and gentle mode of mind. Abandonment opens to the present; and the here and now is not within the realm of desire. Desire operates on the possible realization of what is not here, now. Annihilation attempts to suppress desire; whereas in the here and now, there is the experience of the mind at rest from desire. This is cessation.

Sometimes the desire to get rid of is disguised as non-attachment. In this guise, it causes a certain stiffness and defensiveness of manner — "Don't bother me" — or a tendency not to face up to what is going on and learn from it. The other extreme of the desire to get rid of is wanting to be involved in everything and to solve everybody's problems for them. Getting caught up in the desire to solve everyone's problems is agitating and oppressive too, even if one is not consciously trying to become the great savior.

Some of these forms of desire are subtle and snag people whose intentions are generally good. Trying to get rid of other people's problems can have the same contradictory effect as trying to get rid of your own. Both well-intentioned aims go astray when they affirm that problems actually belong to us. That is, by concentrating on them in a negative way, we unconsciously affirm their reality and lose perspective. We feel ourselves to be flawed, rather than recognize the impersonal and changeable nature of flaws. What is essential is to affirm and encourage the non-problematic side of the mind — the experience of non-greed, non-hatred and non-delusion. This is a Path of self-reliance. However tirelessly, compassionately and skillfully they teach, Buddhas only point the Way: our own stumbling feet have to do the walking. We can help by encouraging the wisdom and purity of the mind rather than by identifying with the weaknesses.

The practice goes deep, and as has been pointed out, the roots of suffering are in viewpoints and attitudes existing beneath the level of conscious

Trying to get rid of other people's problems can have the same contradictory effect as trying to get rid of your own.... by concentrating on them in a negative way, we unconsciously affirm their reality and lose perspective.

49

activity. As we saw in the discussion of Dependent Origination, the sense of self, the "I am," is the wrong view arising from ignorance which then conditions compulsive activity in terms of that self. Whenever we try to get rid of self, we unwittingly reinforce it. For example, if we believe that compulsive habits and desires are "me" or "mine," we may feel we are *this* kind of a person who has a lot of weaknesses, and has to *do* a lot to get rid of them in order to become enlightened or to be a true disciple of the Buddha, and so on. We believe that to get results, we have to do something. We assume that giving up and abandonment are always about *doing* something with body, speech or mind. This attitude can foster real greed for renunciation practices, or great resolutions. And these can strongly increase our sense of identity!

If we think that we don't need to work on our minds, we also miss the mark. We know suffering arises. We can observe the careless habits of self-view which perpetuate the suffering. We should not take these habits personally, but practice with attention to realize the purity of being that does not create them. Patient effort is needed. This means a renunciation of the wish for progress as well as a dispassionate acceptance, not an approval, that what we are experiencing is the way things are right now.

That kind of abandonment gives a fine edge and confidence to the mind. Such stability is likened to a threefold Refuge, the Triple Gem, constituting Buddha—the quality of dispassionate attention; Dhamma—the way it is; and Sangha—the resolute practice. They, rather than the desire to become or get rid of anything, are the guides of the mind through the haze of un-knowing.

Rather than attainment in terms of progress towards cessation, it would be more accurate to talk of purification—not in a puritanical sense or in terms of righteousness, but likened to the purity of water. The metaphor of purity provides a more helpful direction and determinant of good practice. It's not about adding things to one's self-image, or about gaining something that is not already here. It is about losing, not winning; about losing the conceit and the greed and the doubt and the delusions that prevent one from seeing things as they really are and living in accordance with the Truth. The Buddha said his teaching was for those with little dust in the eyes; what is needed, then, is a cleansing, not more makeup.

As the practice of cessation matures, the mind realizes "stream-entry"—a pleasing metaphor. Stream-entry is the beginning of being completely composed upon the Path. With that level of clarity, one no longer has the instinctive need to hold onto the body and its image as one's self. Rather one treats it wisely as a part of nature. Similarly, you're not looking at someone else's physical image as an expression of their enlightenment—or lack of it. With stream-entry, there is no longer any doubt that the Path is based on purity of body and speech, and leads to fruition. Doubt about the connection to the foundation of practice through the Buddha, Dhamma and Sangha does not arise. With this mature understanding also comes a more balanced attitude regarding the use of techniques, conventions and practices: one can use them sensibly, avoiding the extremes of either slavishly following them or rebelliously rejecting them.

If the Path is cultivated to the point of the cessation of self-view, the desire to become something else is completely irrelevant, and so it is forgotten. What is involved is a lightening of the heart, not an intensification of one's self-preoccupation, opinions and convoluted reasoning to justify objectionable conduct. The Path is straight and clear, of one quality in its outward form and its inner essence, without paradox, noble, uplifting, beautiful in the beginning, beautiful in the middle, beautiful in the end.

When suffering fades out, when desire is relinquished, what is left, what is present? There is the cessation, the rest from desire. Stewing away with some hankering or desire is not our fundamental nature. Yet we have to train the mind to attend to those peaceful spaces, however momentarily they may be experienced. To experience this — even briefly — to get a real taste, gives one the confidence that there is, now, no suffering.

> *Bhikkhus, this mind is luminous, and it is only defiled by transitory defilements.*
> (Anguttara Nikaya: [I], Ones, VI)

Non-suffering is our true nature; it's not something that has to be added. And that is what the cultivation of the Eightfold Path is about — it is a way of bringing the mind's undistorted nature into full consciousness. That cultivation is broad as well as sharp, peaceful as well as energetic, as the next section of the Sutta points out.

… we have to train the mind to attend to those peaceful spaces, however momentarily they may be experienced. To experience this — even briefly — to get a real taste, gives one the confidence that there is, now, no suffering.

Idam
kho
pana
bhikkhave
dukkhanirodhagāmini
paṭipadā
ariyasaccaṁ
ayameva
Ariyo Aṭṭhaṅgiko Maggo
seyyathidaṁ
sammādiṭṭhi
sammāsaṅkappo
sammāvācā
sammākammanto
sammā-ājīvo
sammā-
-vāyāmo
sammā-
sati
sammā-
samādhi

8

THE FOURTH NOBLE TRUTH:
The Great Way

Idaṁ kho pana bhikkhave ... sammādiṭṭhi sammāsaṅkappo sammāvācā
sammākammanto sammā-ājīvo sammāvāyāmo sammāsati sammāsamādhi.
Bhikkhus, there is the Noble Truth of the Way leading to the Cessation of
Suffering. It is the Noble Eightfold Path: namely, Right View, Right Inten-
tion, Right Speech, Right Action, Right Livelihood, Right Effort, Right
Mindfulness and Right Concentration.

This illumination portrays a mandala—an image that can be used
to concentrate and compose the mind for tranquillity and reflection. It is based upon a Celtic stone in Scotland which has four
arcing motifs which I have adapted here into eight. Actually, you
can see that it's all just one line going around. Similarly, the Eightfold Path
has eight limbs but it is only one Path, not eight Paths going in different
directions. You cannot isolate just any one aspect of it and call it the Path,
because it's the wholeness of it which is important.

The symbols within the mandala typify factors of the Eightfold Path.
Right View (*samma ditthi*) is the bodhi leaf representing awakening and
enlightenment. Right Intention (*samma sankappa*) is the lotus flower
which, like aspiration, grows out of the earth of mundane existence
towards the heavens. The third is Right Speech (*samma vaca*), here
symbolized by a star—a source of transmission of light across the vast
spaces between us. The fourth is Right Action (*samma kammanto*) which
is a hand—the open hand that holds nothing but is available for work in

a selfless way. Right Livelihood (*samma ajivo*) is the hand in a caring and protective gesture — one of nurturing oneself and others with livelihood. The sixth factor is Right Effort (*samma vayamo*), the *vajra* sword — that is, the sense of determination and ability to limit, define and direct oneself. It has four aspects: to prevent the mind from being overwhelmed by ignorance; to cut away at wrong views and habits; to dig the soil for cultivation of what is good; and to maintain vigilance over the Path. This supports and is supported by Right Mindfulness (*samma sati*), shown as a flower to represent the blossoming of the mind's ability to know things as they are. The eighth factor is Right Collectedness (*samma samadhi*), here symbolized by the hand in meditation *mudra* supporting the flower, the pure mind. And that takes us back to Right View, the purity that sees the way things are.

So this is another circle, one in which the interdependence of the links represents a process whereby wisdom is activated and regenerated. As with the other circles, the mandala interlinks in a cross weave as every single factor supports every other factor and is supported by it. This form makes the strongest weave.

In the picture, the Buddha is walking in the world. The image of the walking Buddha implies relationship with the world of events. The Buddha here has one hand raised in the *mudra* of spiritual protection or blessing; this is called *abhaya mudra*, the "fearlessness gesture." The other hand is in the "giving gesture" (*dana mudra*). When the two are seen together, they symbolize a relationship with the world which is calming and benevolent. This formalized image, most commonly found in Japan, is one of many that express different spiritual values.

More detail. Right View is the view, the perspective that arises from fully understanding the Four Noble Truths. That may be the first factor; it is also the last, since to understand the Four Noble Truths requires the practice of the other seven factors. So the Path is really two turns of the Wheel: the first is the mundane — the seven other factors without Right View; and the second is the supramundane — the Path factors with Right View. Mundane understanding is that which preserves the dualistic model of reality: "me" and "the world;" supramundane sees things holistically as "the way it is."

Mundane Right Intention then is the intention not to do harm in the world — to stimulate considerations of kindness, forgiveness and service rather than vindictiveness, grudges and selfishness. Right Speech is speech which is honest, courteous, purposeful and conducive to concord. Right Action is harmlessness, trustworthiness and sexual responsibility. Right Livelihood is livelihood that brings no ill effects to the lives of other beings.

Right Effort is the training to avoid or abandon unwholesome states of mind, and to cultivate and maintain wholesome states of mind. Right Mindfulness is a particular kind of mental attention and recollection that can best be activated through meditation exercises and then developed as a general state of awareness in daily life. The Buddha said that it can be founded upon the body—being attentive to breathing in and out, walking, stretching, standing, lying down; physical and mental feelings; the general state of mind—whether it's moody, depressed, relaxed or elated, for example; or through awareness of mind objects—thoughts, energies, doubts, joy … an innumerable array.

This last foundation is called "Dhamma" when those mental objects are seen, observed and responded to with mindfulness and objectivity. Thus they are understood as phenomena in the universe, as "the way it is," rather than brooded over or delighted in as aspects of oneself. Other key features of mindfulness are that it does not require a high degree of tranquillity, working readily on the ordinary level of consciousness, and that its tone is equanimous. Mindfulness is the kind of attention that sees phenomena arising and ceasing; its focus is on the change and variability of experience. This is what makes mindfulness such a transformative practice. When the phenomena that we take as "our self" are experienced as something passing through consciousness, what happens to the sense of identity?

Right Concentration or Collectedness results from Right Mindfulness. When the mind sustains attention on the changing nature of things, just on that edge, it is not being drawn into judgements about experience. Things are just as they are. This means that the mind is not being stirred up by desires, fears or restlessness, and, in that serenity, it begins to be aware of its own reflective quality. The mind as an experience of consciousness has certain qualities—one is that it "knows," it is sensitive; the other is that it has a wide range of focus—moving from a pinpoint on your body to philosophical speculations to poignant memories in a matter of moments. We all recognize these aspects, but normally the attention of the mind is limited to objects that bring up interest or aversion. But when we no longer linger upon them, the mind is freed from the limitations of those objects, and the habitual pattern of moods and reactions that accompany them. The "knowingness" becomes a clear sensitivity, and the range becomes boundless. This is quite delightful, and so certain attachments are inevitable unless concentration is linked to Right View.

It is here that the wholeness of the Eightfold Path becomes such an important teaching. Mindfulness will help to undercut the attachment to the delights of these meditative highs, because the nature of mindfulness is non-absorptive, and it notices that the highs also come and go. Then the less elevated aspects of the Path—the ethical training—are of further significance; they encourage a fine sense of discernment with regards to the conventions of human life. Dispassionate discernment, rather than absorption, is the tool of insight. If we are to respond to life as it happens with its instabilities and vicissitudes, we cannot remain absorbed in anything for too long.

The dilemma that everyone who experiences or inclines towards meditation has to resolve is, "How do I keep this sense of concentration going in my daily life?" The simple answer is by concentrating more completely on whatever one is doing. However, this is not always a realistic answer,

The Buddha made a point of expounding a universal teaching, not one for hermits alone.

as anyone living with telephones, business schedules and other human beings knows. Things often happen too quickly. Nor is the answer just about getting away from all that. The Buddha made a point of expounding a universal teaching, not one for hermits alone. A more complete answer lies in the second turning of the Wheel, the supramundane Path, or life lived beyond self.

The supramundane Path "begins" with Right View which results from getting beyond the compulsions of desire through living according to ethical standards, and training the mind to notice its own nature. A stillness is perceivable when the movement of mind objects no longer captures the focus of attention. This stillness may amount to the first taste of Nibbana and has its effects on the intentions and motivations of one's life. You want to get back to that stillness, so you want to cultivate the ways that lead to freedom from the demands of the identity; you want to give up self-ness in body, speech, and mind.

The other factors of the Path are configurations on this theme. What is it that wants to manipulate people or impress others; what is it that wants to possess things and have its own way? Does that lead to permanent contentment or not? Is it comparable to the boundless ease of the mind at rest? Cultivation of the supramundane always looks at the dukkha of desire for things in terms of self. The result is an increase in personal modesty, gentleness and tolerance of others.

This is a very realistic Path, not a belief.

This is a very realistic Path, not a belief. You have to see for yourself what is really preferable. But most people have never found the possibility to test the Nibbana option; so some assessment of life lived under the normal set of assumptions has to take place. You have to *know* suffering for yourself, and come to the Fourth Truth through the other three. There are no short cuts.

As has been noted, this way is not the pretty route. It requires a good amount of personal motivation; but there are some encouragements. This teaching, the Dhamma, is part of that; the fellowship of those who practice the Dhamma—the Sangha—is a great help; and there is the Buddha.

The Buddha was a remarkable person. In some ways, it seems only natural that, having realized the fullness of Nibbana, all the compassion that a boundless mind is capable of could manifest through him. But that he was also able to devise a system, to formulate a teaching beyond systems and words, and then to tirelessly propound many variations around this theme of suffering and the cessation of it, is quite extraordinary.

The Buddha's own life was spent walking through the forests, villages and cities of what is now Bihar and Uttar Pradesh in Northern India, teaching and being available as a reference and example for many people. He never spoke or acted in any way other than the way of Dhamma. Thus, he became a living icon of the teaching—he himself said that whoever saw the Dhamma saw the Buddha.* Conversely, he remarked that the death of his body should not pose a problem for anyone because the Dhamma-

---

* As for example, in his advice to Bhikkhu Vakkali. (*Samyutta Nikaya:* [111], Elements, 87)

Vinaya would be alive to support the practice as long as people wanted it.

In my own practice, I like to think of "Buddha" in terms of the ways in which I apply the teachings: when I apply myself rightly, there is a calm and benevolent presence. And when I see Buddha images and reflect on the gestures they make, sitting, standing, walking or lying down, they help me to recollect the humanity of the Path. I am left feeling a deep sense of gratitude, respect and joy. For those who wish to be trained, the Buddha is still an available presence today. How many other people do we carry around in our minds—without even wanting to? There is plenty of room there for the Buddha; and the Buddha always encourages us to practice for the realization of unconditioned happiness.

This Path is a whole way of living; it's not a little time that you carve out of a busy day. Nor is it a matter of going somewhere for a day or a year until you "get it." That's still the habit of self and desire. The prefix *"samma"* implies a kind of completeness in which one is giving oneself without bias or expectation of gain. It is the spirit of entering into things for their own sake, to see them as they actually are, not as the habitual designations by which we value them. Another way of looking at the Eightfold Path is as a state of communion. At its mundane level, it is wholesome; at its supramundane, it is holistic; and, as such, it is the experience of consummation in a gentle and selfless life. This is why the true spiritual life is called the "Holy Life."

Another reflection on what is "Right" is that it is real for each individual, not just an ideal; it is the variable level of what we can sincerely commit ourselves to. If we cling to it as an ideal of what we should be, it's not "Right." There's not much point in making it into something to be done only for an hour or so while we have enough willpower; the Path should be something we can actually live and work with. As long as we give ourselves to it fully, then that level will always rise to complete fulfillment. But the here and now of it is that we cultivate the Path in a way that allows us to appreciate and respect our efforts, and to have enough confidence to continue. Then the Path begins to cultivate itself. This sets the tone for what is "Right" and gives each of us a sense of rightness or balance. Then we know without elation or dejection what has been cultivated and where attachment still remains. We follow the examples of the teachers, but we also have the confidence to walk this Path ourselves.

This Path is a whole way of living; it's not a little time that you carve out of a busy day. Nor is it a matter of going somewhere for a day or a year until you "get it."

9

LIGHT ON DUKKHA

Idaṁ dukkhaṁ … cakkhuṁ udapādi ñāṇaṁ udapādi paññā udapādi vijjā udapādi āloko udapādi.
There is this Noble Truth of Suffering: …
This Noble Truth must be penetrated to by fully understanding Suffering: …
This Noble Truth has been penetrated to by fully understanding Suffering:
such was the vision, insight, wisdom, knowing and light that arose in me
about things not heard before.

With these words, the Buddha goes on to deepen the significance of what he has just outlined. The repeated phrases of this section point to a penetration of the meaning of the Truths. In some ways, nothing new is declared, but here the Truths are gone through in twelve stages, three to each Truth. In each case, the first stage is a fuller reflection on the import of bearing the meaning of the Truth in mind; the second stage demonstrates the way of practicing with that Truth; the third fully penetrates the significance of that Truth. Together, the twelve stages define the practice.

The most striking feature of this section (particularly evident when chanted) is that there seems to be similar results both from each successive level of understanding as well as from applying oneself to each of the twelve aspects of the Four Noble Truths. The understanding that there is suffering or that suffering has been abandoned are described alike as "vision, insight, wisdom, knowing and light" (or "enlightenment"). Together, these present the Truths and "Awakening" in an interesting way:

could it be that the mind that can see dukkha is operating in the same liberated mode as the mind that sees the cessation of dukkha? Since it appears to be so, how are we to define Awakening?

Could it be that we don't progressively "become" Awake? In a sense, we already "are" Awake, but our wrong ways of interpreting things keep blurring the picture. There is only one thing that all twelve stages have in common, apart from being symptomatic of enlightenment — they all present a highly subjective experience without mention of self. They are all expressed as: "There is; it is to be; it has been." The unenlightened perspective surely is: "I am; I should; I have… " If I was a mathematician, I could probably draw up an equation based upon these data which concludes: "I am" = "unenlightenment."

The description of the practice of the Four Noble Truths does not suggest a process of *becoming* enlightened. It seems that a particular viewpoint is sustained, and understanding arises through it. The viewpoint is a focus upon dukkha in an objective, dispassionate way. This affects intention — the mind inclines towards understanding Truth rather than experiencing calm, stimulation or happiness. The way the mind works is that intention guides and sustains the quality of attention. So when the intention is to penetrate the experience of dukkha, attention gathers onto that feeling and investigates it. This leads to a most powerful insight because it reveals that dukkha is structured, created and not absolute, and therefore possible to be dismantled or not created.

In brief, the sequence as it appears — because words have to appear sequentially — does not indicate a progressive quality in terms of awareness but of the way that awareness sweeps through the experience of dukkha and fully maps out the predicament of the five aggregates. In speaking of the Way, the Buddha said it was one of deepening realization, but the essence of that realization is not delayed in time.

> *Whoever sees suffering, sees also the arising of suffering, the cessation of suffering, and the Path leading to the cessation of suffering.* (Samyutta Nikaya: [V], Truths, III, 10)

A common recollection of the Dhamma chanted in monasteries every day is of the teaching being likened to a lamp or the sun illuminating the world. The extension of practice is one of bringing that light to bear on all aspects of the khandhas. Then the Path is one of bringing consciousness into accord with Ultimate Truth.

The sequence of illustrations that cover this fourfold exposition on practice uses repeated motifs. At the top center is the symbol of the self. It is an interweave of lines that appear to create a solid form, but which is mostly empty space woven by one line that manifests as two creatures. These two signify un-knowing and desire. This subject undergoes transformation in how it appears throughout the sequence. It is not eliminated but turned into a source of radiance by the practice of Dhamma. The bottom center image is a reflection or further comment upon the top center

Could it be that we don't progressively "become" Awake? In a sense, we already "are" Awake, but our wrong ways of interpreting things keep blurring the picture.

image. In this first picture, we have the human paradox—the physical scenario of mortality played out against a backdrop of something more boundless, radiant and pure. We intuit a possible Deathless, immortal or liberated state. In a way, all our desires are sublimations of the yearning for freedom. The picture on the bottom suggests that the circling twelve-headed fiery Wheel of Dependent Arising is getting in the way. But notice, there is a light rising behind that skull. And someone with sharp eyes can see that the very form of fiery heads proceeding in a clockwise direction intrinsically creates a twelve-headed form of the radiant blue backdrop interconnecting with the clockwise circle. Going anti-clockwise, and purely because there is a Dependent Arising, is the Dependent Ceasing: "With the cessation of ignorance is the cessation of 'sankhara' … the cessation of dukkha."

However, the general mood of this illustration is one of being bound up. That is what the intertwining of the borders suggests. Liberation seems a long way from the experience of dukkha. We don't feel very inspired or liberated by the statement "there is suffering"; after all, what is enlightening about that?

The clue to liberation is hinted at in the expression used. The formulation of the words is slightly unusual: it's not the way that the average person would formulate the experience; they would probably say "I am suffering" or "She is suffering," etc. In such a case, the unstated implication is that something has gone wrong for that person and we should do something to stop them suffering. The instinctive response to stop the suffering is firstly to see it all in personal terms, and secondly, to postulate non-suffering and then to bring it about. So the movement is one of identification and desire.

However, based upon that appraisal, one might question if any such attempts can abolish dukkha in the way that the Buddha uses the word. With reflection, one may assume that, ultimately, we cannot get rid of "suffering;" that the best that can be effected are temporary alleviations of the problem through medicine, counseling, aid and amusement. This is the despair of existentialism. These methods of alleviation are so instinctive that even to question them brings up the response: "You mean, you can just coldheartedly sit back in a state of inertia and say, 'There is suffering'; and that any attempt to do something about it is just unawakened desire!"

On the other hand, the approach of the Buddha's teaching is based upon giving up the defenses, distractions or complaining that dukkha normally evokes in us; it feels like giving up the self that hides behind the defenses or goes elsewhere or does the complaining. To see if the method works, give it a test—not on the suffering that we can get rid of temporarily like discomfort or hunger—but on the dukkha that we can't do anything about: for example, the dukkha of birth, aging and death (which we cannot control); then the dukkha of being separated from what we love and having to face what we dislike (a pattern which we can alter in detail but not in a fundamental way); and the dukkha of living as a separate individual in a world with which we must come to terms and which is bounded by the

In a way, all our desires are sublimations of the yearning for freedom.

61

passage of time and the limitations of physical existence. Such subjects would be a worthwhile test; and in fact we have nothing to lose in not attempting to alleviate them.

What happens when we approach our fundamental predicament with close attention to the way it *feels*? As human beings, we have to get old and die. That feels like *this*. We feel frightened; and that is like *this*. When we reflect in this way, isn't this conducive to a sense of stability and calm? Does this not give rise to a "knowing of the way it is" and hence, the possibility of relinquishing impossible expectations and notions of the way it "should" be? And when we have no notions of how things should be, doesn't that make us clear and sensitive, more fully alive? In one who maintains clarity and openness, a strength of heart is available that we forget we have.

What becomes apparent is that the pain of death and grief is really the pain of not wanting it to be this way, not wanting to be experiencing these feelings. And the real internalization of the dukkha comes through trying to be separate from these feelings, trying to get rid of them. When we can accept separation and loss as a natural part of life, then the real soul-destroying sense of alienation and "Why me?" does not arise. When we realize that we're all subject to dukkha, then the pettiness, the jealousies and the grudges disappear. And we find, sometimes to our surprise, that we can cope with life's changes. In the peace of not-suffering and with the presence of knowing and clarity, there are new, real and relevant possibilities of what we can do. Instead of feeling hopeless and agitated in the presence of death, we can be with it in a loving and peaceful way.

The young have the dukkha of feeling they have to conform to the authority of those who are older, the dukkha of being restless, not having a good position, needing to prove themselves, having a lot of sense-desire and being anxious about the future. The middle-aged experience dukkha through the increased pressure of responsibilities, having a position to maintain, getting stuck in habits, losing some of their vigor and initiative and being anxious about the future. The elderly experience dukkha through not being able to keep up, loss of position and role in society, feeling unwanted, dimming of the sense faculties and being anxious about the future. Then there's always the regret over past actions, the limitations of body and mind and the sense of needing to find some meaning in life. So there is dukkha; but isn't it a relief to know that *it's not my fault?*

What happens when we approach our fundamental predicament with close attention to the way it feels?

I recall people hearing these teachings in monasteries and Dhamma centers and meeting others who had come to the realization that "there is dukkha." The response is generally: "So it's not just 'me' who feels like that!"—And sometimes even elation at having come out of the dull cocoon of confusion and self-questioning: "Why *me?* Why did I get this bad deal?" Having birth traumas, being damaged as a child, being jilted, losing a job, being betrayed, getting sick, having your mother die, getting shortsighted, going grey, losing your husband, being manipulated by your boss, and the rest of it, is dukkha. But when these are seen as non-personal—as aspects of a common experience—there is an opening of the heart to something more serene, less demanding and more compassionate. Our "own" stuff doesn't seem so much then.

Isn't it strange that sometimes the greatest sense of solace is to know that you're not alone, and that you won't be ostracized? So it's not that there isn't any dukkha, but now we know the pitch, and our heart feels free from that; what has changed is the perspective — a perspective that we call Right View, the view that is not-self. As has been described, Right View is the basis for Right Intention and Right Action; so it doesn't mean that we won't try to change or improve our experiences and circumstances, but that our actions will not be compulsive, bitter or arrogant. Consider the actions of exploitation and even wanton destruction of life that come about through the wish to make things better — for "me" and "mine."

To know "there is dukkha" is a radical step. The common myth that is perpetuated in society is that the normal person is happy, balanced and integrated — otherwise there is something wrong; maybe they're mentally unstable. We're even alarmed by unhappy people. Everyone in the media is smiling and cheerful; the politicians are all smiling, cheerful, confident; they even make corpses up to look smiling, cheerful and confident. The problem arises when you don't feel cheerful and confident, when you can't live up to one of the images of the model person. This happens when you don't have the right appearance or status symbols, your performance doesn't make it and you're out of touch with the latest trends; or maybe you are just poor, someone that the society doesn't want to acknowledge. Unhappiness, then *is* a sign of failure. Others think, "They're not happy, maybe they didn't do enough. And maybe they'll want something from me; so better steer away from them."

But "there is dukkha" brings us all together. The rich suffer from the fear of losing their wealth and security, and the mistrust of others — or even the guilt of being more affluent. The poor suffer from material need and the degradation of being treated as second-rate; and the suffering is compounded when those positions are taken as personal identities. It's the difference between "an enslaved person" and "a slave." As long as those circumstances are taken to be identities, we adopt the degradation or bitterness, or the conceit and paranoia that each entails. Then the dukkha of circumstance becomes a permanent feature of the heart and mind and affects our attitudes and actions. Is a poor person, for example, someone who has little money; or is it someone who does not have a good proportion of what the society's model for a happy human being has? Isn't their experience of suffering compounded out of being rejected, and therefore feeling inadequate, bitter and depressed?

On a recent pilgrimage in India, I met many people with very little cash and only a few old clothes; but they were not carrying poverty around as an identity, so they weren't suffering from it. I met a Sikh temple attendant who lived in one room with his wife and four children. His only furnishings comprised a bed, a stove and a cupboard. They were not embittered or depressed; far from it. They were in touch with something more reliable

The common myth that is perpetuated in society is that the normal person is happy, balanced and integrated otherwise there is something wrong;... they even make corpses up to look smiling, cheerful and confident.

than material good fortune. There was the dukkha of lack, and yet not of suffering. That's the way it is; the social model (at the village level at least) is not the person who is happy because of what they own, but who lives according to principles of *dhamma*.

When people live in accordance with Dhamma, then the limitations, the needs and the lacks, are acknowledged and effort is put into obtaining the necessities of life through what material comforts are available. In cases of real deprivation, surely a major contributor is the greed and exploitation of others; and that comes from the identification with material excellence. If we could all accept the experience of limitation on our resources and comforts, if our standard of living were not so high, there would be less people who felt "poor." Maybe with more sharing, there would be less severe physical deprivation. Instead of having a golf course in desert regions, refrigeration, air conditioning and 48 T.V. channels, we could try to accept the limitations that acknowledge "there is suffering."

It's not just a matter of everyone feeling wretched, but of learning to know and accept that this realm is one of limitation; to wake up to how it is; and where the real problem is—dukkha puts us in touch with the heart of what motivates our lives. The practice is one of sharpening the attention to catch our instinctive reactions of blaming ourselves, blaming our parents or blaming society. In this way, there is a focus on that recurring mood and the knowing of it as a mood; not to deny it, but to know it as it is. Then there is the realization of that which is not-suffering, that which is knowing and insightful. This way of insight can help us to cope with dukkha even on a small scale in daily life situations such as when we feel bored or ill at ease; so instead of trying to avoid these feelings by buying another fancy gadget, we can look into the heart and develop a gentle and nourishing response to any sense of inadequacy.

Hence dukkha is to be understood, looked at and investigated in order to find its roots in the heart, and what connects our conscious motivation to the Awakened mind. Rather than denying that there is any dukkha: "Life's great! I'm going to Hawaii, and I'm going to have a good time!", we recognize that the constant need to be entertained, to progress or to be appreciated by someone is a sign of not being fully at ease with ourselves. Again, the instincts leap to the defense: "What's wrong with going to Hawaii, getting ahead in life, or having a loving relationship?" In itself, nothing. Where the dukkha is depends upon what has motivated those impulses and we can only know that for ourselves. Relationships tend to go wrong when we *need* something from the other person; they seem to work when we support one another. The most productive activities are the ones that ask us to develop in ourselves. Knowing this, we can use the dukkha, the inevitable misunderstandings and inadequacies, to develop new perspectives or, at least, tolerance in ourselves.

If inadequacy is taken as a personal attribute, the dukkha is driven deeper and life can be lived in a very wretched or distracted way. Through dukkha not having been understood, there's a kind of despair about the

This way of insight can help us to cope with dukkha even on a small scale in daily life situations ... so instead of trying to avoid these feelings by buying another fancy gadget, we can look into the heart and develop a gentle and nourishing response to any sense of inadequacy.

human predicament —when will we ever get rid of the social injustices and the violence and the unfairness? Why is it that the law and order campaign is a failure; that the civil rights movement is not working; that emancipation and independence do not necessarily bring about contentment and opportunity; that Communism was a failure; that the American Dream went wrong; that better pay and better working conditions have not produced the Utopia? Because we haven't understood dukkha, that's why. None of these ideas is wrong, and they have not been without some good effects, but they don't rule out-self view. As long as that view is maintained, the system is always going to be used for selfish aims — by some, at least — or for noble intentions by others, but based upon personal perspectives of what is thought to be good for someone else.

To have understood dukkha is to have known that taking the five aggregates as a personal identity is the problem. Thus, understanding comes about through one's own dispassionate awareness to bear upon how, where and when it hurts. When one takes the five aggregates as a personal identity, it follows that there is the desire to be someone; hence the identification with race, nationality and sex, and all the desires and prejudices that accompany these. Subsequently we identify with those desires and perceptions; and we believe that that's what we are. So we expect our bodies, mental and physical feelings and perceptions of ourselves to be contented. Waking up means we accept that it can't be that way. Then we can stop suffering over it and sift our attention and intention beyond self-view. That is the essence of liberation. It is just one point. To have understood the point thoroughly means that this seeming imponderable mass of human confusion and pain has a source that can be abandoned.

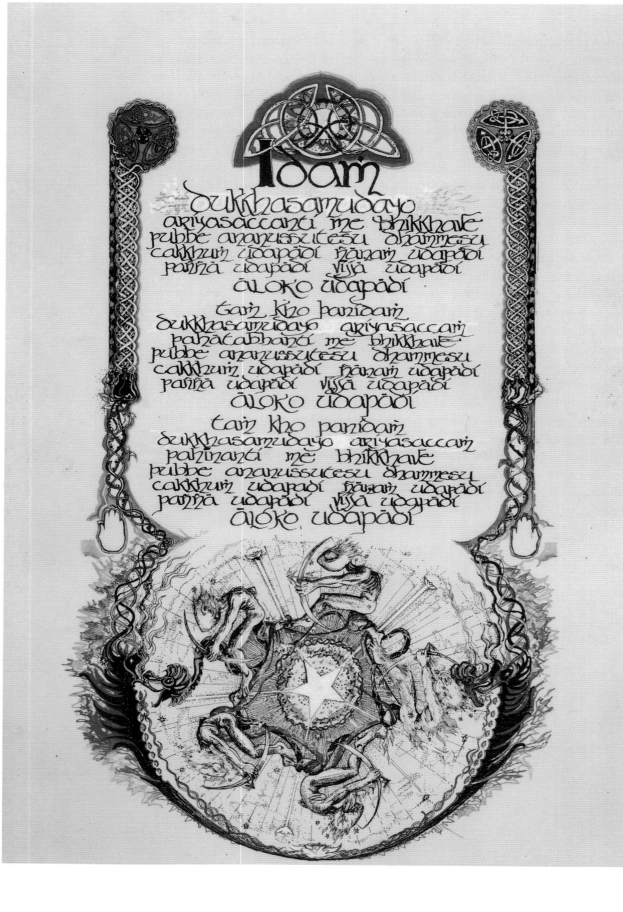

10

ABANDONMENT

*Idaṁ dukkhasamudayo … cakkhuṁ udapādi
ñāṇaṁ udapādi paññā udapādi vijjā udapādi āloko udapādi.*
There is this Noble Truth of the Origin of Suffering: …
This Noble Truth must be penetrated to by abandoning the Origin of Suffering …
This Noble Truth has been penetrated to by abandoning the Origin of Suffering:
such was the vision, insight, wisdom, knowing and light that arose in me
about things not heard before.

The Buddha then repeats the threefold analysis that he used for the First Noble Truth to explain the practice of the Second Noble Truth. The theme here is of abandonment. The insight of the Second Noble Truth is that there is an origin to dukkha; that the origin is to be penetrated by abandonment; and, in its third and final aspect, that it has been penetrated by abandonment. Notice here that the penetration is successive, but the abandonment is not. One doesn't become more abandoned; abandonment, letting go, is the timeless mode of the Awakened Ones. Abandonment is not something to be done in order that something else may follow and it's not done for a certain length of time until one has let go enough and can resume holding. After his enlightenment, the Buddha's realization that he'd abandoned the origin of suffering was not an implication that, since he had gotten rid of suffering, he could return to the normal way of being. Abandonment is not "getting rid of"; it is not an unpleasant medicine that one has to take until one is cured, but a joyful, fruitful way to live. Having abandoned old attachments, one lives with non-attachment. This on-going "abandonment" is the ease of not holding. It is the abiding place of the wise, the place of continual emptying and being beyond holding things in terms of their form or how they are felt and perceived. As long as we hold on, we want things not to age, not to change from the state we like or have grown accustomed to. And that is not possible.

In this painting, the frame of knotwork has opened out a little compared with the previous one. This is a reflection that the tangle of dukkha changes, it is really not the fundamental structure of our being. The mainstays of suffering are portrayed in the black (ignorance) and red (desire) serpentine figures coiling down from the top. These borders emanate from a threefold nuclear motif at top left and right. In the case of the red, left, it is desire (*tanha*) in its triple aspect—sensual desire, desire for becoming and desire for annihilation. On the right, in the black corner, we have the three aspects of un-knowing in action (*asavas*)—sensuality, becoming and delusion. However, at the bottom left and right are the hands of the Buddha in the gesture of protection.

At the top, the interwoven "subject" of the painting is seen as separate from the forces of delusion; there appears to be something pure blooming within that cross-weave of powerful energies. In parallel, at the bottom, a pure central radiance is surrounded by fiery forms. This motif depicts, in symbolic terms, the six sense bases—the five external senses of eye, ear, nose, tongue and body, which surround the sense base of the mind. They have drawn bows with arrows because they are hunters and warriors; they shoot out to seize that which is pleasant and unpleasant (for different reasons, of course). The external senses are depicted as being on fire, bound by the serpents of un-knowing and desire, whilst the mind is bright and radiant with lotuses of purity emanating from it, though surrounded by fire.

This use of fire is a reference to the Buddha's third sermon, the "Fire Sermon" (Adittapariyaya Sutta; *Vinaya Mahavagga*: [1], 21). Its theme is that: "All is burning … the eye … ear … nose … tongue … body … mind are burning with the fires of greed … hatred … delusion … with birth, death, sorrow, pain, lamentation, grief and despair." It was one of those "fire and brimstone" talks about where the real fires were and how to put them out. The metaphor of fire is a powerful one. It was used because the Buddha was talking to a group of fire-worshipping ascetics. Yet, sure enough, the origin of suffering—the feeling that we want to have something, become something or get rid of something—has the power to get us heated up. It also has the fire-like quality of consuming our attention and producing a lot of smoke that blinds our sense of perspective.

This smoke-screen effect is the force of ignorance which plays a major part in keeping the fires unrecognized. Our consumer society has standardized desires to the extent that we call them rights and we expect them to be fulfilled by life. Yet, it is quite clearly the case that the level of consumption of the earth's resources in terms of energy and raw materials

Abandonment is not "getting rid of"; it is not an unpleasant medicine that one has to take until one is cured, but a joyful, fruitful way to live.

68

is too high. And ironically, a good proportion of consumption is actually created by the need to get a break from the stresses of a consumer society that demands so much. It is not an "abandonment" society—except maybe the abandonment of sense restraint. So there's a lot of desire hidden in the ways we perceive and create expectations as a society. When this demand is accepted as the common norm, it never gets checked: "Please be the way I want you to be. I want privacy but connection to all the modern conveniences. I want my team, my family, my country to always be the winner and not let me down. I'd like my monastery to be popular and all the monks and nuns to be wise, happy and serene; and the teacher to be inspiring, but not so much that I feel intimidated; to be strict, but not severe; funny, but only at the right times; and to be there when I want him or her and not to be there when I don't. And I myself would like to be just right, always calm and assured and profound and light and … " The real conflagration is in the mind; the desires of the other senses are merely functional. It is in the mind that you can feel the heat rise, often just over issues and opinions.

But the mind does not have to be on fire like the external senses; the senses are just that way because they are bound to the slow consuming flame of bodily life, functioning in order to support bodily needs and instincts. Although the mind can produce the craziest, most outrageous desires, it always has the power to reflect on that heat. We may choose to ignore it, but this kind of knowing is clear, undeluded and Awakened. Something knows when we slow down or feel "burnt out" that this is the origin of suffering. The one who ignores awareness blots that knowing out as soon as possible.

For instance, an ex-military man was telling me about the common use of alcohol to relieve some of the extreme tension caused by the fear and aggressive conditioning of army life. You drink to get rid of the stress; go to bed in a befuddled state and then wake up the next morning feeling ghastly and confused. The anxiety over what happened last night and the need to try and pull yourself together for the morning is so stressful that you reach for the bottle of Vodka/Scotch under the bed. Soon your body develops the shakes and you need a drink to settle your nerves.

The Group of Five to whom the Buddha addressed this sermon did not have a drinking problem; hopefully, the majority of spiritual seekers will also not have to work through that one. But note the kind of suffering that desire can put you through, the desire to become something or the desire to get rid of. Here is an extract from the Buddha's description of his unenlightened asceticism:

> *I thought: 'Suppose, with my teeth clenched and my tongue pressed against the roof of my mouth, I beat down, constrain and crush my mind with my mind?' Then as a strong man might seize a weaker by the head or shoulders and beat him down, constrain him and crush him, so with my teeth clenched and my tongue pressed against the roof of my mouth, I beat down, constrained and crushed my mind with my mind. Sweat ran from my armpits while I did so. Though tireless energy was aroused*

Our consumer society has standardized desires to the extent that we call them rights and we expect them to be fulfilled …

in me, and unremitting mindfulness established, yet my body was overwrought and not calm because I was exhausted by the painful effort. (Mahasaccaka Sutta; Majjhima Nikaya: Sutta 36)

"Not my problem," comments the average contemporary meditator. Yet within the context of their own values, people do experience the same kind of stress with the desire to stop their incessant thinking. And the alternative course of desire is wide open: the "retreat junkies" obsessively tinkering with situations—wanting the right setting, the right diet, body work, enough relaxation, suitable doses of calming music, eclectic spiritual teachings from which to select the one that is exactly suited to their personal tastes, and a format that does not require them to give up what they don't want to. Contemporary spiritual training can be clever in a technical, manipulative way. It produces a great deal of one kind of knowledge—knowledge of how subtle body energies work and how they can be directed; knowledge of the structure and conditioning of the psyche and how to bring out the most fortunate moods. But it all leads to further perpetration of "me" and "mine" and "my wants." This technical knowledge is precarious—dependent upon sustaining circumstances. It is not free. The symptoms of suffering are being allayed, but its origin is not being abandoned. Technical know-how is not the knowing that abandons the origin of dukkha.

The Second Noble Truth hinges upon the First; suffering has not been "understood" nor looked into. But when we do look into it, the root becomes evident: the problem lies in self-view. This self-view is conjured up out of a consciousness moored to the needs of the body and operating from a desire mode. Our ways of relating to the world get created from the early experiences of helpless, dependent bodily life when consciousness is taught to be constantly on the look out for bodily needs and discomfort; and the impression arises that there is a *mental* or immaterial "me" that needs things. But what the mind really needs is wisdom, for wisdom is the most sustaining food. And the good news is that we already have it. We just have to cultivate wisdom in simple ways like knowing what our body really needs and how much we can expect of it.

So abandonment is not rejection. It is an unwillingness to hold onto assumptions and habits when they are no longer relevant or helpful or when they cause dukkha. With the presence of seeing or knowing, there is that which sustains the mind by itself. In that sphere, there is no need. Through encouraging investigation and thereby activating wisdom, these Noble Truths lead us to something incomparably more worthwhile than this mass of dukkha. That is why these Truths are fine, noble, pure and rare.

The more that our perceptions of how things should be or of how we'd like to be are abandoned, the more Truth can enter the mind. The perceptions based upon self-view are that I like to feel that I'm going in the right way, that I have my bearings, that there are people I can rely upon, and fixed systems that won't let me down, and that my body is healthy and not being corroded by some chemical additives in the food. Above all, I want my mind to be clear, reasonable and in control. But that's not the way it's going to be, is it? This system runs down; sooner or later one of my organs will mutiny and cause me pain. Probably, my memory is going to fade. There's a good chance that if I'm attached to mental clarity and agility, I'm going to get upset and frightened when it goes; and maybe I'll get put in some home with other senile rejects. It is better to abandon physical and mental states as something to identify with. Let go of those perceptions that the self-image depends upon. Then attention can focus upon the present and be free from bias. Things are known in themselves and actions are done because they are Right and not to bring about my imaginary future.

> *Thus, Bahiya, you should train yourself: 'In what is seen, there is only the seen; in what is heard, there is only the heard; in what is sensed, there is only what is sensed; in what is thought, there is only what is thought … ' Then for you … there will be no 'there,' where there is no 'there' … there will be no 'here' … and because both extremes are not, this indeed is the end of dukkha.* (Udana: 8)

It is an insight into non-dualism, the Way of realization.

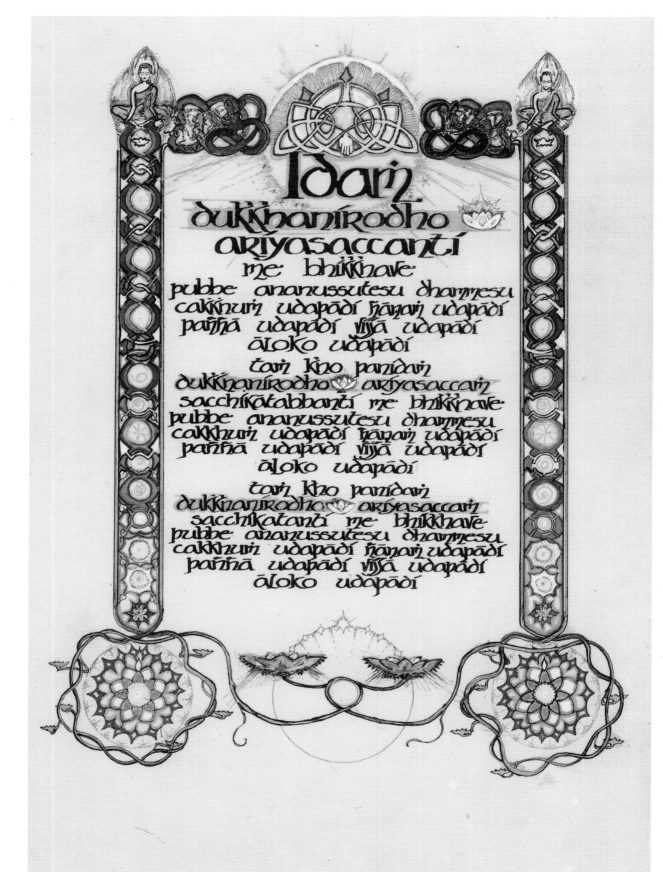

11

REALIZATION

Idaṁ dukkhanirodho … cakkhuṁ udapādi ñāṇaṁ udapādi paññā udapādi vijjā udapādi āloko udapādi.
There is this Noble Truth of the Cessation of Suffering: …
This Noble Truth must be penetrated to by realizing the Cessation of Suffering : …
This Noble Truth has been penetrated to by realizing the Cessation of Suffering:
such was the vision, insight, wisdom, knowing and light that arose in me
about things not heard before.

Here the Buddha talks about realization; making the spiritual ideal of Ultimate Peace real. The images in the top of these paintings have been developing progressively from the first one of a closed-in frame of knotwork. Here, the twin coiling forms of ignorance and desire are separate from the central interweave at the top. In the first picture of this sequence, the central interweave at the top was the tangle of self-view with its twin heads of ignorance and desire. In this picture of realization, the energies that support self-view have undergone some changes. Now, within the interweave, the radiance of true being and the earth-touching hand of Tathagatas confirming Suchness appear.

In the upper corners, the serpents have been replaced by Awakened Ones whose arms are spreading out to send forth Truth and to open to the world of circumstance. The knotwork of the borders has become a setting for images of light and purity. It culminates in the two lower corners where a six-flowered loop (of the purified sense-consciousness) is centered on a motif that represents the radiance of enlightenment. In the center, two more flowers represent wisdom and compassion—the two aspects of Buddhas that are not really separable. The thin blue circle, a simple line around an empty space, represents the abiding of Tathagatas, suggestive of the clarity of form and the spaciousness of not-self, in perfect balance.

In some ways the Noble Truths are mundane and in some ways supramundane. Remember that mundane doesn't mean worldly but the dualistic sense of oneself operating in the world. Consider then, what is the essence of this mundane understanding? Herein, one recognizes that the self-centered appetite for things to have, to control or to become is not appeased through gratification. This is the First Truth. Consequently, it is the very need and hankering for gratifying experiences and irritation with what we find disagreeable that are the source of our suffering. From this we develop insight into the Second Truth. Then we understand the Third Truth—part of the solution is found in simplifying one's needs and expectations, and learning to appreciate one's innate sense of being. If we are scrupulous with the ethical side of our life, the mind is freed from remorse and negativity. Meditation helps us to calm down and be more centered, and we begin to experience the fullness of the Fourth Truth. This is the experience of the Four Noble Truths on a mundane level.

As we grow more attuned to the need for full awareness, a natural sensitivity arises allowing the delight and joy of simple things to leave a greater impact. Cultivating loving-kindness and patience are also intrinsic features of the Way out of Suffering. By such means, we no longer bring problems into the world or into our own minds, and we generate good kamma, many blessings and skills. This is what is called a deliverance in terms of time. It has to be realized, activated and made real. It is not enough to theorize about it. And it has to be worked at individually by all of us for ourselves, with our own habits, weaknesses and strengths.

However, deliverance in terms of time is also temporary. One of the major difficulties is that our habits are often very strong, and it seems that they never relent. Just refraining from appeasing self-centered appetites does not make the appetite die down; in fact "withdrawal symptoms" can stimulate them all the more. Just when things seem to be settling down nicely, old habits suddenly reappear.

Life as a bhikkhu is a good example of what I mean because it heightens and projects the complexity of the problem. This life-style involves a good deal of limitation on activity and sensory experience. But it's not just a question of moral conduct—like refraining from lying or aggressive activity or sexual infidelity (which are good moral standards for people in the world). Bhikkhu life is also the enactment of an ethical norm as a foundation for reflection—for oneself and others. When I became a bhikkhu, I didn't know all the reasons for doing so, it just seemed right at the time: to practice meditation and live in a peaceful environment. So I took the opportunity to live in a situation that was conducive to Dhamma, where I could stay as long as I liked with adequate accommodation and food. It wasn't five-star, but I didn't go to the monastery for the food or lodging, or to have personal relationships, and entertainment. I'd done all that stuff and not been content. And now, having been given the opportunity to practice and hear the teachings with adequate support, I felt a sense of honor to fit in with the system and not disrespect it. And anyway, I thought I'd probably get what I needed from the practice quite soon and then I could go back to doing things in the normal way, according to my tastes.

As the weeks passed, I began to settle in. My ability to concentrate improved quite a bit, but thoughts started to drift through … I wondered how long I should sit, whether or not to move when the body hurt (to be sensitive) or maybe to sit it out (and be resolute). " … Sensitive or resolute, which is better? Maybe I'll endure for a while, and eventually build up a greater ability to tolerate pain … but it would be nice not to have it, and it's natural not to want pain … whoops, better get back to concentrating on the breath, the mind is wandering … not as good as yesterday … temporary setback … resolution … Breathing in … note the sensation in the abdomen … breathing out … flowing out through the nostrils … Wonder how long before you don't feel pain? … It would be nice to go for a walk now, stretch the legs, I could do that mindfully, yes … but that's giving in, you sneak! … Maintain discipline … one hour sitting, one hour walking … wearing out the forces of desire … How long does this go on for? … It's half an hour since I sat down … evening, dinner-time, cooking smells in the lane … normal people are enjoying themselves doing normal, blameless things like having a meal, pleasant company, nothing wild or crazy … yes, when I get out of here I'll be much more restrained, I've learned my lesson … no more wild scenes … and … what was her name? She was a lot of fun really, despite the temper … and … whoa! If it was all so great, why did you leave it! Mindfulness to the rescue again! Resolution … get back to the breath … breathing out … amazing how far your mind can travel in a matter of seconds … scientists reckon that the alpha rhythms of the brain travel at … how many cycles per second? … Maybe I could do this whole thing much easier with a biofeedback machine; definite improvement on these primitive Asian meditation techniques … one flicker away from samadhi and you get a bleep! Maybe when I get back to England … now SHUT UP! That's it, cutting through delusion … breathing in … breathing out, here and now … easy now … lighten up on the thinking, just bare awareness … like a naked ascetic: bare awareness, good one that, eh? It'd be nice to live on a tropical beach where you didn't have to wear clothes … Goa … done *that* too … what's the point? … Get down to it! Right, half an hour more and I'll call it quits for the day,

The monkey mind

give myself a little treat … like what! I guess I could walk round the hut and look at the moon … Big deal! … Easy now, "Nibbana is the highest happiness," here and now, open to the moment … don't repress … That's better, flowing along real smooth … you don't have to live as a monk to do this, it's just non-attachment, living with a smile … Taoism's the answer really, then you can have music, sex in a non-attached way … Who are you kidding! Breathing in … then long slow breath out, deep and slow … nice, and only twenty-five minutes left … God, my knees hurt! How long does this go on for?"

It's the real thing, all right. I suppose one of the benefits of living in a Buddhist monastery—and one of the torments—is that you have the example of the Buddha, and generally other living beings with some easeful, loving and wise qualities. And you realize what a blessing a skillful life is to the world compared to just following selfish desires. The benefit is that you feel it must be possible to work this dukkha out in a way that is not brutal or repressive; the torment is not being able to find that in yourself. At a certain point, the Path out of suffering seems to take you back into it again. Calm, and the understanding that following desire is not reliable, together produce all kinds of conflicts with one's habits. That conflict seems to create as much dukkha as blindly following one's desires. Then something has to shift.

For this you have to go beyond self-view, and develop the supramundane Path. What happens is that you begin to look at your dukkha in an impersonal way. It's true, different people have different mind stuff to work with, but essentially there comes about a realization that the core of the feeling of dukkha comes from something we *all* do: we take things personally. And you can't stop taking things personally just as an idea. The practice involves cessation, letting go of "self" through directly knowing "self." This must occur by feeling out and examining some pretty well-established positions. "I'm going to do it" is one of them; "I can't do it" is another; and the list goes on through every kind of self-view about "I'm not worthy/good enough," "It's not good enough for me," "I have a lot of kamma to work out," and "I have to get rid of self."

In the course of practice, all these self-views come and go continuously until, gradually, the realization of their impermanence begins to sink in. The practice is one of sustaining that attention and that realization. When the habits of mind discharge all these views, if one can keep to a straightforward, non-fanatical, steady practice and not cop out into some philosophical attitude about it all, the Way begins to take shape on its own. The Way is not-self, it is not made by controlling the mind through the will.

Of course, the Way is born out of personal effort, but it is effort of a particular kind—the effort to be mindful. For supramundane freedom, mindfulness is directed towards what we term "self"— in ourselves. The practice that is central to the supramundane Path is called *satipatthana*, "The Foundations of Mindfulness," described in detail by the Buddha in two Suttas of that name (e.g., *Digha Nikaya*: Sutta 22). One of the essential

It's true, different people have different mind stuff to work with, but essentially there comes about a realization that the core of the feeling of dukkha comes from something we all do: we take things personally.

and repeated expressions of this cultivation is a "knowing" that is non-dualistic. For example, "contemplating body as body;" "when walking, he knows he is walking;" "knowing feelings in the feelings." Furthermore, one is encouraged to know: "a hating mind as hating;" "a deluded mind as deluded;" "a developed mind as developed;" "an unsurpassed mind as unsurpassed." Even the hindrances are to be contemplated in this non-judgemental way — noticing greed, hatred, dullness, restlessness and worry, when they are present, under what conditions they arise, how they can be abandoned and the way that prevents them from arising.

This brings us back to the same mental mode as with the contemplation of the Four Noble Truths; an almost disquieting serenity with what surely should arouse our passions. The pragmatic contemplative recognizes that it's natural enough to have strong feelings, but they don't solve the problem. And it's not that one isn't *doing* something about it by meditating — the "knowing it as it is" approach requires a keen attention, but in the quickness to follow the moment as it is, there is no comment being made. The monologue of self which normally attends our actions and thoughts like the audience in a theater, alternately hissing and booing at the villains and cheering the heroes, is steadily reduced each time that we bring the mind back to the object of contemplation. The theater empties. And the mind begins to notice the silence and abide more in that. Energy is withdrawn from the proliferation of feelings and perceptions around mental and physical objects and the hindrances fade out. When there is attention without self-conscious concern over the mind, the mind begins to clear in a light and peaceful way.

The watchfulness or "knowingness" becomes a common factor of experience. It can be present in any circumstance and it can be directed to cover each moment of experience. So in one way, it is timeless and beyond circumstance. Its fleeting nature is actually our fleeting attention to it — mainly because we're not always interested in being Awake. Being Awake doesn't usually seem so important — until, of course, you feel dukkha.

Those who endeavor to practice begin to experience a dispassion behind the movements of mind. The practice is sustained through realizing the dukkha of *any* position held as self. One comes to see that the dispassion has always been there, only it wasn't *realized*. After the love and the despair and the tears and the excitement, one always comes back to the knowing. We tend to practice from the unenlightened position of: "I'm doing it. I'm going to develop, improve, get rid of, be wise, be more of this and less of that." Self-view leads to becoming which brings us to more dukkha. All these attitudes can free us from selfishness, but ultimately their value is that they bring the real problem and the Way more clearly into awareness. The supramundane Path begins with the priceless realization that "there is dukkha" which is unavoidably bound up with the sense of self. For ultimate deliverance, to have really known what the experience of self-view is, the mundane Path is a necessary prologue.

It takes some skill to get past the desire for attainment, but in searching

After the love and the despair and the tears and the excitement, one always comes back to the knowing.

for that Truth that is unconditioned, not supported by circumstances, we can know when we are still holding on. You'll notice that even attainment of refined conditions is unsatisfactory. There is a story of Venerable Anuruddha, a renowned bhikkhu, who sought the advice of the Arahant Sariputta. Anuruddha had developed some remarkable qualities which he described to Sariputta: he had the "divine-eye" with which he could see the ten-thousandfold world-system, he had great energy and resolute mindfulness; yet, he said, his heart was not at peace. Venerable Sariputta replied:

> *Well, Anuruddha, as to your statement about seeing the ten-thousandfold world-system, that is just your conceit. As to your statement about being strenuous and unshaken and so forth, that is just arrogance. As to your statement about your heart not being released … that is just worrying. It would indeed be well for the Venerable Anuruddha if he were to abandon these three conditions, if he were not to think about them, but were to focus his mind on the Deathless element.* (Anguttara Nikaya: [1], Ones, 281)

So what and where is "the Deathless element?" Well the only thing that does not pass away is that which does not arise. This is difficult to describe. But one can talk about that Wakefulness, that knowing itself that the Buddha encourages us not to become, not to achieve or add to, but to realize. It has always been here, but we have been using it in the wrong way. We have been using the awareness of the mind to seek out and create perceptions and feelings that foster our sense of being a separate identity. All that arises and ceases is born and dies. But the "knowing" of it does not. An untrained mind will attend to the *objects* of knowing — that which arises and ceases; a learner will be strengthening the power of the knowing; an adept will be proficient at focusing on that "Deathless element." Realization awakens to the Truth that has been caught in that process. Then one is not bound to reacting in compulsive identity habits.

When we cease to activate these habits, the mind experiences real, complete, ordinary peace. One comes to recognize that a liberated life is just a matter of sustaining the perspective of not-self in the silences and bustles, the pains and the pleasures, the successes and the confusions of life. Ultimate deliverance, then, is not bound to time nor outside of it. In order for cessation to be ever-present, it has to be a way of living that goes beyond the self-view. It is a Noble Path because it has to be selfless.

12

CULTIVATION

Idaṁ dukkhanirodhagāminī paṭipadā . . .
cakkhuṁ udapādi ñāṇaṁ udapādi paññā udapādi vijjā udapādi āloko udapādi.
There is this Noble Truth of the Path leading to the Cessation of Suffering: . . .
This Noble Truth must be penetrated to by cultivating the Path: . . .
This Noble Truth has been penetrated to by cultivating the Path:
such was the vision, insight, wisdom, knowing and light that arose in me
about things not heard before.

This illustration shows a more dramatic change of style. Cessation is only the beginning; it should not be taken as a final deliverance. Having insights and then making too much of them can be an obstacle. In a moment, a great sense of realization may dawn and the mind can become very clear and peaceful. That may occur for a few minutes or even days, sometimes without practicing anything at all. There is the cessation. Some people still try to understand the meaning of a mystical experience of oneness that they had a decade ago. In a sense, it has subsequently spoiled their practice because they continue to remember that experience, and wish to repeat it again; or wonder whether it was really valid and where it went; and are unable to start afresh.

Sometimes people turn up at the monastery claiming to be Arahants (enlightened ones) and Bodhisattvas. The Arahants are difficult enough, they don't want to fit into the routines and help out and they expect special treatment; but the Bodhisattvas are even worse, because they feel obliged to tell you how you've got it all wrong, and want to set up a teaching program. We had a Bodhisattva at Chithurst Monastery once but he couldn't tolerate anything cooked in a teflon-coated pan or any processed foods like white sugar or white rice, so he left.

Not everyone becomes so deluded, but people do have valid insights into not-self and experiences of cessation that get distorted. It's easy to get attached to insights, and to assume that you have become something. I recall in the early years of my practice having what seemed to me to be realizations of Truth and then the mind going on about them incessantly; sometimes it would take days for the mind to clear and relate to the here and now. I was so full of these great insights that I would get lost in thoughts and mental states and forget to clean my hut. Sometimes I'd feel that the experience of cessation or insight was just a fantasy but it was not necessarily the case. The problem was either taking cessation as self, or thinking one doesn't have a self, or sundry permutations on this theme. As the Buddha put it:

> *This is how he attends unwisely: 'Was I in the past? Was I not in the past? How was I in the past? Having been, what was I in the past?' (And similar patterns for present and future) … one of six kinds of view arises in him: the view 'self exists for me' … or the view 'no self exists for me' … 'I perceive self with self' … 'I perceive not-self with self' … 'I perceive self with not-self.' 'It is this my self that speaks and feels, and that experiences here or there the ripening of good and bad actions … '* (Sabbasava Sutta; Majjhima Nikaya, 2)

As the last of the above views points out, the self-view affects our activities, motivation and sense of achievement. It becomes extremely helpful, then, to live in a way that constantly asks something of you and trains you to relate to the here and now without self-consciousness. It is equally helpful to see the whole process of life as one of not gaining anything, even liberation. Then that whole goal-orientated way of thinking is discouraged. This, in a nutshell, is the practice of sustaining insights and letting go: the cultivation of the Fourth Noble Truth.

Insight into this Truth gives rise to Path Knowledge: knowing there is a Way rather than having a one-off experience that becomes something personal and part of one's self-identity. Put into a proper perspective, the experience of cessation brings about a greater willingness to work within the world of conventional appearance, limitation, restrictions, things going wrong, things going right and so on. The Awakened mind sees all that dispassionately. Knowing there's nothing to be liberated from except ignorance gives much scope for living insightfully.

> *This is how he attends wisely: 'This is suffering,' and 'this is the origin of suffering,' and 'this is the cessation of suffering,' and 'this is the way leading to the cessation of suffering.'* (Sabbasava Sutta)

In this picture, the upper lines that before were a cage have now turned inside-out to form what is reminiscent of a sun, and also of a dance. This reminds me of the image of old-fashioned dances where people formed

Cessation is only the beginning; it should not be taken as a final deliverance. Having insights and then making too much of them can be an obstacle.

circles with interlocked arms as seen from above. Along the sides, flowers again … eight of them in a flowing motif that is symbolic of the Eightfold Path. Down at the bottom is the Buddha, walking with the mudra of teaching in the world which was explained in the earlier frame on the Eightfold Path. Behind him is a triple-armed figure that is a symbol of virtue, meditation and wisdom: the threefold aspect of the Path. All around are animals, plants — all that is begotten, born and dies — and it is through this world that the Buddha is walking in a serene way.

The Buddha described his own experience of fully Awakening in a particular way. It wasn't just a momentary flash but a thorough review of the way the mind works, and, with each realization, the Buddha later commented: "But I allowed no pleasant feeling that arose in me to gain power over my mind." The night under the Bodhi tree culminated in the realizations of the Four Noble Truths as well as the insight into the origin, cessation and Path leading to the cessation of the *asava*. *Asava*, which I have previously translated as "un-knowing in action," literally means "outflow." The implication of the word suggests that, like a leak in a dam, it has the nature of creating further and more damaging outflows. Scholars' minds have strained to find a suitable equivalent in English to fully convey its meaning. The archaic "cankers" doesn't mean very much nowadays and the relatively inactive-sounding "taints" is quite common. Perhaps with further explanation, "outflows" will be the most useful term.

In this context, the Buddha described three outflows — three ways in which the mind rushes out in avalanche mode. These may be listed as: the outflow of sensuality or belief in the sensory "description" of reality, the outflow of becoming and the outflow of ignorance. The mind rushes into those modes of perceptual activity the way that water heads towards the sea down a gradient. Although there is volition, no *conscious* effort is necessary; because of this, by and large the outflows go unnoticed. Those who have no interest in Awakening will generally find themselves not questioning the veracity of the responses and perceptions that their sense faculties make with objects. Such is the power of the sensory outflow (*kamasava*).

Despite the changing and unsatisfying nature of sensory experiences, we find ourselves falling in love with new and refined ones. Exquisite states of mind bowl us over in the same way that glamorous movie-stars used to. As in the case of the "Arahant" and "Bodhisattva" above, and in my own experience, interest in mental stimulation is one of the causes for grasping at insight. One can become quite intoxicated with thoughts or with the mental feeling of bliss or confidence that may come with insight. Spiritual adepts can become skilled at producing and even radiating such feelings. They may even be convinced from the refinement of the feelings that they have realized enlightenment. But when the outflow of sensuality is still active and one is *moved* by feelings, refined or otherwise, what one is experiencing is something other than the freedom of enlightenment.

Becoming is a powerful instinct that has already been explained. In its latent form as an outflow, it gives rise to the mood that looks for, or dreads, results instead of appreciating the present. So we are never able to appreciate the quality of our efforts or our stillness. This is not to suggest that we should be inactive, but that our activity can be appreciated for its goodness of intention and the skillfulness of its enactment, rather than be dogged by the nagging Furies of targeted goals. It is important to understand that this "outflowing" energy to get ahead and make things the way we want them to be is by no means all that we have access to. It is quite normal for people to apply themselves to a task for its own sake without the compulsion to become something or any hope for reward; we call it pure love or devotion.

Another more helpful recollection for our active side, is of the spirit of play. This avoids the pitfall of emotional attachment. Play can employ a lot of energy, concentration and mindfulness. It doesn't have to be inane or fatuous. Drama itself arose out of a religious enactment, and came to represent archetypes and models of human behavior that would have an instructive quality. Similarly, art and poetry were originally sacred "play," sometimes bringing forth the finest qualities that a person had in order to portray aspects of the human situation. The spiritual path is play in a like fashion—an enactment of the highest values, of the faculties of Wakefulness. In this, becoming something is completely irrelevant; one doesn't believe that one is "enlightened," nor that one is not. The self-view is not being engaged. And the spiritual path is the supreme play because the script and the stage, or the raw materials, are our lives. Play is also adventurous and challenging and the personal fulfillment is dependent on the balance between commitment and dispassion. Then there is the necessary energy and the application without the burden of self-consciousness: the self has been consumed in the purity of the action.

When we use the insight into play, the plot and the scenario of our activity are not crucial—it's how we act within them that is important. Bringing the stage into the theater of the mind, we can develop skill in working with thoughts and feelings, activity, calm or confusion. This is liberating. Living in the present does not mean to consider nothing other than the tip of the nose, but that we are able to know plans about the future and memories as arising now, and having only a notional, "penciled-in" existence. Do we find ourselves panicking or procrastinating? Failures and successes can be appraised and learnt from rather than stored up in memory. This is why, in Dhamma practice, the reference is to "skillful" and "unskillful" rather than "good" and "bad."

The key problem again is ignorance, un-knowing. This is the third outflow, requiring no conscious effort and no attention. Ignorance is the view of a mind that has not been matured by insights into the Four Noble Truths. For example, notice how surprised we are, and sometimes even shocked, that things go wrong, that there are misunderstandings, that pleasant relationships come to an end. Yet that is *always* the way it is. Why do we assume otherwise? Because of this outflow, this irrational assumption. This is ignorance, the refusal to develop a mature response to dukkha. As we have seen, the shock of dukkha triggers off defense mechanisms in the psyche—the desire to have and to hold on. From that is inferred an identity in terms of the five khandhas. This is what supports all the difficulties of life. Attachment to the five khandhas sets up a self opposed to dukkha and blocks the insight that could transcend dukkha. In that way, this outflow embeds dukkha in the psyche where it is ignored and left to foster and stimulate further outflows. Hence the enormous emphasis, as in the Satipatthana teachings, on applying clear "knowing," knowing even greed, fear and doubt in an impartial way. That knowing has no self-interest yet uses the mind keenly and without distraction. We replace, in a moment by moment way, ignorance with knowing.

The Way of cultivation is described in terms of an Eightfold Path. Throughout his teaching career, the Buddha gave many methods and elucidated numerous factors that would support Awakening. But in this Dhamma tour of the Eightfold Path, our scope is limited to guidelines of action, meditation and developing an understanding that is selfless. Cultivating these in terms of daily life requires a dynamic and on-going teaching—ideally with reference to a trusted spiritual friend. The painting attempts to convey this as the way to a joyous life. Although the encouragement to sustain "knowing" as the principle for Awakening may sound ineffective and the reflections on sense-restraint may appear quite chilling, a mind that does not flow out into proliferation and grasping at what is ephemeral is both glorious—and normal.

They do not repent over the past, nor do they brood over the future; they abide in the present: therefore they are radiant. (Samyutta Nikaya : [I], Devas, Reed, 10)

The Buddha and his enlightened disciples, who had realized the cessation of dukkha, impressed people by their serene countenance: "cheerful, clearly rejoicing, with minds like the wild deer." They did not drag themselves along in life, faded-out and fed up with everything. It could not be that way: as you begin to see how suffering is compounded, you know that the cessation of suffering could only be realized by a sharp and agile mind and a gentle, patient heart. When the mind is liberated from craving and stops trying to set things up for oneself, then it radiates compassion, kindness, serenity and joy at the well-being of others. The fire of desire has become a light radiance rather than a consuming flame. This is the natural mind—the way we act when we are not confused or distracted; when we are truly at ease, our inclination is to be loving and wise.

As you begin to see how suffering is compounded, you know that the cessation of suffering could only be realized by a sharp and agile mind and a gentle, patient heart.

yāvakīvañca me bhikkhave
imesu catūsu ariyasaccesu
evantiparivattam dvādasākāram
yathābhūtam
ñāṇadassanam na suvisuddham
ahosi

neva tāvāham bhikkhave
sadevake loke samārake sabrahmake
sassamanabrāhmaniyā pajāya
sadevamanussāya
anuttaram sammāsambodhim
abhisambuddho paccaññāsim

13

THE HOST OF MARA

Yāvakīvañca me bhikkhave ... abhisambuddho paccaññāsiṁ.
As long, bhikkhus, as these Four Noble Truths in their twelve aspects were
not seen clearly as they are, I did not declare to the world—with its devas,
maras, and brahmas, with its samanas and brahmins, its monarchs and ordinary folk—that I had realized the complete and perfect Awakening.

In other words, here the Buddha is telling the Group of Five that
he didn't teach this until he had actually put it into practice himself.
The Buddha has already penetrated the Four Truths in their twelve
aspects. From that perspective, this picture looks back to what it
was like before having had those realizations. It is also a portrayal of the
problems that beset all contemplatives, bearing marked similarity to the
spiritual ordeals of mystics of all religions. Two intertwined serpents
representing desire and ignorance completely encircle the center where
the Bodhisatta* is seated in meditation surrounded by a provocative horde
of demons and fellow-humans. These two serpents form a screen that
prevents the Bodhisatta from seeing the Four Noble Truths, represented

---

* "Bodhisattva" (Sanskrit) is more commonly found, but I am using the Pali version of
this word to connote the Theravada use of the term. In Theravada, "Bodhisatta"
applies to someone inclining towards Buddhahood. There is only one Bodhisatta in the
world system at any time. In Mahayana Buddhism, there are many Bodhisattvas in
each world system postponing final realization to help other beings who have not yet
penetrated ignorance and craving. This is indeed an inspiring idea.

by the four emblems in the corners of the square framing the inner circle.

The center of the painting is congested. This represents the way difficulties of the mind seem to a sincere but unenlightened contemplative. Activating the aspiration to be free from attachments makes the mind more keenly aware of their presence, and of the difficulties encountered in relinquishing them. It entails putting forth energy in ways that do not gratify the outflows of the mind. When the outflowing habits are no longer catered to, their unresolved energy starts to throw up a lot of fantasy, doubt, and longing. The instinctive flow of energy towards self-view creates ideas and feelings that are constantly seen in terms of self. Further-more, the very process of outflow and attachment is identified with — one feels that one *is* an attached person: "Is this the right Path for me?"; "I shouldn't have such doubts"; "I shouldn't repress doubts"; "Why am I a repressive person?" and so on. These all contribute to the sense of self, which is an oppressive, congested feeling. Even a relatively insensitive person feels shut in when selfishness, self-consciousness or any of the more developed creations of self-view are operating.

The unenlightened practice is to smother one set of self-images with another: drive oneself hard to prove that one isn't lazy; be austere to prove that one isn't greedy; be indulgent in order to be a more fun kind of person … keep becoming somebody to suppress the doubts, guilts and anxieties that are an inevitable feature of self-centered life. The mental congestion gets pretty dense. That's why the realization that "there is suffering" is such an important stage. The time for this realization ripens when the energy of the outflows has waned enough for the mind to recognize that there is a lot of stuff to be resolved. Some people haven't enough space to see that yet.

The experience of the hindrances is not all bad news. It is a sign that the mind is bringing to light unawakened habits that need to be known insightfully. As it is taught in the Satipatthana Suttas, the first contempla-tion of Dhamma, of the way things are, is the contemplation of the five hindrances. These are sense-desire, ill-will, dullness, doubt and restless-ness. Contemplation of these is a matter of noticing their presence, their arising and passing, and what causes their arising and passing. With mindfulness, the mind can focus on how it is being pulled by desire or aversion, and see that desire hinges upon the need to gratify, defend or annihilate the self. Hence the forces of greed, aversion and delusion are always founded on self-view.

Although one can alleviate and dispel them in obvious ways — such as cultivating detachment, kindness, concentration, alertness and investiga-tive reflection — the hindrances always come back until self-view is aban-doned. As long as one imagines that the personal realm of the five khandhas has to be something that one feels fulfilled by, there is always going to be the sense of need, uncertainty, disappointment or even bitterness within that realm. To gain the dispassionate perspective that frees the mind from this view is a life's work; not necessarily because it takes a long time but because it is strengthened by the variety of experience that a human life

The experience of the hindrances is not all bad news. It is a sign that the mind is bringing to light unawakened habits that need to be known insightfully.

presents. All things, even the pleasant and commendable things that we think we are or ought to be, must be released from ownership. Here the image of the Buddha's life is again worthy of reflection.

The traditional image of the Bodhisatta attempting to realize Awakening portrays him seated in meditation beset by a whole horde of demonic forces and energies called the host of Mara. Mara, the demon, the figure of death, the deluder, appears frequently in the Pali Canon. Although he is generally presented as a separate entity, there is the strong suggestion that Mara is an aspect of one's own mind. This is backed up by the way that his host have names akin to the Seven Deadly Sins of medieval Christianity. It's the way that Mara speaks in the mind that gives him his deluding quality. Mara says things that appeal to the sense of self like: "Take it easy. There's a nice palace in Kapilavatthu waiting for you, which is much more pleasant and useful than wasting your time here." Sometimes Mara is critical: "When are you going to face up to your responsibilities and get a decent job instead of sitting under this Bodhi tree contemplating your navel? What kind of a Bodhisatta are you with all these crazy thoughts going on in your mind?" And sometimes congratulatory: "Well, you're really enlightened now, you don't need to deal with this world of unawakened idiots." Mara is always persistent and cunning: "O.K., this *is* the voice of delusion; but it keeps on going and you're never going to shake it off." Mara is the force that identifies us with conditions. The first thing that Mara attacks is the faith that there is a Way and the confidence to keep practicing it. Without faith the energy of aspiration dies, there's no mindfulness, no concentration and no insight.

The enlightened response to this voice of Mara is to say, "I know you, Mara—I know this is just a delusion." This is the unshakeable confidence in the power of mindfulness that the Bodhisatta demonstrates by remaining cool and unmoving in the midst of the demon host. Even after his enlightenment, the Buddha was assailed by Mara. One example was when the Buddha had paced up and down in meditation for a great part of the night. The Buddha washed his feet, entered his hut, took up the lion's posture (that is lying down on his right side, placing one foot on the other, mindful, clearly aware, and attentive to the thought of getting up again). Then Mara, the Evil One, approached and came into his presence, addressing him with these words: "What, do you sleep? For what reason do you sleep when the sun is risen?"

The Buddha's response (in slightly different words) was: "I sleep but there is no entanglement of craving in me. What, Mara, is there here for you?"* In other words, "So what, I'm resting! What's it to you?" Here, Mara assumes the form of the nagging inner tyrant of the mind that is always ready to take the darkest view of our behavior.

At other times, Mara's approach differs. Mara is not fussy as to how he chooses to entangle you with self-view. Mara can justify sensual indul-

---

* A rendition of the substance of *Samyutta Nikaya*: [1], Mara, 1, 7. In this chapter, there are many other incidents of Mara trying to weaken the confidence of the Buddha.

gence as "freedom to open to the sensory realm;" he can call self-hatred "being honest and firm." It is impossible to name all the constituent members of Mara's army, but the generals of the army have been identified as Sense Desire, Boredom, Hunger and Thirst, Craving, Sloth, Cowardice, Doubt, Obstinacy, Worldly Gain and Fame, and Conceit [See *Sutta Nipata*: 436-8 (Padhana Sutta)]. They have one thing in common — they all stampede the mind towards self-view through identification with sense-data (*kamasava*), becoming (*bhavasava*) or denial of dukkha (*avijjasava*).

On the outside of the central panel are the Four Noble Truths, which the Bodhisatta hasn't seen because of this veil of ignorance and craving still surrounding his mind. The core of all of the obstructions to enlightenment is the triad of greed, hatred and delusion. If we work inwards, the symbols of these manifestations of Mara begin to appear. At the bottom of the inner picture is the hog of delusion. The hog is wearing spectacles which represents the love of abstract speculative thought such as, "What if everybody sat under a Bodhi tree, who would milk the cows? If the Dhamma is here and now, why do anything special to realize it? Isn't spiritual practice a self-centered manipulation of the mind?" Despite the ingenuity of its questions, the hog itself remains caught up with ineffectual opinions.

Here, the hog is portrayed carrying a lot of books. These represent love of intellectual understanding. Intelligence can be deluding! People can become so enamored by ideas that they fail to notice whether these have any good effects. Ideas can be used to justify fanaticism and brutality towards other beings. Attachment to ideas can divorce people from direct experience where sensitivity, virtue and peace are found. The thinking mind, if followed blindly, will make one feel that one is getting close to Truth — here represented by the key that the skeletal figure on the left is proffering — but in fact the thinking mind is merely fascinated with the feeling of knowing and having interesting thoughts buzzing in the mind. So delusion can be both an extremely intelligent yet ignorant quality — ignorant of the laws of cause and effect or of what is for the well-being of others. Filling one's mind with a lot of ideas can be one way of blocking out the awareness of how things are.

The skeleton on the left is riding on the cockerel of greed. This skeleton has several sets of arms to suggest some of the objects that greed can pick up. The most obvious one, represented by playing the lute, is the attachment to sweet and flowing sensations. Beautiful sounds are included, as well as all the things that stir the emotions. We like to feel aroused and think: "Maybe enlightenment is a permanently high state of sweetness and light." Another hand is offering the key of knowledge to the hog of delusion: "Maybe if we had more ideas and knowledge, we could develop a syncretic wisdom of the ancients and the moderns — psychotherapy, Kabbala, Gnostic Christianity, Abhidhamma, neo-Platonism, Taoism — that would give us the sum total of enlightened knowledge. After all, we wouldn't want to be narrow-minded!" With this approach, we tend to get

It's not that one should approve of or do nothing about evil, but one's actions to remove the demons must come from a positive aspiration rather than from hatred.

confused and never bring up the kind of resolve needed to keep practicing any one of these Ways through the highs and lows of inspiration and boredom. It's an eclectic kind of delusion.

Notice the religious insignia on Mara's coat, and the set of hands clasped in prayer. Greed can also affect our inclination towards spiritual experiences, insights and practices. We can want to saturate our minds with meditation techniques, arcane knowledge, ritual empowerment and devotional exercises, and miss the point. Mara can make anything into a substitute for knowing how all phenomena really are. The telltale sign of Mara operating is that the mind has to keep active in order to sustain the fabricated quality of delusion. No matter how hard we try, we can never get enough, and the ignorant mind keeps wasting the opportunity to look at that very experience of "not enough" as the First Noble Truth. Yet that looking is what turns practices and techniques into tools for liberation. It is only the ability to reflect on even religious phenomena as relative, conventional truth, not literally the Absolute One and Only, that brings the mind out of the spin of desire and ignorance.

Coiling over the Bodhisatta from his left side is the serpent of hatred, with a wrathful ascetic seated on its head. There are many things that can irritate the mind and cause feelings of hatred to arise. Some of them are occupying the bottom right hand corner of the picture—figures involved in acts of violence. These are the grossest forms of mental defilements: lust and hatred—the things from which one recoils with the most horror. The ascetic figure up here is bashing them down, saying to the Bodhisatta: "Why don't you do something about this? You've got to take steps to wipe all this out." And the Bodhisatta is listening to that voice in the mind as hatred. Hatred of hatred, hatred of greed or hatred of lust is itself an unskillful root. It's not that one should approve of or do nothing about evil, but one's actions to remove the demons must come from a positive aspiration rather than from hatred. Unless positive energies of wisdom and compassion are brought into the mind, negative states are created, and there is no end to it. So meditators are encouraged to practice listening to their grudges and wrathful indignation with a welcoming, calm mind. Having no negative feedback, the demons fade away. This can provide a foundation for Right Action with regard to working with other people's anger also.

Further within the circle are more personal images that might have haunted the Bodhisatta's mind. At the bottom, on the hog's back is his son Rahula (the name means "fetter") crying out to his father. The figure astride the cockerel of greed is bringing up the memory of Siddhattha's wife, Yasodhara—beautiful, gentle and devoted. How could he abandon them? Behind the Bodhisatta's right shoulder are the figures of his father, Suddhodana, and his stepmother Mahapajapati. Suddhodana is offering the crown: "Come home, son, and rule Kapilavatthu. I'm getting old, we need you." Meanwhile, on the Bodhisatta's left are his five samana colleagues. Some look shocked that Siddhattha has abandoned the path of

The telltale sign of Mara operating is that the mind has to keep active in order to sustain the fabricated quality of delusion.

asceticism. Some declaim him saying: "You're all washed up, Siddhattha. You couldn't hack it as a prince, then you backed out of spiritual life too!"

Notice that they are all convincing, and all are personal. Their personal quality is what makes them convincing. The notion of boundless, timeless Awakening doesn't have the same emotional impact as the image of being a comforting presence for your son in his formative years. Most of us take the personal world as reality and base our actions upon it. And yet, Siddhattha had fully understood the personal realm. His early considerations were that all beings were subject to old age, sickness and death. His leaving the family was an enactment of what was ultimately inevitable: separation from the loved. And it was undertaken for the sole reason of rigorous self-inquiry—the aspiration to find a Truth that would set people free from the fear and despair of mortality. No matter how good a son, husband or father Siddhattha would be, his family would experience suffering, aging, disappointment, separation and death. Siddhattha himself was not secure from death—how could he accept the position of being a refuge to his family, when he couldn't even be a refuge to himself? How could he be the leader of a group of spiritual seekers when he had no Truth to follow?*

The insight into "there is suffering" begins to reveal the core of the existential problem of humanity which arises from taking the five khandhas as an identity. Desire systems issue forth from that false assumption. Wanting to have something, be something or get away from something; wanting someone else to be or not be something—all that arises out of self-view is dukkha. Mara is always right there saying that dukkha can only be shifted by changing the circumstances. Then if you change the circumstances (Mara says) everything will be all right. Siddhattha will be perfectly happy, Suddhodana will be perfectly happy, Yasodhara will be happy, and Rahula will be happy. Mara makes you forget that the personality realm is unsatisfying and changeable; that it can't be a haven of bliss even with a good measure of cosmetics and distraction.

Even those of us who are not intent on complete Awakening, but just want a little more peace of mind, need to know about the host of Mara. Whenever one is meditating, a quite responsible and reasonable idea will come along and start to poke: "The lawn needs cutting, you know! I really ought to get out and cut that lawn. Am I just being irresponsible by sitting here meditating? After all, the lawn does need cutting." Maybe the lawn does need cutting, but does it have to be right at this minute? But the voice of Mara goes on and says: "Well I can't really practice now anyway with that on my mind. Mow the lawn now, then I'll meditate later." Once we

---

* It is interesting to note that if Siddhattha had left home in order to fight for his country, our sense of moral indignation about him "deserting his family" would not be aroused. We have accepted that it is a noble and honorable thing to fight "the enemy"—causing death, bitterness and grief, but not to "fight" the spiritual enemy—giving rise to wisdom, compassion and an ethical path. We must also note that, after his enlightenment, the Buddha did return to Kapilavatthu to give the teaching that brought many of his family to complete enlightenment.

begin, we find that there are endless numbers of things that we ought to do. If we believe it, we find ourselves caught in the spin. And Mara says: "Well, I'm too agitated to meditate now anyway, maybe I'll just relax for a while … or maybe tomorrow … or maybe when I retire." When we reinforce these habits of mind, we establish that the conditions required for meditation are of being calm and having nothing going on in the mind. So we miss the opportunity to insightfully investigate the thoughts and drives that really affect us, the very ones that need to be understood. Game, set and match to Mara.

But for insight, one doesn't need to experience a great deal of calm or have lofty thoughts. Insight is based on looking into the way it is now. The more convincing and habitual the mood is, the less it should be heedlessly followed. The ordinary, unquestioned habits and assumptions are the very ones that we need to see as impermanent, coming from conditioning and not from a fundamental self. Otherwise, meditation becomes an irrelevant and fruitless hobby.

Of course, if the lawn does need cutting, there's a time for this. But recognize that there are always responsibilities and things to do, and many of them are based on good reasons. Then consider whether it will ever stop, and can it ever be done? I mean, can the lawn ever be finally cut? As soon as it's cut, it starts growing again; then you're back mowing the lawn. Is one's life going to be a round of cutting lawns? Is this what you're born for? To work for the welfare of all lawns, or the garden, or washing the car, or fixing the house, walking the dog, and so on? Maybe one should consider more clearly the amount of responsibilities that are undertaken and their purpose. There has to be an ability to look steadily at the compulsive drives within oneself and question their validity.

Not that we should blindly reject social responsibilities. They help us check whether our intention is to get away from something (which we can never do anyway) or to get to some pleasant comfortable space. Any trace of self-interest will always bring up greed, rejection or delusion. However, complete enlightenment is a higher goal and more fruitful for all beings than that of being a good person in conventional terms.

These restless, distracting hindrances are what the host of Mara are about. They make us think that the real world is the world of sense-data, becoming and self-view — the world of the outflows. The aim of insight is to practice in the presence of the host without suffering. Instead of feeling alarmed, ashamed or infatuated by their presence, one develops the ability to dispel them temporarily. That gives rise to an understanding that they are visitors, and not-self. With this confidence, undistracted energy arises in the mind, and, with that, zest and joy. Such spiritual factors lead to the full Awakening of the mind, to true peace. Then the need for position and states of being or the rejection of the sense realm — all that which is the expression of the outflows — can be abolished.

Notice how the forces of Mara completely hem in the Bodhisatta. Yet the Bodhisatta is sitting quite coolly, serene and peaceful; not trying to push away, reject or run away from them. The Bodhisatta is listening, turning his eye inwards—alert and upright to the way things are, to the pain and sounds of the world, the belief, despair and hope of it. And he is remaining on one spot—the place of knowing. When he has fully Awakened, there will be no Siddhattha, no Kapilavatthu, no Bodhisatta and no self in the realm of birth and death; only the Awakened Purity. Hereafter, he will be called "Buddha," the One who knows the Way it is.

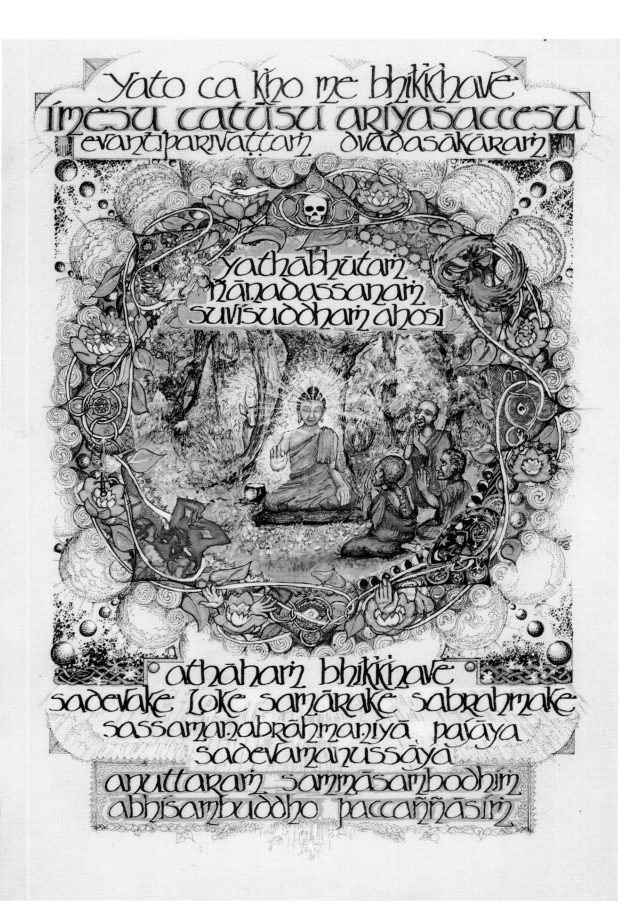

yato ca kho me bhikkhave
imesu catusu ariyasaccesu
evantiparivaṭṭaṁ dvādasākāraṁ

yathābhūtaṁ
ñāṇadassanaṁ
suvisuddhaṁ ahosi

athāhaṁ bhikkhave
sadevake loke samārake sabrahmake
sassamaṇabrāhmaṇiyā pajāya
sadevamanussāya
anuttaraṁ sammāsambodhiṁ
abhisambuddho paccaññāsiṁ

14

NIBBANA, THE UNIVERSAL POTENTIAL

Yato ca kho me bhikkhave … abhisambuddho paccaññāsiṁ.
But as soon as these Four Noble Truths in their twelve aspects were seen clearly
as they are, then I taught the world—with its devas, maras and brahmas,
its samanas and brahmins, its monarchs and ordinary folk—
that I had realized the complete and perfect Awakening.

The position of the Buddha is the same here as it was in the last illustration. He hasn't moved, but something about him has changed. His eyes are wide open, he is teaching the Dhamma, and he looks more vitalized than in his previous state as an unenlightened Bodhisatta. Also, everything else in the world has changed radically. The experience of the host of Mara has been transformed into that of an attentive universe, delighting in the Dhamma. All this has come about through the Buddha having clearly seen the Four Noble Truths and understood their implications.

To use another phrase, he has realized Nibbana. Nibbana is often held to be the ultimate goal in Buddhism, and yet it is rather ill-defined. It is considered to be remote, indicative of a superhuman vision that sees the illusory nature of the world, and hence, is free from grieving about its misfortunes. For many people, this gives Nibbana about as much appeal as an anesthetic—and a difficult-to-obtain one at that.

What does the word Nibbana actually mean? It is a term that was applied to a fire; when it is no longer burning, the fire has "nibbana'd"—

the elements on which it was based are no longer in a state of combustion. This may seem like sterility and lifelessness from the viewpoint of the fire, but from the perspective of the elements it means life and potential. The Nibbana that the Buddha pointed to was in the mind, when the fires of greed, hatred and delusion are extinguished. Nibbana, then, is the ease and joy that is realized through the cessation of those fires.

> *If … greed, hatred and delusion are given up, one aims neither at one's own ruin, nor at others' ruin, nor at the ruin of both, and one suffers no more mental pain and grief. Thus is Nibbana realizable even during this life-time, immediate, inviting, attractive and comprehensible to the wise.* (Anguttara Nikaya: [I], Threes, 55)

As it is based upon dispassion and cooling, the realization of Nibbana cannot arise from getting heated up about the host of Mara, or from denying its existence. It comes from replacing the compulsive movements of desire and ignorance with mindful energy and insight. Nibbana is the experience of space in the mind where previously everything was densely stuck together in regenerative congestion. In that congestion, a self is imagined that, now and then, longs to escape from the oppressive host of inner voices, feelings, doubts and desires. So, to one who practices insight, the idea that Nibbana is a selfish goal doesn't make sense, for the mirage of self evaporates as the fires cool. And the means of bringing that about is the self-less Eightfold Path. Essentially, the practice cultivates a purer and wiser response to faults and attachments than the "counterattack" or "defense" moods adopted by the self-view — and typified by the ascetic perched on the serpent of hatred in the last picture. Rather than fight the host or get away from them, you have to liberate the host of Mara from all delusion — from all the hatred and fear and belief that binds them with self-view.

What is it like when the approach to life is free from the force of ignorance? What happens to motivation when there's no self to gratify? Who is there to defend? What about the search for some state of happiness? And does this in itself mean that, with Nibbana, there will be no happiness and no motivation so that we exist in a state of neutralized apathy? Well, when we investigate happiness, we note that it is normally experienced in those moments when we feel we have enough; or we have a beautiful experience that blots out the aches and pains and troubles or makes them seem insignificant. Then sometimes, there's a relief when something painful has ended, and the irritations associated with pain and the resistance to it cease. All these forms of happiness and ease arise when desire temporarily stops. In the case of Nibbana, the Buddha brings about happiness in the direct and total way. The Buddha's Nibbana isn't through a temporary alleviation, but by a complete abandonment of the self upon which desire and discontent grow. Hence Nibbana is a nonspecific "happiness," not related to any particular circumstances; therefore, it is not subject to change.

To bring that about requires a deep sense of motivation, but one that

Rather than eradicating what is individual and particular, Dhamma practice allows us to experience a changing uniqueness — because life is not held within compulsive self-patterns.

goes beyond the reach of self. Liberation can only come about through letting go of the hosts of Mara which are always manifesting through our unenlightened attitudes towards ourselves and the world. To liberate all those beings, forces and memories may seem like a task of hopeless gallantry, but insight brings the whole process down to the subtle point of self-view. When one isn't acting from a position of self, its fabricated needs and desires have no footing upon which to stand. When this is experienced, even for a short while, there is vitality, ease, and life seems full of potential. So the energy of life gets released from the constricting "self" pattern into the total, universal pattern.

The serpents of ignorance and desire have turned into a garland of lotuses — the Eightfold Path — woven around the Four Noble Truths. Radiance pervades the world-system, here depicted by many planetary forms. These represent every permutation of the external and internal worlds: every person, every individual quality or form that is held as having separate existence. Here, the worlds are seen as part of a totality; their separateness has blended into a pattern. This, rather than uniformity, is a useful model of the experience of individuality in the context of not-self. Rather than eradicating what is individual and particular, Dhamma practice allows us to experience a changing uniqueness — because life is not held within compulsive self-patterns. Then all personality and separateness can be seen and respected without attachment, and it all fits together. Our apparent identity is one of being a localized experience of the changing universe. In fact, all harmony, all true fitting together without force, is dependent on some practice of not-self. Notice what such harmony in life actually feels like — there's space, buoyancy and potential in that feeling. Yet we can only experience that by understanding and letting go of our own attachments and views, not through being with "harmonious people."

The Buddha commented that he did not contend with the world; the world contended with him (*Samyutta Nikaya:* [III], Elements, 94). The exemplar of total harmony, he is at the center of this painting as a focus for all the worlds, an access point for all beings, no matter how varied. Four primary character types encircle him outside of the particular expression of individuality (the circle of bhikkhus) and within the more universal formulation of the whirling worlds. From top right, proceeding clockwise, these are: the solar power, represented by a mythical fire bird, the *garuda;* the lunar power, represented by the water snake, the *naga;* the power of earth, represented by a satyr, ogre, or *yakkha;* and the power of ether (space and sky), represented by an angel or *devata.*

Normally these exist in opposition to each other. *Garudas* attack and devour *nagas.* The conflict of these two refers, in one sense, to the cyclical drying-up of the rivers by the heat of the tropical sun, and, in another sense, to the discord so often experienced between the rational (solar) and the irrational (lunar) aspects of the mind. The rational has the capacity to remove phenomena from their context and sees them in an abstract light.

Throughout his life, the Buddha spoke sincerely and compassionately to every kind of human and non-human being: to yakkhas and devas and nagas as well as fierce bandits, sophists, distraught widows and proud monarchs.

A rational mind can classify a parrot as a bird and study its characteristics to develop principles about birds, feathers, and flight. However, it sees a parrot as separate from its tree, its habitat and the creatures that prey on it, and puts the parrot on a perch in a cage in order to "look after" the poor brute. The irrational flows along with the rhythms of Nature like the moon and the water. However, although it may feel a sense of unity with Creation, it can't get any perspective on the manifold world. It tends to meander and lack the vision of the rational. And so we spend our day looking at parrots instead of learning about flight.

The Earth characteristic here is also irrational; instinctive and spontaneous rather than intuitive and cohesive. It is characterized by its separateness; it is lumpy and fixed—yet occasionally volcanic and giving little warning of its vast upheavals. On the psychological level, the satyr represents a disruptive element in the irrational realm. It is the urge of spontaneous creation, the force that does not conform and flow according to generally held feelings. So it is in opposition to the cohesive Water element, either blocking it or being eroded by it. Their conflict is just like the emotional conflicts between men and women.

The massive substantiality of Earth is also opposite to the formlessness of the Ether represented by the angel of the next vignette. Psychologically, Ether is the aspect of the rational that looks towards balance, and the propriety of universal perspectives. In the overwhelming burst of Earth's spontaneous creativity, there's not much possibility for cool objectivity about what is right or suitable. Earth's expression is in terms of "what I want now, the way it feels for me." Ether is cool and mobile, but lacks immediacy; everything is possible, but nothing ever takes form. Lacking form, it tends towards an indifferent passivity to the forces that can move through it. Hence its presence is also frustrating to the soaring drives of the solar intellect; just as diplomats are a nuisance to people with a sense of mission.

When such forces operate independently of each other, they create an assembly point for Mara's host. They become harbors for self-view. Pride and conceit gather around the fiery Sun; moodiness and inconsistency collect within the watery Moon; stubborn wilfulness settles into the firm Earth; and aloof dilatoriness drifts and blows around in the space of the Ether.

Despite the great differences between these psychological characteristics, the Buddha-mind is a point of harmony that they can all reach. We can all contemplate these energies whenever they manifest. The Buddha sees dukkha in taking a position of one against another, and he abandons this. Throughout his life, the Buddha spoke sincerely and compassionately to every kind of human and non-human being: to yakkhas and devas and nagas as well as fierce bandits, sophists, distraught widows and proud monarchs. Knowing the Dhamma, that all phenomena are only conditioned configurations of an Unconditioned, he saw all these appearances as part of the way it is, and thereby did not make conflict with them. In this enormous act of faith, mindfulness and selflessness, the Buddha gives up any position in the conscious world—apart from to know it. This is Nibbana's cooling of desire and attachment. And in the internal psychological realm, it is the Buddha of our own mindful wisdom that allows characteristics to harmonize with each other. In the wholeness of knowing, there's room for the rational and the irrational, the spontaneous and the orderly. Then we can learn from life, how it actually is—not from a fixed position of how we take it to be.

When our aspiration is to realize Nibbana and to liberate all beings, we can reflect on all positions and archetypes. For example, consider the Earth and Ether characteristics as the respective values of individual experience and expression, and conformity to principles of universal Truth. When these are mutually respected by a mind that is not attached to any position, then the individual can be seen as enriching and giving meaning to the universal, and the universal as establishing a frame of reference for the individual. So in a religion, if the orthodox established viewpoint suppresses the individual, the religion loses its immediacy and its vitality. But the traditional expressions of Truth have to be respected to create a foundation for the individual. If this is not done, there is no common ground for dialog or transmission through time. Worse still, each individual becomes their own cause and God, and represents a new tyranny of *my* way and *my* view being the only way.

Unenlightened beings cling to their views and perceptions. Our conscious world is full of positions and attitudes that we alternately favor and despise. It is peopled with friends and enemies; those we are attracted to and those we are repelled by; those to whom we feel loyal, such as "my family;" and those we feel separate from and take no responsibility for. We can act in good and bad ways, we have bodies with masculine or feminine features, and we can be grouped according to racial type. We have minds that formulate things according to differences. But in emphasizing differences or seeking to establish ourselves as identities, we add to the sum total of divisive and conflicting energy in ourselves and in the world.

We may dismiss our intuitive side and repress the rational or lose contact with rational discernment. We may attach to traditions or to not having traditions. We may adopt a viewpoint and neglect others—or even cling to the view that one shouldn't have a viewpoint. All these become sources of identity, and as long as we hold on to views about ourself or each other, no matter how valid they seem, we prevent the possibility of being liberated from self. Then there is the teaching of the Buddha:

> *"What is the teaching of the samana, what are his views?"*
> *"According to my teaching, Sir ... there is no contending with anyone in the world, because of which the Pure One is not obsessed with ideas as he practices. He remains unattached to sense-pleasures, without confusion, free from regret, empty of the desire to be something or to be nothing. This is my teaching, this my view."* (Madhupindika Sutta; Majjhima Nikaya, Sutta 18)

Because his mind has realized Nibbana, the Buddha was content to teach using the viewpoints and conventions of the time rather than create another set of polarities to establish "Buddhism." So he taught within the conventions of the Vedic culture—kamma, Dhamma, Nibbana, heaven realms—to the societies of samanas, brahmins, monarchs and ordinary folk. His way of teaching was often to ascertain what his audience's position was, and, from that position, expound a Path to Ultimate Truth, the experience of no conflict, no suffering, Peace, the Unconditioned, Nibbana. So he taught the Way independent of any personal position or philosophical viewpoint, presenting themes that relate to the way that human beings in general experience and live their lives.

The fundamental position that we can all reach is the basis of the Buddha's teaching: we all suffer and nobody likes it.

The fundamental position that we can all reach is the basis of the Buddha's teaching: we all suffer and nobody likes it. The nature of the human realm is that we are sensitive and affected by everything. Because of this, we tend to take positions for or against different experiences; these positions harden into the boundaries and habits of self. All that creates separation, loneliness and conflict. Yet we all want to get off this one-way road going nowhere, and the wish to get beyond the self-view can bring us together. The practical effects of that must be for the welfare of everyone: cultivating no-self for ourself alone is by definition an impossibility. So the realization of Nibbana is to be shared, available for those who no longer want to be men and women, mothers and sons, samanas and lay people, Asians and Americans. When there is Awakening, ultimately there is no position to take, no separation.

In this illustration, the Buddha is beginning to proclaim the universal law that will balance out all the polarities of humanity. Seeing yourself as separate from everything else is an illusion. Acting in that way brings pain, restriction, fear, disappointment—dukkha. Listen to the world as it is and find the balance in your own mind. Find the place where there is no ignorance, no avoidance of the way it is. Abandon the desire that things be your way. For each one who does this, there will be harmony, serenity with the difficulties, and delight with what is pleasing. Such a balance will immediately benefit the world and provide the inspiration for others to cultivate the Way.

Ñānanca
pana me dassanam
udapādi
akuppa me
vimutti
ayamantima
jāti
natthi dāni
punabbhavo'ti

15

UNSHAKEABLE FREEDOM

Ñāṇañca pana me dassanaṁ udapādi
akuppā me vimutti ayamantimā jāti natthidāni punabbhavo ti.
The knowledge and the vision arose in me:
"Unshakeable is my deliverance. This is the last birth. There is no further becoming."

Finally, the Buddha asserts that his Awakening to Truth is not just a momentary vision; it's no passing thing. What makes him so sure? After all, everyone experiences certainties that don't always prove reliable. How many relationships begin with the conviction that "You're the one for me;" only to find out a year or two later that "You're not"? In the places where I've lived as a bhikkhu, quite a few people have come to the monastery with the absolute certainty that they are going to be monks or nuns, and this is the only way to live. Not many of these people make it through the preliminary stages. It's not that they're lying, it's just that they don't always understand the nature of conviction.

Conviction based on belief and affirmation is unreliable. Belief by its very nature needs to be constantly affirmed. Left unattended it wilts. When religion is based on belief, the adherents must keep on meeting to tell each other how wonderful it all is or go out and convert someone. Getting fresh converts boosts one's own belief to no end. But why is there this demand to believe? Does Truth or God, really *need* to be believed in?

When inspiration initiates and promotes conviction, it aims to preserve a particular feeling, role or image. The image then easily becomes a stereotype. Familiar examples we all know about are: the loving couple—always sharing and caring, growing together through life; or the serene, gentle monk—abiding in the peace of non-attachment, delving into the profundities of the mind, composed and wise. As ideals they are fine but one can't expect to realize them without going through the trials posed by the things that challenge them. With regards to monastic training, confronting the hindrances, living together with other people as they go through their changes and growing pains, and the duties of maintaining a monastery as a place for people to practice, all involve something other than liking the idea of peace and mental refinement. Inspiration alone doesn't usually provide the practical know-how to help you see the need or appreciate the means for discerning effort. If you're just interested in inspiration, it's generally easier to dump one idea and find another idea, situation, partner or cause, than go through the work of bringing the ideal into the realm of reality. Continuously switching loyalties is the samsara shuffle which is based on desire for a particular condition, a certain place, a scene, a mood, an atmosphere, a role or a particular state of mind.

The Buddha looked at the fundamental conditions of life—the conditions of the body and mind—and not special or fascinating ones. Rather than approving or disapproving of any of them, he looked at the inherent nature of them all. All phenomena are caused. They arise dependent on conditions. Mental phenomena depend on interest, belief and other supporting conditions which include some form of desire. All of these are subject to change and can only be temporarily sustained. For this reason, things are unsatisfactory. It follows that no condition can be an Absolute Truth, nor can it be the true quality of a person or any living being. Whether the "self" is being masqueraded as a voice in the mind (myself), or a bird on a branch (some other self), it doesn't matter. All conditions which arise are impermanent and not-self. Yet an unenlightened mind sees the world from the perspective of conscious experience based in desire/ becoming and birth/death. The experience of self, which the mind holds instinctively, goes against all reason.

Just consider what gives rise to the conviction that one has an identity which is found within a body. Not the *thought,* but the emotional conviction, "This is my body." Isn't that conviction based on attachment to bodily pleasure and pain? The sense of actually *being* a pleasant bodily feeling is ecstatic, however impermanent. It feels like a higher, more unified sense of being than the diffuse bric-à-brac of ordinary consciousness. It *feels* like the real thing. Unfortunately the experience is fleeting, and is a set-up for being put into the firing line of receiving unpleasant feeling as the real thing. Hence the violent swings that sensual indulgence puts you through. From another perspective, there can be pleasant and unpleasant *mental* feelings based on the body. Being told that one's body is wonderful or disgusting is liable to cause a certain amount of identification. Yet if one's

When religion is based on belief, the adherents must keep on meeting to tell each other how wonderful it all is or go out and convert someone.

reference point is that this body is mostly made up of protein chains of hydrocarbon molecules or of flesh, bones, nerves and various kinds of liquid, there isn't a sense of "self." And this factual description is more accurate than the value judgements our emotions believe in.

What about the mental processes that give rise to the belief that we *are* our thoughts? Belief in the states of the mind is really based on aspects of interest (either through desire or aversion): "I approve of these states — they are 'me'; I disapprove of these — they are also 'me.'" Then the good me has to get rid of the bad me. And despite my efforts to get rid of it, the bad me keeps popping up like a jungle guerrilla. When we think the campaign is too tough, we look for another cause to believe in; we switch to another set of thoughts, interests and attitudes. With the mind, the very *creation* of phenomena is conditioned by the mental act of believing that they are aspects of our self. When you take the "special and personal" labels off; when what we experience is the same as everybody else, all phenomena amount to nothing much. And in one way, they are all the same: they are all impermanent, dukkha and not-self. And as such, they no longer emotionally bind the heart. When that happens, the wizard's spell is broken. That "disenchantment" with conditions is what the process of insight awareness is about.

From where does the Buddha see things? Isn't that yet another position that the mind can attach to? What is the Buddha's wisdom based upon? What happens to it when he dies? If we use the Buddha as a sign, the no-position of the Awakened Mind can be made clearer. In considering the Buddha, one can't really say that the body is the Buddha, nor are the feelings, or the sense-consciousness, or the ideas, thoughts and so on. The world of the khandhas is what is seen and not grasped by Buddhas. But Buddhas have the five khandhas. So all we can say is that the existence of Buddhas can only be designated in relationship to them; and when the five khandhas cease, we can't make any more designations. So Ultimate Truth can't be contained in any concept. Can you conceive of the inconceivable? Not being conceived, it can't be born; not being born, it can't die. Being beyond birth, death and all conceiving, it has no position and no characteristic. It has no "self."

When we can't hold onto the Ultimate Truth, and everything else is dukkha, the problem becomes one of sustaining the motivation for practice. Maybe if we were sufficiently high-minded, we could sustain endeavor without the support of developing something, making progress or feeling happier. But that isn't how it is. One's practice *should* be to carry out every action with a one-pointed attention to do the thing right, irrespective of personal cost or gain. Moreover, the various pleasant or unpleasant feelings that arise in the body and mind *should* not be adhered to. Nor *should* one cling to the peacefulness of the neutral feelings. To abandon such preferences however, requires the mind to be constantly in touch with the ground of consciousness within which phenomena arise. To do this requires a major change, not only of energy and attention, but of ingrained value systems. Most people's problem is that their mind still remains unconvinced of the value of Nibbana. Whatever the theory, when it comes down to the actuality, we are still turned on by the sensory world despite getting burned by it. How does one develop the taste for the Unconditioned? Is it just through being disillusioned with everything else? This sounds like a pretty grim prospect....

However, the insight teachings of the Buddha are practical and instructive rather than inspirational. For this Path, aspiration comes from faith rather than belief. Faith is the quality that sustains the heart without the need to have something else to hold onto. It is akin to courage or the willingness to try something out. Dhamma practice has to begin with this, otherwise there is no real giving of oneself, and no personal inquiry. With one moment of faith, we practice one moment of letting go. But one moment of Dhamma has a furthering quality. The practice is one moment at a time, and yet very firm and supportive. The Buddha explained it as a natural process:

> *Bhikkhus, for one who is virtuous ... there is no need to wish: 'May freedom from remorse arise in me.' Bhikkhus, it is in accordance with nature that freedom from remorse arises in one who is virtuous. For one who is free from remorse, there is no need to wish: 'May joy arise in me.' Bhikkhus, it is in accordance with nature that joy arises in one who is free from remorse. (And similarly joy is the foundation for rapture, rapture for calm, calm for contentment, contentment for concentration, concentration for insight, insight for dispassionate realization, realization for liberation.)*
> (Anguttara Nikaya: [V], Tens, 2)

Motivation without selfish desire, attachment or becoming is a matter of sustaining the Dhamma, and letting the practice bring up our fundamental wholesomeness. In brief, we develop qualities in which we can trust. The cultivation of Dhamma, remember, has two Paths—the mundane and supramundane. The mundane Path begins with setting up conditions like living honestly, without intoxication, aggression or greed. These are favorable for peace of mind. Moral integrity is the best foundation for meditation. Then meditation makes your mind more calm and clear—and these are pleasant and fruitful conditions. Moreover, if you sustain the practice, it gives you the insight to realize that the mundane is ultimately not good enough, and that there is a supramundane.

The supramundane practice is based on the same moral conditions, but brings the mind's attention to the self-view—the judging, wanting, comparing, complaining, besieged ego that is trying to find exactly the right situation for itself. It uses conditions in the body, the mind and the world for reflection on the unsatisfactoriness of seeing things in personal terms. The supramundane Path in its entirety is aimed at shifting the mind to fit the world rather than expecting the world to fit the mind. The certainty of that Path is quite different. It's not based on propping up one's faith with *attachment* to conditions—such as great teachers, lots of fellow-disciples and scintillating teachings. Those things if they are around are a bonus. But

Faith is the quality that sustains the heart without the need to have something else to hold onto. It is akin to courage or the willingness to try something out.

when the teacher has confessed to a drink problem and everybody leaves except you and the janitor, you can keep going—if your practice is based on your own insights. The unshakeable insight isn't dependent on having a series of inspiring perceptions to believe in. Perceptions are dukkha, and the need for belief is dukkha. True insight has a delight and uplift based on not holding onto the conditions of the body and mind. It is called the Unconditioned. And it has the taste of freedom.

> *Just as the great ocean has only one taste, that of salt; even so has the teaching and discipline only one taste, the taste of liberation.* (Anguttara Nikaya: [IV], Eights, 19)

Let's take a look at the painting for some further reflection. The Awakened One sits in the meditation posture in a nonspecific place in this world system. The central picture is framed by many faces, some animal, some human. These represent the many births of the Great Being, the Buddha to be. If there is no self, what is it that goes through a series of lives? The Buddha firmly rejected *reincarnation*— which is the theory that an immaterial being is contained within the body, and, after the break up of the body, goes to another body. He once sternly rebuked a bhikkhu who asserted that the same consciousness carried over from one life to another (Mahatanhasankhaya Sutta; *Majjhima Nikaya:* Sutta 38). This, of course, is a form of self-view. Yet on other occasions, the Buddha would talk about a person's future destination after the death of the body or about his own previous births.

The apparent contradiction only becomes resolved when we understand the Buddha's use of language on the one hand, and, on the other, insightfully investigate the process of life. Regarding the use of language: birth is the arising of the five khandhas which we experience as self. Using "self" and "I" as conventional terms for ease of expression, we can talk about the self-experience being born. However, the practice of insight points to form arising dependent on consciousness, which in turn is affected by intention and attention, and so on. So nothing has separate existence. Aspects of an interdependent, conditioned whole mesh and interact with other aspects in a field of conditionality that we can liken to a kammic biosystem. For this reason, in accordance with the Buddha's own usage, I refrain from using the word "rebirth" which implies that some thing that was before pertains in the future, and simply refer to "birth" (*jati*). That keeps our inquiry within the linguistic and experiential framework of the Buddha.

In a kammic field of interdependence, no thing is really born; but through the coming together of the five khandhas is the appearance of a unified and separately existent self. The continuing factor of birth after birth then is not the elements, but what brings them together. What holds and merges energies, elements and forces into apparent independent units? It is that which serves as the continuum for "further becoming" upon which birth is dependent. Obviously desire, the inclination towards separative existence (*bhavatanha*), plays a key part—as does attachment (*upadana*)—while ignorance bars the insight into interdependence.

When we examine the experience of life with insight, we might see that the "coming together" is experienced in a moment-after-moment fashion as the co-dependent arising of consciousness and name-and-form.* In this way, when we see something, it can be noted as a moment of visual consciousness arising dependent on the eye organ and contact. A feeling and a mental perception arise, which is mind consciousness arising as the mind receives the eye's message. With the perception arises the mental formation, the thought of the visual object. Then, dependent on interest/desire and the lingering of attention or attachment, a whole range of perceptions and feelings proliferate, compounded out of associations, memories, inclinations—in brief, attachments—and this experience gives rise to the impression of a separate self who sees and thinks.

> *Visual consciousness arises because of eye and material shapes; the meeting of the three is sensory impingement; because of sensory impingement arises feeling; what one feels, one perceives; what one perceives, one reasons about; what one reasons about, one proliferates over; what one proliferates over, becomes the source of the array of perceptions and obsessive thoughts that assail one in regard to visual objects of the past, future and present.* (Madhupindika Sutta; Majjhima Nikaya: Sutta 18)

Using the references of Dependent Origination, it is the proliferating power of ignorance affecting the "kamma-productive activities" in mental consciousness (*avijjapaccaya sankhara, sankharapaccaya viññanam*) that is the condition for birth. This can also be expressed as the activity of the outflows. The accumulative effect, the *vipaka* of this, affects the kammic field in which consciousness continually arises. The more that the mind is allowed to dwell and be activated in ignorance, the more patterns are established on ignorance, and the accompanying desire and attachment get established where consciousness arises. The net result is that consciousness keeps getting re-established in the same old patterns. To this extent, there is re-birth. Nothing is really re-born, but a pattern persists—a kind of kammic blueprint or genetic code—upon which consciousness and name-and-form get established.

> *In that way, Ananda, kamma is like a field, consciousness like a seed and desire like sap. For beings that are hindered by ignorance and fettered by craving, consciousness is established on a low level. So it is that further becoming and ongoing birth are brought about. Thus, Ananda, is existence.* (Anguttara Nikaya: [I], Threes, 76)

To use a simile: if we apply a burning match to dry paper in the presence of air, a flame will arise on the paper. The flame has not left the match, nor has anything passed from the match to the paper. The second flame has arisen bearing certain similar characteristics to the first, and related to the

---

* i.e., *rupa* (form) + *vedana* (feeling) + *sañña* (perception) + *sankhara* (intention, attention and contact) + *viññana* (consciousness)—that is, the potential to receive impressions through the senses based on a psycho-physical organism

first through action (kamma) initiated by some volition or desire. The paper (form) is dry and has the potential for combustion (the arising of consciousness); what we have to remember is the essential presence of oxygen (becoming) which is the continuum of the transmission.

The pattern of birth is then established on desire, attachment and ignorance. So the "stickiness" of consciousness is a result and a cause for the accumulative processes of attachment and becoming that give rise to self-view. So, although the process of birth is selfless, the "glue" that binds the khandhas together, the *upadana* or attachment, is nourished and developed by the results (*vipaka*) of kamma. Before the whole scenario gets too depressing and fatalistic, we should remember that the whole birth/becoming process only pertains to the field of kamma. And as the Buddha says, there is the Unborn. We could liken this to the space within which action and form occur. How can we know that? Simply because we can observe action and form, desire, attachment and becoming.

This must be the case in order for there to be a clear way to fully see desire, attachment and becoming. In the Buddha's accounts of his own Awakening, this complete review of the process of kamma and birth was not a sign of being totally enmeshed in it, but rather of a mind that was transcending it.

It must also be considered that the way out of kamma is by cultivating enough good kamma for consciousness to arise with the requisite faculties for enlightenment. Good kamma binds the sense of self in more sensitive, refined, loving and peaceful states; bad kamma does the reverse. Although both kammas are adhesive in essence, good kamma will sensitize the mind until its reflective powers can see through the accumulated whirl of phenomena, and the appetite for further birth palls. And good kamma *feels* good. It's good to feel free from remorse, clear and compassionate towards others.

> *Kamma performed without greed ... hatred ... delusion ... is skillful, praiseworthy; that kamma has happiness as its fruit, that kamma leads to the ceasing of kamma* ... (Anguttara Nikaya : [I], Threes, 108)

Although the spirit of selflessness is not measured in terms of some mental feeling, we have already seen that Buddhas do have feelings; they feel the bliss of concentration, the pain of physical sickness. In the presence of Buddha wisdom, feelings are made light and non-obstructive. The process of cultivating good kamma, which is inspiring and leads one on, is the subject matter that is illustrated by the border of this painting. Although ultimately there is no "rebirth," there is "further becoming"—the process of *kamma-vipaka* stimulating the arising of beings in the plane of time, birth and death. Some of these beings are depicted in the border.

The Buddha, in describing his own Awakening, recounts seeing, during the first watch of the night, the stream of cause and effect that had led him to that point. His mind had become so clear that he was also able to see the stream of cause and effect extending into a great range of his past lives and

... the way out of kamma is by cultivating enough good kamma for consciousness to arise with the requisite faculties for enlightenment.

111

that of a great number of other beings as well. In looking at his own circumstances, what stood out was the consistent perfection of good kamma through *paramita:* spiritual acts that go beyond the normal motivation of personal gain. The ten perfections of kamma are: generosity (*dana*), morality (*sila*), renunciation (*nekkhamma*), wisdom (*pañña*), energy (*viriya*), patient endurance (*khanti*), truthfulness (*sacca*), resolution (*adhitthana*), benevolence (*metta*) and equanimity (*upekkha*). The story goes that the recollection of this wealth of goodness was one of the foundations for repelling the host of Mara. Fully knowing his aspiration and inner worth, the Bodhisatta was able to stave off any doubts that might assail him as to his intention and resolve.

This presentation of the value of good kamma is very helpful. It indicates that the mind can be weaned from sensory gratification, becoming and ignorance. As the Buddha's teachings grew more popular, the practice of perfecting kamma was illustrated by means of hundreds of fables, called Jatakas, about the previous lives of the Great Being. In each of his previous lives, whether he was a monkey or a brahmin, a prince or a hermit, he perfected one of the ten *paramita.*

For instance, in one life, the Great Being was a hermit who lived in a cave practicing patient endurance. At that time, the King of that country liked to go out in the countryside enjoying himself, hunting and drinking and eating, as is the way with kings. Generally he took his 150 wives along with him. He probably expected them to coo in awe when he came back with a dead stag. Anyway, they were out together one day, and the King decided to go off and chase some deer, leaving his wives with the servants and the baggage in a nice picnic spot. After a while, the ladies got bored and decided to go pick some flowers and look at the scenery. Well, they came across the hermit sitting in his cave, radiating gentleness and serenity. These ladies were intelligent and cultivated and they were moved to respectfully inquire as to what his practice of dhamma was. So he told them he was practicing patience. They, having had to put up with the behavior of the King for many years, could easily relate to the practice of patience and were very uplifted to realize that being patient with life was spiritually strengthening. This event set them thinking.

Meanwhile, the King came back from the hunt, hot and tired and expecting to be received by his adoring wives and told how magnificent he was. Nobody was there but a few servants looking after the baggage. "Hummph!" snorted the King, and when the servants told him that his wives had gone for a walk, he stomped off in the direction in which they had gone. Coming to the hermit's cave, he found all of his wives engaged in rapt conversation about patient endurance with a little man in a loincloth. The King's instincts and ways of assessing situations were pretty basic. Out came his sword. "Practicing patient endurance, are you! Let's see what you make of this!" And with two swishes of his sword, he sliced off the Great Being's ears. The hermit remained unmoved in body and mind. "Oh yeah?" roared His Majesty and sliced off the Great Being's nose. Still, the hermit kept cool. Off came the arms and legs as the King tried to shake the hermit's resolve to no avail. The King perhaps started to consider that there was something unusual about this hermit, or maybe he was getting tired; anyway he asked the Great Being why he was doing this practice. "Your Majesty," replied the sage, "I wish to become a Buddha and discover a Dhamma for the welfare of all beings. In this lifetime, I have resolved to develop the *paramita* of patient endurance towards that aim. As you have helped me to perfect that quality today, when I do attain to complete Awakening in a future life, you will be the first one to whom I will transmit my Dhamma. Now if what I am saying has any truth in it, may my arms and legs and severed members be joined back to my body." In a moment, his body was restored to its former appearance. The King, it is said, dropped his sword and prostrated on the ground in a gesture of humility and respect. Many lifetimes later, he was born as Kondañña.

Another good example of a transcendent virtue is equanimity (*upekkha*). In one Jataka, the Great Being decided to perfect this *paramita*. He lived as an ascetic, sitting out in the blazing sun all day and going naked in the chill of the night, sleeping on thorns and rocks, drinking water from puddles and eating leaves. All this was intended to develop equanimity. He did this for eighty years, constantly testing the body in order to become equanimous to pain and discomfort. However, as asceticism is a negation of the body and inflicts unnecessary hardship, it leads to a birth in Hell. So when the ascetic died, he went straight to Hell. As he saw the gates of Hell loom up ahead of him, he thought, "That life was a complete waste of time. Oh well, never mind." And at that moment, he perfected equanimity and immediately went up to the heavenly realms.

Such stories give you another perspective when your boss is hollering at you for something that wasn't finished yesterday. It helps you to remember what you can get right, what you can take with you and where your real home is. To remember that feels good and gives you strength when times are hard. When the reflections on insight, cessation and Nibbana lose their appeal, having such a fable in mind helps one find the

We have to "touch the earth"—leave the illusions and hopes behind and get in touch with how it really is now.

aspiration to keep going in face of the stuff that life brings up. And the results are good. Life can give you spiritual strength and a sense of purpose if its mundane routines are highlighted in this way. For example, to be patient, generous, kind, moral and wise are qualities to perfect; any action that brings these perfections into the world has the capacity to Awaken the transcendent side of the mind. When you rise to the occasion, the result is that you feel good in yourself.

In the first watch of the night, when Buddhas Awaken to some aspects of transcendent Truth, they realize their true lineage. It is a spiritual lineage—an evolution of wisdom and purity. It gives them the foundation from which to view the khandhas, the outflows and the host of Mara as not-self. That foundation is not a personal position or an identity. It is a transcending position, established not on any personal quality, but on qualities we can all develop and that take us out of our personal concerns and limitations. Being patient is definitely not-self. It does not appeal to the outflows or the self-view; to them, it seems like a waste of time, and even a humiliation. The transcendent, supramundane Path is always a giving up of self. Yet giving up self becomes a far more stable and unshakeable foundation than anything that comes through the processes of gaining and becoming.

It is said that in the second watch of that night, under the Bodhi tree, the Buddha came to understand the laws of cause and effect that determine the future of all beings. This deepened his compassion and understanding of not-self. In this picture, the Buddha is portrayed seated above a knotwork figure. The knotwork represents the links of cause and effect, of temporality, in which the Buddha is no longer operating. His perfection of good kamma has led to the end of kamma. He is depicted touching the ground, calling the earth to bear witness to his *paramita.* The hand is painted in some detail, whereas the face has no detail apart from a gentle smile. This represents the "change of lineage" from the realm of personality (we normally identify with the face) to that of transcendent activity within the field of cause and effect—the cultivation of *paramita.* That hand reminds us that realization of Truths only comes by getting in touch with fundamental things like our actual feelings and beliefs. We have to "touch the earth"—leave the illusions and hopes behind and get in touch with how it really is now. We don't need to contact a special set of perceptions and feelings but we must develop an unwavering contact with the ones that arise ordinarily. Thus another meaning of a "Tathagata" is "one who has come"—a Buddha, having seen through cause and effect, willingly enters into it out of compassion for other beings, beings still held in the belief that they *are* the process of cause and effect.

All we can know is that we *are*—although the definition of what we are is subject to views and opinions. Is it possible to leave that Suchness, that "Is-ness" of being, unconditioned by our attempts to define it? Is it possible to abide in that apparent emptiness until we taste the freedom that enriches it? It is an act of trust. And the Awakened Ones can abide trusting in emptiness because of the rich store of *paramita* that has given them supreme confidence. With that, they repel Mara, and come to full understanding, not purely of themselves but of the way it is. Through this, in the third watch of the night, the Buddha came to realize the Four Noble Truths, the Way of living beyond self.

The illustration depicts, in the center of the Buddha's body, a mandala — a spiritual theme formed into a symbol for the purpose of meditation. This particular mandala represents the union of male and female as the polarities of the universe. We can list what goes under those polarities: active/passive; constriction/expansion; form/space, and so on. As in the previous painting, the main theme here is the harmonizing of all positions. When there is unity, there is no "other" to flow towards, or away from. When there is harmony based on a fundamental resolution of all the potential dualities, there is no possibility of desire for one of them. There is no taking a position in the masculine to be drawn towards or away from the feminine. This point of resolution is the supreme liberation, the irreversible termination of the outflows because there's nothing to flow out to.

The Buddha has lived it out. Now he is no longer fooled by any condition, any position, or any "self." Hence he is no longer convinced that anyone is really that which is born and dies, because it becomes obvious that that true being or Is-ness is more than a matter of temporarily holding to a position. With this insight he can live with total sensitivity and compassion in a world of suffering beings, without anxiety or despair. As he does not take or hold any position regarding conditioned phenomena, he has all the possibilities of relating to them. His mind is open, free from bias, self-interest, unresolved traumas and the rest of it. Nor is he biased toward not experiencing conditions. It's not the case that he doesn't bother with the phenomenal world either. His liberation from suffering is, therefore, a source of faith as well as an inspiration for practice for all beings.

Homage to the Tathagata!

16

WHAT KONDAÑÑA KNEW

Idamavoca bhagavā … yaṅkiñci samudayadhammaṁ sabbantaṁ nirodhadhammanti.
Thus spoke the Blessed One, and the Group of Five bhikkhus were gladdened
and they approved of his words. Now while this discourse was being delivered,
the untarnished and clear insight into Dhamma arose in Venerable Kondañña thus:
"Whatever has the nature to arise, has the nature to cease."

When the Buddha finished speaking, the Group of Five were delighted by the scope and the clarity of his teaching. Now during the course of this talk, there arose in Venerable Kondañña the clear and pure seeing of the Dhamma "that whatever has the nature to arise, has the nature to cease." This does not mean that he had a spectacular vision. Here, the view of wisdom is summed up in the simple phrase, "whatever has the nature to arise also has the nature to cease." That's the way it dawned upon Kondañña.

His realization was not just a mimicking of what the Buddha said; it is not to be realized through the logic of words but only by putting into practice what has been said about dukkha, attachment and desire. This is why Kondañña's utterance is profound; he insightfully, gnostically saw the holding onto the world wherein dukkha is conditioned and is let go of. In order to recognize that everything—even the very thoughts and emotions that one has—just comes and goes means that there is dispassion and detachment, a clear seeing of how things work. Attachment means that we give thoughts or feelings a significance that they would not have if they were seen as passing phenomena. With attachment there is no independence from the immediate circumstances, no space to see things objectively. So we go up with the ups and down with the downs, falling into despair about being depressed, and we then languish in that mood.

Or, perhaps, we try to deny our depression. If we manage to deny and bury it, that depression can become embedded in the psyche and manifest as a negative or cynical view of life. If we try to blot out the dark side of our feelings with forced highs, we may end up frantically grasping at the sensory world in order to distract ourselves and prevent more depression. If we fail to notice that the highs, the gains and the happiness are impermanent, we feel disappointed when they end. Our heavens condition our hells, and our hells are strengthened by the memory or the possibility of heaven somewhere out of reach. To know in the heart that sadness and pain are impermanent is a profound relief from the suffering they bring and from the kamma of trying to avoid that suffering.

Instead of grasping and assuming, "I thought that, this is my idea, what a great insight!" he recognized that those very thoughts and perceptions arise, mature, wane and end.

Such was Kondañña's insight. Also instead of grasping and assuming, "I thought that, this is my idea, what a great insight!" he recognized that those very thoughts and perceptions arise, mature, wane and end. So there's no attachment to the insight—even the emotional delight is, after all, something that arises and ceases. This coolness leaves the mind very clear and free from preoccupation or statements about "me having attained" something. Its lasting value is that it brings us to liberation from self-view.

This painting attempts to make a little more out of that cool insight, "whatever has the nature to arise has the nature to pass away." The theme depicted in the center of the picture is the changing nature of all phenomena. To be more fully conscious of the phenomenal world involves a deepening of the mind's receptivity. This leads to a deepening of awareness rather than an increase in the analytical framework by which one classifies (and remains separate from) phenomena. In the course of exploring consciousness, a huge amount of psychological and emotional conditioning comes to light. It is the result (*vipaka*) of kamma in the near or remote past. This conditioning so much affects our experience of the world that it can no longer be separated from that experience. Kamma and its results define our personal "world"—the realm of conscious experience. This world is called *loka* in Pali to distinguish it from the objective world, called *jagati*. The catalysts of time and place and particular events tend to trigger off experiences of elation, despair, contentment or inferiority, whose roots are in the kamma-saturated consciousness. Those who begin to investigate the mind can often experience this whole range of moods and feelings while apparently "doing" nothing special.

In the practice of insight, we see that the felt quality of an experience is variable: one person can react to another as menacing, a second would find that person charming. Our feelings and perceptions of the world fluctuate not only between different beings, but also within ourselves. Whatever change we perceive in the external world is small compared to the minute-by-minute — or even faster — way that the realms of mental perception and mood can change. Processes within consciousness are in a constant state of arising and ceasing to generate new forms. The very complexity and variety of that flow of phenomena is mesmerizing; it keeps us from noticing that it has the nature to arise and cease. However, although it changes, the world as an experience in mental consciousness can be contemplated and understood clearly as a number of "realms." The world of ordinary consciousness — that which is affected by sense desire — can be classified as sixfold, and appearing within a larger world system (or galaxy) of birth and death. This galaxy includes everything that has the will to become something, to exist as a self — even including those beings who seek out formless realms of *jhana.* * However, this painting is limited to the presentation of the worlds within the sensory sphere (material sphere) in which we can take birth. It is called the Six Realms of Existence.

Traditionally, these Six Realms are painted encircled by the twelve links of Dependent Origination, which I explained in the Second Noble Truth. The tradition dates back to the time of the Buddha when one of his chief disciples, Maha Moggallana Thera, who was a specialist in psychic powers, made frequent visits to the various heaven and hell realms. The story goes that he employed supernormal powers in order to learn how the beings in each of those realms experienced states of happiness or anguish dependent upon their actions in a previous life. They had to stay there until the *vipaka* (effect) was exhausted, whereupon they would take birth in another plane. Even the happy realms presented a tenuous security from the restless movement of the whole cycle of existence or *samsara.* He explained all that he had seen, and it was felt that people should be informed about this. So it was suggested that a picture be made, and copies hung up in the entrance of every monastery for all to see.

Generally the painting shows Yama, Ruler of the Dead, holding up a mirror. In the reflection of this mirror, we see the Six Realms. It's to be understood that Yama is very fair. When people die, they go to see Yama, and he asks if they paid heed to the messengers that he had sent to the realm of humans to warn them about mortality — old age, sickness and death. He then asks them to recall any of their good deeds and these are written down; then the bad deeds are recounted. He rejoices when someone has lived skillfully and made good kamma. They are then conducted to the fortunate realms while those who lived in bad ways go to the unfortunate realms.

People who are near death say their whole life flashes in front of their eyes; it seems that Yama is present in our minds. We judge ourselves. Who could know us better? Actually, the Six Realms are not about Divine Judgement; they portray the laws of kamma operating in the sensory realm — a map of causes and then inevitable effects. Cosmology, like myth, is a convention. It depicts broad and immutable truths that are beyond our power to affect. We can create good kamma or bad kamma; but all kamma

---

* i.e., resulting in birth in the brahmaloka .

is going to have its effect, (*vipaka*), and all of it comes up for review. In fact, we create so much kamma that Yama visits us while we're alive, and we are temporarily despatched to heaven and hell accordingly. Yama stops visiting when, through insight, we stop creating kamma through no longer basing our actions on the "me and mine" of self-view.

> *If you give up looking at yourselves as a soul [as a fixed and special identity], then you will have given yourselves a way to go beyond death.* (Sutta Nipata: 1119; trans. Saddhatissa)

I've modified the traditional picture to accommodate this section of the Sutta. Here, I use the image to depict birth into mind states in this life. In the center is Kondañña, reminding us that the realms can only be realized and understood as impermanent by those who are centered in themselves and hence, also at the center of the realms. He is sitting right in the middle of it all — looking rather haggard it is true; but actually recognizing all this stuff, and, seeing it as conditioned phenomena, he lets it arise and pass away.

The other four of the Group of Five monks are looking outwards, thinking: "Oh, that was a really good teaching!" They may be gladdened and respectful, worshipping it all, but they haven't actually seen it in themselves — it's still out there. To them, perhaps the concept of change refers to the realm of Nature, the four seasons, symbolized by the changing state of the plant life in the four quadrants of the picture. To see change in such a way is a useful reflection; it reminds us that our bodies too must go through seasons. However, understanding the change of Nature doesn't have the same impact as the insight that the realms of our perceptions and feelings are bound to change. This insight brings the experience of transiency into this moment and into what we take ourselves to be. And when we experience who we are as a constant flux, the sense of identification with any phase or aspect of that flux is undermined.

> *Maintain in being ... the perception of impermanence for the purpose of eliminating the self-view; for when one perceives impermanence, the perception of non-self becomes established; and when one perceives not-self, one arrives at the elimination of the self-view, and that is Nibbana here and now.* (Udana: [IV], (i); Anguttara Nikaya: [IV], Nines, 1)

The lowest realm, the pits, is the bottom left-hand side of the wheel. According to tradition, there are eight major hells, each with sixteen auxiliary hells, each of which has innumerable minor hells. They range from the most pleasant and commodious hell, Sanjiva — where beings are killed and then brought back to life in a continual cycle — down through hells of "black rope," of "crushing and smashing," of "screaming," of "great screaming," of "fires," of "great fires," to the lowest of them all, Avici Hell. This is the realm where matricides, patricides, murderers of Arahants, those who cause schism in the Sangha, those who have raped a nun and those who have shed the blood of a Buddha spend incalculable periods of time. It defies description. Anyway the kind of person who is humble enough to take guidance from this book isn't liable to go there, and anyone who is due for a spell there probably wouldn't heed the warning. Avici is the realm of suffering without respite. Other hells offer you a moment's break, like the space between having one shovel of blazing coal tipped down your throat and the next. It's hardly a vacation, but if you've just come out of Avici, in a lesser hell you'd probably feel that things were coming up roses. That's how bad Avici is. So I haven't attempted to paint Avici, just one of the ordinary hells — a river of fire symbolizing what it feels like when you're really burning up with anger or violent hatred or pain.

Opinions differ as to the next realm of decreasing order of misfortune. Some say it's the animal realm. Perhaps it isn't a neatly stacked system. Anyway, the next one that I'll deal with is the realm of the Hungry Ghosts (*peta*). Abiding as a hungry ghost is like being in a barren desert craving food and water. They have great fat bellies, but very skinny necks, which makes it impossible for them to get enough to eat. They're always in a state of craving. That's the place for swindlers, cheapskates, people who oppressed the poor and totally selfish beings. If you're addicted to drugs or liquor, this realm is the place you're headed for. The telltale signs of the *petaloka* start to manifest for those who are even psychologically dependent on drink or drugs. In that "hungry ghost" realm of addiction, there's a lot of coarse selfishness, squalor and neglect of the body, and a mind that inclines to self-pity. The reflection here is that if you're always thinking about yourself, it usually degenerates into whining about the bad deal you got and feeling hard-done by. There's a lot of that complaining in the human mind anyway, especially wherever material values are prevalent. It doesn't take much to tumble into the realm of the Hungry Ghosts. Conversely, when we expect little and bring forth our inner strength and resources from ourselves, we feel very full.

The animal realm is also an unfortunate one. For those who are fond of (some) animals or regard them as pure and innocent, reference to the animal realm as a lesser abiding can seem unfair. I'm not condemning animals — in fact, the Bodhisatta took many animal births and lived skillfully within those limitations. However, animal life involves severe limitations. Most animals spend their time in a realm of fear — they fear death and starvation. They are bound to a particular habitat which they cannot farm or improve very much. They are at the mercy of the weather, the forces of nature and human beings as well as predators. And they are constrained by territorial

Petas, hungry ghosts

121

and breeding instincts which put them through all kinds of trials. Some can latch onto finer or more comfortable modes of existence and ways of living skillfully, either through their own conduct or as a result of association with human beings. Yet, this association can be utterly wretched as when animals are kept for food, or are treated as passive objects of someone's moods and whims. In the context of the Six Realms, the animal world symbolizes the volition that is associated with reproduction, eating and killing. Animal kamma is, more or less, what you have to practice with in having a physical body. However, the kamma is not always so severe: selfless and kind actions seem to be possible in some animals. It's a bit gross at times, but it's not an unworkable position.

A slightly more fortunate realm is depicted at the top right. This is the realm of the *asuras* or Jealous Titans. They once lived in a lower heaven until Inda, the *devata* king of the lower heavens, threw them out for being so rowdy. Now they are at the bottom of Mount Meru (in the background) while most of the *devata* are in palaces up on the hill. Although some of the Titans have palaces and pleasure parks, they are jealous of the greater splendor of the deva realms and the blissful, carefree lives of the *devata;* so they war on them. It is actually only their envy, anger and aggression that deprive them of the happiness of the heavens. Humans can empathize with the *asura* realm: like *asuras,* humans can believe that it's their right to have whatever they want, and become petulant when they feel that somebody else has got a better deal. The love of power is an *asura* trait; and a human one too — there are those who like to attack the innocent or the defenseless, because in some ways they are envious of that purity and hate to be reminded of it. Their relative good fortune manifests as a seeking something higher and more refined; their unhappiness comes from the way they try to attain it. We don't have to wait for the death of the body — in this very life we can notice that acting on such impulses is a ticket to the *asura* state of being.

The world of humans comes next. As a venue for working out liberation, it is more fortunate than that of the *asuras* because Buddhas and their teaching arise there. It is the perfect place for enlightenment, though in sensory terms, it is less pleasant and refined than the next realm up. We'll come back to it in a moment.

Above the world of human beings is the *devaloka,* the six "heavenly" realms of refined sense-pleasure. These range from the ones where the pleasure is mostly derived through living in places that are visually and physically delightful to a refined bliss that is largely of a mental nature. This vignette is a picture of a *gandhabba,* a heavenly musician. In the lower *devaloka, gandhabba* play to the devas (more formally known as *devata*) only when they are asked to do so and stop when not wanted (unlike musicians of the human realm). Deva means "shining one" and also applies to beings outside the *devaloka.* The "formless gods" or Brahmas are a kind of "superdeva," belonging to a higher stratum of existence within the world system of birth and death. Special humans, such as Awakened Ones, and even kings and ministers (perhaps as a politic gesture) are referred to occasionally as "deva." As in all states of being, the state of consciousness is the determinant, and that of the *devata* is more sublime and refined. It's not so refined that it rules out quarrelling and arguments and jealousies in the *devaloka,* or the need to protect the realm against the *asuras.* And also, eventually, there is death. If you've noticed, human happiness and success have those characteristics too.

The human realm (center left) is the strangest of them all, the one that really stretches the imagination to believe in. The human realm is the most kamma-productive realm. The human mind can move between the Six Realms with relative ease. It is possible for a human to be fully established in a miserable or blissful realm by living either in depravity or in a kind and scrupulous manner. They have the choice. It takes a little time—during which the body has to die away—but nothing compared to the innumerable millennia it would take to get from a middling hell to a not even top-rate *devaloka.* The kammic potential of humans is so powerful that they can even get previews of the other realms, and assume the corresponding characteristics, just by inclining their intentions and activities *within* the life-span of the body. So humans are sometimes like hell beings, sometimes like hungry ghosts, sometimes like animals, sometimes like *asuras* and sometimes like the *devata.* No wonder human beings are so confused!

Perhaps it is due to this almost constant confusion that human beings have the urge to get beyond all these realms—unlike other beings. Humans can never become fixed in anything for too long. Even one of the nicer and least-demanding hell realms requires a tenancy of tens of millions of years; and the heavenly realms are of like duration (in the *brahmaloka,* the smallest unit of time is trillions of years). Human beings can have previews of all of these, and the opportunity to reflect on the possibilities of becoming anything in the light of impermanence. This is one aspect of Kondañña's realization: that all the realms of becoming arise and pass away. And as they are impermanent states which offer no respite from becoming something else, they are unsatisfactory. That kind of perspective allows humans the opportunity to cultivate the very state of awareness which can notice and not be drawn into self-creative kamma; and in knowing that, be set free from all the restless delusion of becoming.

But the human realm is a strange one. It is here that Buddhas always arise and give most of their teachings. It is the perfect place for seeing the need to abandon all possibilities of becoming; yet most humans feel they just have the wrong blend. Yama constantly sends his messengers to remind humans of the limitations of becoming and that the human mind can experience the Six Realms readily. And yet … humans get stuck into being human. When they do, they don't use their agile minds to contemplate the common characteristics of phenomena. Instead of cultivating the serenity and vision that frees them from *samsara,* they hatch out new permutations of semi-heavenly, semi-animal, semi-hellish experiences (such as power politics, sport, romance and entertainment) instead of

… the human realm is a strange one. … It is the perfect place for seeing the need to abandon all possibilities of becoming; yet most humans feel they just have the wrong blend.

123

abandoning becoming. This, then, is the drawback of all that kammic potential—humans don't often consider the option of transforming it. They are always restlessly creating this, trying that, rejecting *this* with all the refined discrimination of a *devata;* then grabbing *that* with all the blind instinct of an animal; feeling the pitiful yearning of a hungry ghost; and yet, like an *asura,* rankled at the prospect of another human getting a better deal.

Perhaps the most important thing that Kondañña had to realize is that the True Life is one of *being,* not of becoming. This involves a profound letting go—the abandonment of identification with any aspect of the world of birth-and-death. However, after hearing this teaching, Kondañña only attained the first stage of enlightenment; his realization still needed to be developed. The Sutta doesn't say what he had not let go of. Perhaps there was still an attachment to the sense of being the watcher, which appears changeless and could be mistaken for self. This may have been the case because soon after teaching this Sutta, the Buddha gave a teaching specifically on the characteristic of not-self. With that further elucidation of the Truth, all five of the Group attained liberation.

One might say that the first stage of enlightenment is the realization that there is no self within the sensory realm. If one also understands that there is no self *outside* of the sensory realm, then the abandonment goes a little deeper. There is nothing to become in the sense sphere *or* away from it. Just as there's nothing to be found within it, none of it has to be rejected.

> *A man with nothing in him that he grasps at as his and nothing in him that he rejects as not his.* (Sutta Nipata: 858)

The sage as the "watcher" of the Six Realms is only a position; it's not self. The Six Realms are to be known without condescension, condemnation or denial. Condemnation is an aspect of self-view: we think that certain people really *are* evil, and we feel glad when they are punished. Awakened Ones, on the other hand, experience the sense of regret that people become deluded and generate so much suffering. But what they *know* is that all realms of becoming are impermanent. The Buddha commented that even Devadatta, who had tried to kill him and succeeded in drawing his blood, would, after languishing in the Avici Hell, eventually exhaust that *vipaka* and realize Buddhahood. He was just going through a bad patch.

Hence, the serenity of Buddhas is in the timeless present where nothing is rejected. The Awakened One experiences harmony in it all: there are the dark and the light, the positive and the negative sides of existence—all aspects of the way things are. The Buddha expounds a teaching that can fit all people and bring them out of their attachments; hence he is the bestower of blessings. The Blessed One puts sensory things in their right place; at the right time and in suitable ways, he teaches what is for the happiness and welfare of beings, and what actions and mind states are best avoided. This understanding applies to all the cycles of Nature—the rhythm of creation and destruction. One learns how to generate skillful states within the limitations of Nature. For our confused and conflicting world, this understanding is indeed a blessing.

In the letter "B" of Bhagava, I have drawn the Buddha with a giant cobra coiled around him. This alludes to the story that after his enlightenment the Buddha was encircled by a giant hooded snake, who protected him from severe weather. This signifies that the Awakened mind is protected from the violence of Nature when it has understood how to bring its own nature into balance. Those who live wisely and mindfully find themselves abiding in the most advantageous conditions that human and personal kamma will allow. From this, two possibilities arise—either complete liberation, or, if attachments still remain, birth in a fortunate realm.

If you're interested in birth and would like to know more about where the present kamma is leading to, the next few paintings may be helpful …

Pavattite ca bhagavatā dhammacakke bhummā devā saddamanussāvesuṃ

etaṃ bhagavatā
bārāṇasiyaṃ isipatane migadāye
anuttaraṃ dhammacakkaṃ pavattitaṃ
appativattiyaṃ, samaṇena vā brāhmaṇena
vā devena vā mārena vā brahmuna vā
kenaci vā lokasmin' ti

17

HEAVEN ON EARTH

Pavattite ... kenaci vā lokasmin ti.
When the Wheel of Dhamma had been set rolling by the Blessed One,
the devas of the earth raised the cry: "At Varanasi, in the Deer Park at Isipatana,
the matchless Wheel of Dhamma has been set rolling by the Blessed One,
not to be stopped by any samana, or brahmin, or deva, or mara, or brahma,
or anyone in the world."

This section of the Sutta describes the effect of the teaching on various celestial realms. In painting these pictures of the various *devaloka*, I have taken considerable artistic license. The text is very non-committal; it simply states that these various devas hear this, and then having done so, they proclaim it to the beings in the next realm. However, many people nowadays would dismiss the realm of the *devata* as a quaint feature of Buddhist cosmology, a hangover from Vedic tradition or the folklore of the time. The section of the Dhammacakkappa-vattana Sutta which describes the rejoicing of the *devata* that the Dhamma has been taught would then seem to serve no useful purpose, and even detract from the practical importance of the teaching by introducing elements of whimsical mythology. Are they there as signs of a textual aberration or as embellishments on the main body of the Sutta for conventional purposes? Do they add any meaning to the Sutta?

We can appreciate the significance of the heavenly realms by reflecting on the structures and themes of Buddhist cosmology. For a start, Buddhist

To the Awakened, things neither exist nor do they not exist; they have a relative existence, they arise and cease dependent on conditions.

cosmology puts the thinking mind in its place by making it clear that the universe of innumerable worlds is too vast for the human mind to reckon with. Our ability to conceive in rational terms is impressive, but finally inadequate for such a purpose. With the cultivation of the Path, we have to bring forth a different kind of "knowing" — one that is not abstract but related to the mind that can recognize dukkha. That kind of "knowing" is the insightful knowing that recognizes the changing and insubstantial nature of the sensory experience of reality. It is in touch with the quality of volition and kamma. As you come to understand dukkha, you recognize the voice of ignorance that persuasively denies any state of being other than that which is based upon a cursory attention to sensory experience. Through meditation, you can *know* the clinging that supports rational sense perceptions and denies irrational or mythical perceptions. The mind endowed with insight abides in the knowing that is free from such views. To the Awakened, things neither exist nor do they not exist; they have a relative existence, they arise and cease dependent on conditions.

The rational mind has not found satisfactory answers to the questions of the origin, the extent, the structure or the workings of the universe in purely material terms. A Buddhist, understanding the co-dependency of motivation and perception, might very well ask, "Why do you want to know?" Why you want to know, and your view of what you and the real world actually are, will affect how you attempt to find out the answer to this question. If your idea of reality is of being a separate entity in an objectively existing universe, you probably want to know it in order to eventually control and exploit it — the right that self-view grants to humans. So you try to understand the universe by looking at what is far away, not at your mind. (After all, that's not supposed to be part of the universe.) If you want to see the universe through a telescope, fine, but that will only show you a telescope's opinion of the universe, conditioned by the ways of telescopes, and interpreted by the brain. Do you believe in curved space? Or black holes where time slows down and stops? Or distances so vast that it would take millions of years traveling at the speed of light to cover a tiny portion of the Cosmos? Or that the stars are flecks of fire set in the vault of heaven? Or that God created human beings out of mud, having created the rest of the universe in five days?

Personally, I like all those ideas for what effects and reflections they can set off in my mind. But Buddhist cosmology is very closely tailored to fit the Path to the real experience of Nibbana. In this system, the "world" that we dwell in is the realm of conscious experience in which the ingrained volitional tendencies and perceptions of consciousness play an essential part.

Apart from the activity of the self as subject in sensory reaction, memory and association, imagination, judgment and inference, there can be no world of objects. A thing in itself which is not a thing to some consciousness is an entirely unreliable, because contradictory, conception. (J.H. Muirhead: Encyclopedia Britannica, 1944 edition)

No intended actions are without effect in the world of the agent. With this understanding, Buddhist cosmology works, in line with every other form of the teaching: as a guide for conscious experience; to bring the mind out of the realms of attachment to the conscious experience of Nibbana—Amaravati, the Deathless Realm. It offers a reflection on how we are integrated with the universe; it qualifies the teachings on the laws of kamma and birth in vivid terms. Without those laws, our whole sense of purpose and guidance is lost and we exist in a confused purgatory. (The hell realms are the conscious experience of existence without any understanding of morality.) Cosmology also emphasizes the significance of the human realm: it is in the human state alone that good kamma can be created. Beings in lower realms are generally unaware of the laws of kamma and have to remain there until the effects of bad kamma have worn out. On the other hand, the realms of the *devata* are happy, but dependent upon past good kamma which can only be accrued by participating in and aligning the mind with the skillful acts of human beings.

In a characteristically Buddhist way, the highest opportunities do not come to those who have the most comfort and pleasure, nor to those who have the most suffering, but to those of the middling painful and pleasant human realm. The human birth is the most fortunate, having the possibility of immediate realization of Nibbana and of creating good kamma. It is, then, part of the practice of this human realm to share the fruits of their good kamma with all beings throughout the world system who are able to share in it. Most Buddhist traditions have spiritual exercises that, as in Christian prayer, project the energy of consciousness that has been enriched by meditation, generosity, sense restraint, and so on, towards all beings. In Buddhist practice, this is called "the sharing of merit" (*puñña*). Hence, rather than condemning those who are evil or worshipping (or feeling jealous of) the fortunate, we cultivate sharing the goodness of our practice with all beings wherever they are on the Great Wheel of Becoming. Cultivation of the mind along these lines broadens the vision of the practice and transforms the self-oriented thinking and actions that prevent consciousness from flowing towards liberation.

Rather than dismissing cosmology or seeing it as something very abstract, I would encourage a reflective interpretation with a breadth of vision and scope that is missing in meditation techniques. Even with meditation practice, people's basic viewpoint comes from the belief in themselves as ultimately separate beings.

Human beings are born on one of the grosser material planes, and are deluded by it. We tend to get locked into a few limited responses in our dealings with the material world. Rather than bringing forth the subtle beauties that the mind is capable of—such as gratitude, wisdom and empathy with the world of form—much of the response is based upon greed, aversion and ignorance. Although the human mind can experience a profound range of consciousness, from insensitive stupor to ecstatic bliss (simulacra of what is mapped out in cosmology), we also base our attitudes on the assumption (coupled with the denial) that we are incarcerated in a skin bag for a lifetime and then annihilated. With that view, the mind is bound to generate "get it while you can" impulses. True enough, *that* view has a certain reality to it too: it holds up under the dim light of semi-conscious experience. But acting on that assumption certainly heightens the possibility for birth in one of those lower realms of delusion.

As we have seen, there are many worlds in Buddhist cosmology: among these are the realms of celestial beings called *devata* or devas. Such beings make a fairly common appearance in the scriptures of all the Buddhist schools; in fact, the Buddha is known as the teacher of celestial as well as human beings. They are born in the celestial realm, in accordance with the laws of kamma, through having lived human lives full of such virtues as kindness, honesty, harmlessness and generosity. According to scriptural accounts, *devata* are less constrained by material form, having more diaphanous bodies and a consciousness which is intelligent and refined. The subtlety and the skill of the Buddha's teachings appeal to them; and they have a high regard for morality. The Buddha apparently taught the Abhidhamma, the metaphysical construction of the Dhamma, for their benefit and many gained understanding through that.

However, the *devata* find the direct understanding of Dhamma through contemplating impermanence, unsatisfactoriness and not-self even more difficult than humans do. Life on that ethereal plane seems very long so it is difficult for the devas to notice impermanence. The almost constant refined happiness (some devas feel a little under par for a week before they pass away) does not motivate them to have a great urge to practice. Consequently, they are unable to provide a transcendent teaching for others. However, they are sensitive to purity and gentleness. Whenever these qualities manifest, they experience great joy. They all celebrate the proclamation of the Dhamma but few gain the Dhamma eye. It is from the suggestion in the Sutta that they are rejoicing but not sharing Kondañña's insight that this series of paintings evolved.

What relevance has the plight of the *devata* to the struggling human aspirant? Quite a lot when we recognize that the universe, including the heaven realms, is as much a part of us as we are of it. In Buddhist cosmology, heavens and hells are equivalent to states of mind that we can experience within this life-span. As these result from the degrees of refinement of the mind's attachments, the heavenly realms embody the positions that consciousness can adopt in the search for Truth. They provide a perfect model of how the mind can grasp pleasant and inspiring states, and be unable to reflect upon them as changing and insubstantial. It is useful to know about the biases of the high-minded, peace-loving celestial realms when it comes to working with our own well-intentioned inclinations. We have to remember that it is only through non-attachment and insight that we can realize the liberation that is for the ultimate welfare of all beings.

The first group of *devata*, the Bhumma or Earth devas, (pronounced as "boomer" not "bummer") do not have a realm of their own; they abide on the earth, probably under the supervision of the Four Great Kings (who appear in the next painting). Folklore of most countries mention encounters with these beings.

We can see them as representative of the states of mind that find happiness in the beauty of the earth. When one walks around in beautiful countryside on a sunny day and the birds are singing, the grass is green and the sky is blue, one feels an inner happiness. But if one is looking for powerful excitement, or if one has just had a fight, then it is difficult to appreciate the beauty of Nature. It depends on the *kamma-vipaka* in the mind of the individual. An appreciation of Nature requires a somewhat refined state of consciousness which is natural in a calm or gentle mind. This is where the earth devas live.

The devas really appreciate the presence of the Buddha, but with their unreflective minds, they portray him based upon their limited deva experience. So he appears as one of them—a very sunny, radiant being— and the Wheel of the Law becomes just a decorative frame for him. We see them here paying little attention to the Dhamma—the teachings on impermanence, cessation of becoming and the realization of Nibbana. They are enjoying themselves: one of them is riding on a fish, one is sitting on a flower, one of them is riding on a bird and everything is fine in the world. "We'll think about Nibbana some other time; this existence is good enough." This is the *devaloka* of refined physical pleasure. The next one is somewhat different.

bhummānaṁ devānaṁ saddaṁ sutvā
catummahārājika devā saddamanussāvesuṁ
catummahārājikānaṁ devānaṁ saddaṁ sutvā
tāvatiṁsā devā saddamanussāvesuṁ

18

THE REALMS
OF THE GUARDIANS

Bhummānaṁ devānaṁ … tāvatiṁsā devā saddamanussāvesuṁ.
When they heard what the Earth devas had said, the devas of the realm
of the Four Great Kings cried out with one voice: "At Varanasi … "
And when they heard the cry of the devas of the realm of the Four Great Kings,
then the devas of the realm of the Thirty-Three cried out with one voice …

So they all start celebrating. The Earth devas start off and then the devas of the realm of the Four Great Kings join in, and then the cry goes up and up, with each celestial realm being succeeded by higher ones. In the two realms depicted here, guidance and personal responsibility are very important. The *Catummaharajaka devaloka* is the realm of the Four Great Kings who are the *lokapalas* or world guardians. In this sense, they represent the consciousness of the world rather than being comic book superheroes who wear skin-tight leotards and do battle with extra-terrestrial villains with names like Smarg and The Exterminator. The *lokapala* style of guardianship is more befitting to celestials with ethereal bodies.

In the last half of the twentieth century, people began to consider that the planet and all forms of life on it, the climate and the mixture of chemicals in the air and water, might exist in a sensitive balance that is somehow self-regulating. It does not appear to be ruled by a Creator God separate from it, but to say that it is not directed would be the opposite view — the materialistic view that has led to the gross and selfish exploitation of Planet Earth and all forms of life by humankind. Nowadays, scientists are beginning to talk about a self-regulating principle guarding the planet — they call it Gaia; in ancient civilizations, it was Earth Mother or Sky God or Great Spirit; in Buddhist cosmology, it is the Four Great Kings and the *devata* of the Thirty-Three who live on the world mountain, Mount Meru.

The Buddhist emphasis is on mind and consciousness. This, for beings with consciousness, is the access point to the subtle forces that govern the world of Nature. Consciousness is a subtle, localized and highly-developed aspect of creation. Within its immaterial forms are the patterns that abide in the material sphere. Consciousness is the world in which Mount Meru is a symbol for the upright, centered mind, the *axis mundi* — the central pole of our being. If Mount Meru is secure from corruption and upheaval, the world-system is in order. If the human mind is clear and uncorrupted by delusions, hatred, pride and intoxication, then our world is balanced.

In this analysis, the uprightness of the mind implies more than is normally meant by a simple moral standard; it signifies a whole view on the world and on life, in which the ego is dethroned from being the moral arbiter and center of the Universe.

In this analysis, the uprightness of the mind implies more than is normally meant by a simple moral standard; it signifies a whole view on the world and on life, in which the ego is dethroned from being the moral arbiter and center of the Universe. In Buddhist social convention, the ideal ruler, referred to as the Wheel-turning Monarch, was one who was invested with the ten righteous principles or *rajadhammas*. These are: generosity, virtuous conduct, self-sacrifice, honesty/integrity, gentleness, self-control, calmness, non-violence, patient forbearance and conformity to the principles of Dhamma. These qualities are regarded as the proper rulers of the world; whether this is the "external" social world, or the microcosm of our own person. While these principles are firm, Mount Meru — the stable balance within the individual and in society — is secure. When these are decaying, the converse is true, with effects that manifest in wider contexts such as the increase in violent crime, suicide and drug abuse:

> *When people are consumed by improper desires, overwhelmed by corrupt ambitions, obsessed by wrong ideals, the rainfall dwindles. It is hard to get a meal. The crops are bad, afflicted with mildew and stunted. Because of this, many people perish.* (Anguttara Nikaya: [1] Threes, 6, 56; my trans.)

The Buddha saw an intimate connection between the world of consciousness and the natural world; self-view in consciousness always affects the attitudes and the motivations that, in turn, affect the world at large. It doesn't take a completely enlightened being to realize that today's environmental problems stem from greed, and wrong values which manifest as personal wealth pursued at the expense of others.

So the *devata* of the Four Great Kings and the Realm of the Thirty-Three are mostly connected to energies in consciousness. As such, they are frequently mentioned as seeking advice from the Buddha. Sakka (also known as Inda) is the ruler of both realms. In this painting, he is depicted being carried by a *yakkha*, (a kind of genie or ogre), kneeling in front of a Buddha who appears in the regalia of a Wheel-turning Monarch. The Four

Great Kings are immediately above. In the East is Dhatarattha. He is generally accompanied by the white *devata* called *gandhabbas*, the skilled musicians mentioned previously. When they are in charge of things, the East is a serene quarter. Virulhaka is the King of the South. He oversees this quarter with the help of some *kumbhandas*, reputedly gnome-like beings with pot-bellies and short limbs. The guardian of the North is called Vessavana or sometimes Kuvero and he is accompanied by a host of *yakkhas*. The West is guarded by Virupakkha who has a band of *nagas* to back him up. His is quite a team because *nagas* are giant serpents who draw upon and embody the rhythmic flowing power of water and the moon.

These are the four celestial guardians who try to defend the four corners of the world by keeping it free from demonic energies. Like Inda and the *devata* of the Thirty-Three, they are often called upon to defend Mount Meru from the attacks of the *asuras*, the selfish fallen gods of conceit, pride and power. However, like all the devas, they are very much affected by the activities of the human realm. When there's a lot of killing, stealing, lying and greed, that sets up a pretty unpleasant vibration which makes it difficult for them to function properly. Judging from conditions in the world today, these *devata* seem to be sorely pressed to keep the *asuras* and demons at bay. They have a high sense of responsibility and concern for the world, so they rejoice when Buddhas appear in the world to advise human beings how to live wisely.

The next realm above that of the Four Great Kings is the realm of the Thirty-Three, Tavatimsa, which is shown in the lower half of the painting. The realm is variously described as inhabited by thirty-three *devata* or a ruling committee of thirty-three. It is, of course, fantastically beautiful and pleasant. It is a sociable world. There are frequent meetings in the Great Hall; gatherings to listen to celestial concerts, and sometimes guest deities, a visiting Arahant or the Buddha himself drop in to talk on the subject of Dhamma.

This realm is the normal abode of Inda (in Pali) or Indra (in Sanskrit), who was one of the supreme gods of the Vedas — the ancient religious texts, which pre-date Buddhism. Just as the early Christians absorbed aspects of native religions by canonizing their barbaric gods, the Buddhists transformed Inda from a thunderbolt-wielding sky warrior to a righteous monarch, lover of the Dhamma and disciple of the Buddha. In one of the suttas (*Digha Nikaya:* 21 Sakkapanha Sutta), Inda, having recognized that his time was drawing to an end, puts forth renewed spiritual zeal and attains stream-entry. He takes his position as a celestial ruler quite seriously. In the *Jataka* stories, Inda acts as a witness to the Great Being's practices of supreme *paramita*, intervening from time to time to put the Great Being to the test which will enable him to manifest his great virtues. One time, Inda appeared as a hungry Brahmin when the Great Being was a hare and asked him for some food. The hare, having no food to offer, responded by offering his own body as food and throwing himself on a fire to cook (after shaking all the fleas out of his fur). At that moment, the fire went cold and Inda proclaimed the self-sacrifice of the hare, and, as a lasting testimonial, drew the hare's face on the moon. (Remember we're in the realm of mythic truth, here.)

These accounts define Inda as a righteous ruler of realms that are ethically sympathetic to the human realm and interested in its welfare; we should also recognize that Inda, like the realms themselves, plays a part in the human mind. "Inda" is related to the word *indriya*, the five spiritual faculties that govern the contemplative mind. These are faith, energy, mindfulness, concentration and wisdom. If these are not developed in a balanced way, spiritual cultivation is patchy. When "the proper ruler" is present in terms of spiritual practice, or in terms of relationships and duties in the world, the mind is upright and there is a feeling of "rightness." There is a kind of happiness, less gleeful but more flexible and useful, that comes from being balanced and well-guided within oneself. This is the well-being of these celestial realms. However, one has to realize that the extent of this ruling principle is changeable. One can't expect the world to always be under harmonious rule, or the society, or the family. Even in the Sangha, during the time of the Buddha, there was plenty of disharmony, squabbling and corruption; and much the same is true today. In my experience, monasteries go through cycles of inspiration and gloom when people get disillusioned and things become difficult.

Attachment to this realm of social order means that you worship the Buddha as the epitome of everything working out in an orderly and peaceful way. Then you suffer when it changes, and you get disillusioned with Buddhism. But the Buddha never said, "Stick with me and everything will work out well. Believe in me and you will never be disappointed by injustice in the world, or by corrupt monks or apathetic nuns; you're on the winning team." He said: "The conditions that support the apparent world are impermanent; keep practicing diligently." That's the Refuge of the Dhamma, and as you can see in this painting, attachment to perceptions of fairness, rightness and harmony weakens the impression of that Dhamma Wheel.

The beings of these two *devaloka* also see the Buddha in *their* terms, as a being of supreme, though benevolent, power. This kind of Buddha is called a Dhammaraja, the Buddha as king of the Dhamma. He appears in the human realm, too. Giving confidence to Buddhists in the centuries after the Master's decease, such a figure was occasionally carved in stone in the Buddhist kingdoms of India.

From around the first century B.C., Buddhist iconography developed in Northern India for devotional purposes. Gradually there emerged a pantheon of Buddhist saints, Bodhisattvas and Buddhas. This stems from the human mind's natural inclination towards the physical human form rather than towards the abstract "this is the way things are." Kondañña's insight that everything that arises passes away can fail to have much impact on a human mind. You could overlook that in a moment, couldn't you? But that desire to find a guru or a leader or to be able to personify the teaching in a physical form is a very strong tendency for a human being. From this desire to personify the teaching comes the tendency to glorify this human form. In

... the Buddha never said, "Stick with me and everything will work out well. ..." He said: "The conditions that support the apparent world are impermanent; keep practicing diligently."

this picture, we already see the Dhamma Wheel looking vague and faint behind this powerful figure.

So over time — unless there is a community or a good, consistent teaching that keeps inclining towards Dhamma — it's easy to miss the point and get involved with the qualities of the teacher: "I've got to be like that teacher, then I'll be an enlightened being." This again is an example of the origin of suffering rather than the cessation of it because, of course, it's not up to any of us to be like anyone else. But if we apply ourselves to Dhamma, we can be uniquely ourselves and that is good enough; we need not invest this mundane mortal form with charisma. However, to have this kind of confidence in the way it is requires penetration of the Dhamma rather than inspiration from a teacher. The devas don't have that understanding in Dhamma because they can't keep track of things arising and passing away. Devas live for at least ten thousand years so they have little recollection of death. When they finally die, they do so very discreetly. Their twinkle goes out; they're just not seen any more, and everyone says: "D'you remember what happened to … ? Who … ? Oh … peel me another grape." They're forgotten. It's the same with us humans: just consider, when you're feeling captivated, high and inspired, how much do you really remember of everything that arises passes away? You have to be fairly grounded to recognize that even the higher aspects of mind are impermanent conditions.

tāvatiṁsānaṁ devānaṁ saddaṁ
sutvā

yamā devā
saddamanussāvesuṁ.

yamānaṁ devānaṁ saddaṁ
sutvā

tusitā devā
saddamanussāvesuṁ

tusitānaṁ devānaṁ saddaṁ sutvā

19

THE ABODES OF BLISS

Tāvatiṁsānaṁ devānaṁ saddaṁ sutvā yāmā devā … tusitā devā saddamanussāvesuṁ.
When they heard the cry of the Thirty-Three devas, the Yama devas cried out
with one voice … When they heard the cry of the Yama devas,
the Tusita devas cried out with one voice …

This illustration is of the next level of celestial abode that the message was transmitted to. The Yama devas picked up the cry from the Tavatimsa *devaloka* and the Tusita devas picked up the cry when they heard what the Yama devas had said. In the picture, the Yama *devaloka* is at the top, and underneath it, corresponding to the word sequence found in the Sutta, is the Tusita heavenly realm. That's the way I've depicted it to correspond to the way we read from the top to the bottom of the page. Of course, the sequence in the Sutta describes an *ascending* order of heavenly realms.

The Yama devas are those who have gone beyond any kind of unpleasant impingement. At this level, there is no fighting with *asuras*. In the picture, the Yama devas are flaunting the Lord of the Dead; indicating that they feel they have no need to pay heed to his warnings — his messengers of old age, sickness and death don't come to this realm. This is a slight exaggeration, but with a life span of 144 million years, one might be excused a little poetic license. Anyway, here all is very jolly.

The Tusita devas are the smiling, blissful *devata;* Yama *devaloka* plus. The Tusita *devaloka* is where, according to Buddhist legends, the Bodhisatta Metteyya is living. That's the one who will be the next Buddha, and will emphasize loving-kindness in his teachings. Here, he is in the center of the lotus world of Tusita heaven, teaching Dhamma and biding his time with all the Tusita devas being blissed-out around him.

Both of these realms are more refined than the lower *devaloka.* In fact, at this stage, we have left solid ground altogether. The Tavatimsa devas live on Mount Meru, but the subsequent higher realms are in the air and ethereal abodes above it. And the higher you go, the longer the life-span. What does this all mean in terms of the mind?

The ascent to higher realms signifies increasingly refined states of happiness, or happiness created by more refined objects. With the Bhumma devas, it was the joys of the natural world — bucolic idylls, satyrs, fauns and the rest of it. I can relate to that. To enter that level of perception means that the mind is free from remorse, violence and craving for coarse material things such as money or powerful stimulation. To have the Bhumma deva mentality is a sign of some virtue, and the development of wholesomeness. It is even more so with the realms of the Four Great Kings and the Tavatimsa, the realms that relate to the sense of custodianship of the earth and responsibility for the society. At this level, it's not the happy-go-lucky pastoral glee that gives us happiness; but that in us which delights in good deeds, in rightness and being inspired by the wise. Here, there is less frivolity and a steadier radiance from the heart.

At the level that has left the earth altogether, the realms of the Yama devas and on up, the mind has entered the abodes of what is conventionally known as spirituality. At these levels, we are concerned with subtle energy bodies and vibrations, chakras and meridians, sensitivity to the astral and ethereal planes. The Tusita *devaloka* is like the vision and rapture that accompany religious fervor. These come when you absorb into the feeling that *your* teacher is the greatest and is the one who has all the answers. This rapture also comes when your spiritual practice, meditation or faith is going well and there are no problems; it's plain sailing and you feel totally confident that this is the way for you.

There is a more refined happiness available at these levels: one is involved with the quality of mental consciousness, so the physical realities are less relevant. Instead of being concerned with a person's conduct, one picks up their vibrations or their aura. This refined sensitivity is quite delightful, and the more refined the state of consciousness, the longer it appears to continue — since time dilation is another feature of refined consciousness. States of heightened sensitivity, even induced through psychedelic drugs, can seem like an eternity in duration. You forget about impermanence. And this is what is happening here.

The Wheel of the Law that Kondañña saw so clearly — the Truth that everything that has the nature to arise, has the nature to pass away — is fading from view. The central image is the figure of the Buddha as a mystic,

In monastic life, we have to live in a community and have responsibilities ... . This means that we don't get into refined states of bliss for very long, but we do develop an equanimity, serenity and openness of heart to life as it is.

140

and it is to this image, not the Good Law, that the *devata* pay homage and respect. We too can tend to worship the personification of our own values and ideals and lose touch with the teaching that transcends them all. People will quote a teacher out of context or slightly alter the emphasis and omit some qualifying remarks in order to justify their own viewpoints.

When you lose contact with the physical or the mundane realm, delusion born out of attachment to ethereal perceptions becomes much more possible. People will go so far as to neglect domestic and social responsibilities, and consider chores as mundane work that somebody else can do. The idea comes up that if I'm on retreat, I shouldn't have to be disturbed by doing my laundry or cleaning the house: "I'm having an important spiritual experience; don't bother me."

This attitude is another aspect of self-view and becoming. If it is really strong, it can even develop into *sañña vipallasa*, "distorted perception"—overwhelming rapture, visions, intimations of personal destiny, voices from the other shore and the rest of it. In such cases, the teacher will usually assign such disciples mundane tasks, such as sweeping the hall, to keep them in contact with other grounded humans who understand their predicament. It passes. Undergoing this kind of "distorted perception" experience can really upset a person's balance and understanding. Therefore, in contemplative monastic training, attachment to refinement is seen as potentially unbalancing, and any attitudes founded upon that attachment get short-shrift.

In monastic life, we have to live in a community and have responsibilities to each other, to the monastery, to the lay people and to the tradition. We have to perform many mundane duties. This means that we don't get into refined states of bliss for very long, but we do develop an equanimity, serenity and openness of heart to life as it is. As those important qualities can be developed on any plane of existence, one doesn't hanker after some and reject other states of being. All that is needed for Awakening and liberation from the suffering of self-view is a continual reflection on impermanence.

Not that I'm putting down the Yama and Tusita *devata*. It's good not to get stuck on the materialistic and functional plane; it's helpful to refine the mind and realize that the apparent world is dependent on consciousness. The ethereal realms are no problem, provided that one doesn't attach to them. Yet if we attach to such states, no matter how long they may seem to last, when the mystical experience ends or the ethereal body starts to droop, what happens to the so-called "enlightenment"? Gone, isn't it? Then what do you do to get it back?

When I painted this picture, I was on a meditation retreat, and certain colors kept arising in my mind. I was contemplating the feeling or the tone that a color can bring up. Mood and feeling were playing a more important role in my meditation practice at that time. In general, over the four years of creating this series of paintings, as one may easily deduce, there was a development towards tone and overall mood expressed through design

All that is needed for Awakening and liberation from the suffering of self-view is a continual reflection on impermanence.

141

and color and away from the clear definitions of line. Spiritually, I felt part of things, less an observer/analyzer. I also found my mind readily bringing images and form into being. I think I was heading for the next *devaloka,* the realms of creative delight. …

> *Tusitānaṁ devānaṁ saddaṁ sutvā …*
> When they heard the cry of the Tusita devas …

20

CREATIVE DELIGHT

... nimmānaratī devā ... paranimmitavasavattī devā saddamanussāvesuṁ.
... the Nimmanarati devas cried out with one voice ... When they heard the cry of
the Nimmanarati devas, the Paranimmitavasavatti devas cried out with one voice ...

In these two realms, *Nimmanarati* and *Paranimmitavasavatti,* we find the devas of creation and the devas who delight in the creations of other devas. As you can imagine, these are even more refined and long-lived than the Tusita devas. The Nimmanarati devas abide at almost magical levels of consciousness where the mind is so light and unburdened with temporality or form that it can create and sustain images according to its wishes. The Paranimmitavasavatti devas are one step further on from having to make the effort to create images of existence; they merely abide in the enjoyment of what has been created. They never question the purpose or result of these creations, but appreciate them for their own sake. The mortal earth realm has been left far behind and with it such considerations as impermanence, purpose, cause and effect. They rejoice to hear that the Dhamma has been taught, but it is probably because they perceived the flash of light and heard the rejoicing from below. This is a happiness that could easily lead to indolence and decadence, and, fittingly enough, one of the two monarchs who rule over the

Paranimmitavasavatti realm is Mara—the lord of delusion, whom we have met many times before. The other monarch is in another quarter of the realm and doesn't even know of Mara's existence. It seems to me that there's a very clear message here about this kind of bliss.

Creation is a magical act. It is the ability to produce simulacra of living or non-living entities, and even images of principles and thought. Creation ranges from physical procreation to everyday speech (whereby whole realms of experience are reproduced in the mind of another) to literature and the fine arts. The arts can use mundane objects but, through metaphor and other forms of craft, evoke higher meanings and implications in the mind of the reader/viewer. These meanings may be reflections on the significance or purpose of life or the relationship of the human to the universal. Creation should, therefore, be seen as a sacred act. In mythology and ancient civilization, it was sacred; creative acts were presided over by deities and attended by or prepared for with rites, ceremonies and priests who were there to move the minds of the participants away from the instincts of self. Art was a magical act, originated perhaps to evoke and commune with the spirits of the creatures that were painted—as with the cave paintings of creatures of the hunt at Lascaux. Poetry and literature established the values, the inspiration and the aspiration of the society. What an ecstasy of stillness for those creators, and what awe and rapture for those who reviewed and were enriched with their creations!

This creative impulse can also be traced in the development of Buddhist art. The Buddha himself taught in different styles. One style that was used employed high lyrical verse as a form called *gathas*. The Arahant disciples also left traces of their enlightenment in poetic form, collected as the *Theragatha* and *Therigatha*. These different forms of expression should be borne in mind so that we don't expect everything attributed to the Buddha to fit into a prosaic, rational view. Although the Buddha did not encourage artistic representations of himself, tradition has it that he agreed to the representation of the Six Realms as a teaching device. After the Buddha's passing away, the wish to establish sacred images as icons of the qualities of the Buddha or as visual metaphors for the furtherance of the Dhamma, naturally led to a swelling stream of poetry and visual arts. These forms of expression were very important for the largely non-literate and polylingual civilization of the Buddhist empires. The story of how they evolved and their importance is quite long, but I'll cut it short to fit this painting.

After about 1,000 years in India, Buddhism had developed its literature and commentaries. During that time, many lineages of practice and theory arose and passed away. The more established vital centers of Buddhist theory were in Nalanda, near Bodh-Gaya, where an enormous university housed up to 20,000 students, in nearby Odantapura, and in Vikramashila in West Bengal. In these places, many of the Mahayana and Vajrayana teachings were established. By the eighth and ninth centuries of the Christian Era, they were still flourishing, while all the lands to the west came under the influence of Islam. That meant a later form of Buddhism,

The arts can use mundane objects but, through metaphor and other forms of craft, evoke higher meanings and implications in the mind of the reader/viewer.

the Vajrayana, could only be transmitted due north, into Nepal and Tibet, or across the sea to Indonesia rather than along the now inaccessible routes from Afghanistan into China.

One feature of Buddhism as it appears in Mahayana and Vajrayana forms, is the development of the Buddha from a solitary sage to a principle of enlightenment. This principle is embodied and manifests in many places and over a large span of time. It's a nice thing to think about: one Buddha is good, therefore two are twice as good, and so on. The historical Buddha, Gotama, is reported to have made reference to a whole lineage of 27 preceding Awakened Ones. Some may doubt this, but for the purposes of mythological and poetic truth, there is no reason why one shouldn't have Buddhas everywhere. If their presence encourages the quality of awe and selfless attention to the present moment, if it develops the faculty of faith, if it helps to counterbalance the materialistic concerns of life, it has a purpose. As a historical account, it is not of much use anyway. In the Vajrayana, five Buddha forms have crystallized to convey this universality of Buddha-nature; the number five signifies the four cardinal directions and the center. These are called the five *Dhyani* Buddhas — that is, they are for the purpose of meditation (called *dhyana* in Sanskrit); one can learn to visualize them, practice devotion to them or reflect upon their qualities.

The central one is Vairocana whose name means "radiant." He is generally white and is depicted with his hands in the *Dhammacakkappavattana mudra*. This is the Buddha that proclaims the Dhamma — the Four Noble Truths and Dependent Origination. His position is central; here I repeat the *mudra* throughout the painting recognizing that this (teaching the Dhamma) is still the fundamental significance of a Sammasambuddha — one who is completely self-enlightened.

Beginning on the right and proceeding counter-clockwise, the next Buddha is Akshobya, the Buddha of the East. His color is blue, his epithet — "imperturbable." This is the Buddha at the moment of enlightenment, knowing how it actually is and repelling all delusion. His hand is in the earth-touching *mudra*. This is the "mindfulness *mudra*" much used in Southeast Asia as the epitome of Dhamma practice.

In the South is Ratnasambhava, traditionally painted yellow. Ratna is a jewel, so this is an emblem of the precious gifts of the Buddha mind. The hand *mudra* is that of generosity. Nowadays, this image is generally found in Tibet (and Nepal) where Vajrayana practitioners revere the boundless Dhamma gifts of the Buddha.

The Buddha of the West is called Amitabha. Like Akshobya, this image was established before the Islamic conquest of Afghanistan and Pakistan, and thence, traveled to China and Japan where it became very popular. In fact, a whole school arose based upon devotion to this one Buddha called the Pure Land School.

Herein, Amitabha (also known as Amida) is the Buddha of the Western Paradise. He promises that all who *sincerely* put their faith in him will be reborn in a Western Paradise, and work out their way to Nirvana from there. Of course, the catch is in what you take "sincerely" to mean. I would think it implies a lot more than a few recitations and prayers. Faith is made sincere by effort, mindfulness, concentration and discernment—then it certainly will get you to a pure state of mind. The fact that Amitabha is the Buddha portrayed in the posture of meditation seems to indicate that purity is not attained by paying lip service to the teaching alone. Actually, if used insightfully, Amitabha is a fine transcending teacher. His purpose is to cut, with a mind of faith and insight, the root perception that one is not enlightened and that one has to *do* something to *become* enlightened. As we have seen, this self-view, this identification with the habit-bound mind, can never be transcended by any actions proceeding from the sense of self. So in the Pure Land practice, the meditator abandons that view and proceeds from the basis of being one with the Buddha of bliss. You can't do that by thinking about it—only through faith born of a powerful commitment.

The last of the *Dhyani* Buddhas is Amoghasiddhi, the Buddha of the North. His color is green and his hand is in the *abhaya mudra*, the sign of fearlessness. This Buddha's characteristic is the All-Accomplishing Wisdom which is attained by means of the dispassionate, selfless activity of an Awakened One. Such activity is all-accomplishing because when there is no personal bias, and yet a full commitment to the welfare of others, love and insight operate in an unfaltering way. Amoghasiddhi never demands that people live up to any expectations, can never be disappointed, and hence never gives up on compassionate activity. Content to hold up the Dhamma in the fearlessness *mudra*, he acts as an unconditioned Refuge with no discrimination and no thought of result. Amoghasiddhi is a symbol of the equanimity that is regarded as the highest form of love.

Essentially, these *Dhyani* Buddhas are meant to be objects of contemplation to remind us of the practice and of the mind which gives rise to Awakening. All of these *Dhyani* Buddhas are believed to be offshoots of a supreme *Adhi* Buddha, a cosmic over-Buddha who never actually manifests in any form at all. He remains a potential for Awakening in the universe. All the *Dhyani* Buddhas are manifestations of that one single potential.

Upon these five Buddha-modes, I have evolved twenty-eight figures corresponding to the lineage of the 28 Buddhas described in a Theravada sutta, the Atanatiya Sutta (*Digha Nikaya:* 32), and also in an apocryphal book of verses, the *Buddhavamsa*. There are a few references made in the Pali Canon to previous Buddhas suggesting that Gotama Buddha was not the only one and that he rediscovered rather than created the Dhamma teachings. These references also indicate a continuum of spiritual purity that continues to manifest in the world. Although the lineage of the 28 Buddhas predates the manifestation of the *Dhyani* Buddhas, both serve as a reflection to encourage faith.

These forms and others like them became popular because one can retain them more clearly in the mind. If you are not steeped in contemplative ways of thought, say you are a farmer planting paddy fields behind a water buffalo, the relativity and ultimate emptiness of conditioned phenomena means much less than the idea that Buddha has compassion for you and will help you if you do good. Even for a contemplative, these images give the mind something more tangible to focus upon. And this is their sacredness.

But a creation can also become a hindrance. In order for it to be sacred, we should not be drawn into the creation or into its creator. The highest aim of Creation is to indicate the Uncreated. Poetry that succeeds in this endeavor reminds us of silence and the cessation of thought as the true source of fullness; visual arts remind us of the ephemeral nature of form and its dance with space. However, creations get profaned by self-view and become obsessive and narcissistic. Words and speech are profaned because they are used to heighten the ego sense or to project the ego's wishes onto the universe. Sexuality is profaned into self-gratification and power fantasies. The same is true of religious forms and conventions—we can use them as objects to blindly worship and project our desires onto, or to throw at each other. So, the creation of Buddhas can lead to asking favors of images and making offerings to them for good luck; or to sectarian strife.

All the additions to a religious form can have great vitality in them, but if clung to blindly, they can obscure spiritual goals with cultural and metaphysical incrustations. The development of styles, lineages and conventions is a natural thing like the growth of a plant. While a tree grows, the systems that transport nutrition remain quite delicate. Its life-giving sap is carried through a fine ring of wood between the bark and the heartwood. The heartwood, which is there just to support the mass of the tree, becomes more and more massive, but it's not where the life really is. Of course, the tree needs the support to hold the mass of leaves up, so the heartwood is not useless. But if you want maple syrup, you know where to look.

What we have to consciously aim for, and what we often neglect in the bliss of creation is the Way of transcendence, the Uncreated—that which is beyond form. It is to this that the Wheel of the Dhamma, the Four Noble Truths point. There may be other ways, but this Path is the shortcut. It does not attract energies that entangle and delude. And in this painting, as in many of the cultural and metaphysical accumulations around the Buddha's words, the Wheel of the Dhamma has faded in significance. Here, it is just a few spokes of light emanating from Vairocana's *mudra*. In the realm above, the light is even fainter.

Paranimmitavasavattīnaṁ devānaṁ saddaṁ sutvā …
When they heard the cry of the Paranimmitavasavatti devas …

The highest aim of Creation is to indicate the Uncreated. Poetry that succeeds in this endeavor reminds us of silence and the cessation of thought as the true source of fullness; visual arts remind us of the ephemeral nature of form and its dance with space.

brahmakāyikā devā

saddamanussāvesaṁ

etaṁ Bhagavatā
bārāṇasiyaṁ isipatane
migadāye
anuttaraṁ dhammacakkaṁ
pavattitaṁ appaṭivattiyaṁ
samaṇena vā brāhmaṇena vā
devena vā mārena vā
brahmunā vā kenaci vā
lokasmin'ti

21

FORMLESS RAPTURE

... brahmakāyikā devā saddamanussāvesuṁ ... kenaci vā lokasmin ti.
... the devas of the retinue of the Brahma deities took up the cry: "At Varanasi in the
Deer Park at Isipatana, the matchless Wheel of Dhamma has been set rolling by the
Blessed One, not to be stopped by any samana, or brahmin, or deva, or mara, or brahma,
or anyone in the world."

By the time we reach this realm, we are at the *Brahmakayika devaloka*. The Brahmakayika devas are the assembly of devas who attend the Brahma deities. They occupy the first level of the next "world"—the world of the *Brahma*. The beings in the *brahmaloka* have no sense desire, and a form that is more refined than that of the Six Realms. They have also a correspondingly long life span. They have attained this state of being through the development of absorptive meditation and loving-kindness. The Brahmakayika devas live in a state of devotion to what seems eternal and lofty. All of the *devata* experience happiness and bliss, but the higher the *devaloka*, the more refined the object as well as its resulting pleasure. Here, the object is formless, indefinite. In the realm of the Brahma gods, form is tenuous; yet these realms are also impermanent and subject to becoming and illusions of selfhood.

This realm is equivalent to the mind that enters into a state of very steady happiness born of faith without investigation. This happiness is an oceanic sense of oneness with, and trust in the benevolence of, the universe. Despite the fundamental goodness of this realm, it is subject to delusion. The mind goes to sleep. The object of one's faith—whether it be called God, the Tao, the Dhamma, the One, Ultimate Truth—is conceived in sufficiently remote and indefinable terms to be beyond investigation. It's beyond good and bad or any other definition; this has an element of truth—even Awakened Ones say that Ultimate Truth is beyond designations. With no ill-effects at first, the mind can slip into attitudes that lack discernment: "It's all Dhamma," we think—and lose our sense of direction. There's only the inclination to stay in a state of oneness and rapture for as long as possible, and avoid the more abrasive energies of the sense realms.

Yet the trials and pulls of the sense realms highlight the self-view and the liberation that is realized through abandoning it. Hence the Way of practice is outlined time and time again in ways that are tangible. The Buddha kept his frames of reference linked to states that did not fascinate the mind or act as soporifics.

> *But whatever are the states of which you, Gotami, may know, these states lead to passionlessness, not to passion ... absence of bondage, not to bondage ... absence of accumulation, not to accumulation ... wanting little, not wanting much ... contentment, not dissatisfaction ... solitude, not sociability ... putting forth of energy, not to indolence ... ease in supporting oneself, not to difficulty in supporting oneself; you should know definitely, Gotami, this is Dhamma, this is discipline, this is the Teacher's instruction.* (Vinaya, Culavagga: [X])

These were the words on Dhamma that the Buddha addressed to the first nun, Mahapajapati Gotami (his stepmother and aunt, no less). Applying this reflection within her practice, she also realized Nibbana.

But the Brahma deities have not realized Nibbana. The mind states that determine their existence lack insight and wisdom. Being too deeply absorbed into their own existence, they cannot reflect upon or know the way things are.

In Sutta 11 of the *Digha Nikaya* (Kevaddha Sutta), a question arises in the mind of a meditating bhikkhu as to where the four elements cease. In other words, where is the place beyond all phenomena? He travels, presumably through psychic power, to various celestial realms and is continually advised to seek his answer in a higher abode. Eventually, he comes into the presence of the Great Brahma (which is only the third of the twenty brahma realms, but probably as high up as allows communication!) However, the Great Brahma, surrounded by devotees, can only respond to the question by extolling his own magnificence. When questioned for the third time, the Great Brahma takes the bhikkhu aside and says he doesn't know but can't admit that in the presence of the retinue. And Brahma then admonishes the bhikkhu for seeking an answer to such a question from anyone but the Buddha. The Buddha, of course, puts the bhikkhu right by saying that the question is really: Where do the four elements not get established? The answer is that they do not stick in the mind of someone who has no wish to attach to any mode of existence. When consciousness is in the "rest state" of "cessation" the intentions and perceptions that define experience are not created:

> *Where consciousness is signless, boundless, all-luminous,*
> *That's where earth, water, fire and air find no footing.*
> *There both long and short, small and great, fair and foul—*
> *There 'name-and-form' are wholly destroyed.*
> *With the cessation of consciousness, this is all destroyed.* (Walshe, trans.)

That's what Brahmas don't know, because they are attached to their refined state of being.

The Great Brahma

Fascination with "special" energies, auras and refined powers of the mind makes you feel special and consequently, you invest a lot of interest and significance in those states. Then you find kinship with other special people who are attuned to that level, and, consciously or not, the kinship reinforces your specialness. So you get stuck in a self-view as big as Mount Meru. You don't want to let go of it and see it as just another condition because it's uplifting to be special and fascinating. Surely, enlightened beings must be special and fascinating? No, enlightened beings are the only totally ordinary beings. Everyone else is special in some way or another, with their unique special problems and sensitivities. Enlightened beings are those who realize Ultimate Truth as totally ordinary—as the way it is. However much they demonstrate and praise the qualities of

153

wisdom, they don't think of themselves as anything in personal terms.

> *The wise man does not rate himself with the distinguished, the lowest, nor with ordinary people; calm and unselfish, he is free from possessiveness: he holds onto nothing and he rejects nothing.* (Sutta Nipata: 954; Saddhatissa trans.)

The Buddha didn't even bother to refer to himself as a person at all. When questioned as to who he was; deva, brahma or human, he refuted them all and said, "I am Awake." The quality of Awakeness is brought to the foreground, and the personal form not mentioned. The Buddha constantly notes: "But I did not let the pleasure that came from this realization take over my mind."

That is the great difference between the bliss of Awakening and the *brahmaloka*. The Brahma gods are always affirming their identity and lingering in the bliss of their sphere. The mind loses its discernment and sense of investigation, and the bliss is worshipped in its own right. People love these high states of mind, tend to idolize them, and idolize beings who attain them. But notice in the picture that the Dhamma Wheel has almost disappeared; it's a vague glow and there's a strange *mudra* in the center of the glow that has become a meaningless gesture.

I equate this image with the worship of an Ultimate Being which places the experience of the Ultimate beyond the possibility of personal realization. One can have some experience of the bliss of not being involved with the sense realm from this calm, or simply by believing in this heavenly being, but it limits the direct experience or investigation of Dhamma. So the bliss of the Brahmas is one akin to suspended animation rather than transcendence through penetration of the sense realm. In the long run, the good kamma that keeps the Brahma afloat runs out. Unresolved attachments begin to have their effect, because they have not been transformed through insight into not-self. In formless rapture, we lose spiritual definition to the extent where even morality and reason become secondary to the experience of being with the Great Brahma.

The *brahmaloka* are easy to fake also, because they do not allow any criteria outside of their realm to be brought to bear. They support an attitude of unquestioning devotion. That attitude has an attraction but it means we can be unquestioningly devoted to some fake Brahmas. The so-called Transcendent One may even transcend loftiness: "It's all Dhamma, sleeping Buddhas, fighting Buddhas, drinking beer and watching T.V. Buddhas." That's the interpretation of the formless realms that the unawakened mind can make. We seek out the refined pleasure, but neglect the skillful actions that give rise to those refined states of being.

Those people who make an identity out of refined levels of consciousness are apt to use that sense of being the Great Brahma, the Bodhisattva, the next Buddha and the rest of it for corrupt ends. When this happens, as can be noted in several contemporary cases, self-view keeps justifying the indulgence. The burden of self-view is like a lead weight, and, if left unchecked, it can drag one's consciousness down to the realms of Hell,

The brahmaloka are easy to fake also ... "It's all Dhamma, sleeping Buddhas, fighting Buddhas, drinking beer and watching T.V. Buddhas."

generally with a few fascinated disciples in tow.

Devotion takes many forms, some of them refined and some coarse. I've seen people get into devotional highs over football teams. However, whether it's high or low, devotion without investigation produces a rapturous energy in the mind of the devotee, but not much else.

And investigation without devotion falls short of the full appreciation of Dhamma. Instead of that wholehearted knowing that unifies heart and mind, without devotion we cultivate an intellectual analysis of conditioned phenomena—the structure of the world and the self. Some aspect of our mind is always standing apart; the result is a lack of heart—and a "self" acting as an onlooker. Even dedicated insight meditators get stuck at this arid level—and may suddenly abandon their decade of practice to sit at the feet of a guru who offers great presence and expects complete surrender to his will. To go beyond the pitfalls of the absence, or misdirection, of devotion, we have to abandon our intellectual detached stance, and leap, in faith, not to a person but into the center of the apparent world. With insight, devotion helps us open to conditions and stop hanging onto our perceptions, and can take us beyond our self-view. Without devotion, we remain on the sidelines of Truth; if devotion is fettered by ignorance, it breeds attachment to objects of faith—special people, rituals, hobbies— even football teams.

The wise use of devotion is not to form or formlessness, or any level of sensual or non-sensual becoming. These are the shortfalls of the *devata* mentality. But when faith is balanced by wisdom and concentration is balanced by energy, and when that balance is preserved by mindfulness, our insightful knowing can penetrate the changing and unsatisfactory nature of appearances and not seek to gain, become or annihilate anything. Then a fortunate fruition of the spiritual faculties takes place:

> *When these five faculties are maintained in being and developed, they merge in the Deathless, reach to the Deathless and end in the Deathless.* (Samyutta Nikaya: [V], Faculties, VI, 7)

The Buddha, as the teacher and human exemplar of enlightenment, is a catalyst for our faith, but the giving of ourselves is to the Dhamma that we can experience through this body and mind. Complete cultivation sustained through body, speech and mind is the supreme devotion.

> *Whatever monk, nun, male or female lay-follower dwells practicing the Dhamma properly, and perfectly fulfills the Dhamma-way, he or she honors the Tathagata, reveres and esteems him and pays him the supreme homage.* (Mahaparinibbana Sutta; Digha Nikaya: Sutta 16)

To make that offering, we have to return to where we are, seeing it no longer as self and the world, but as the realm of Dhamma.

Complete cultivation sustained through body, speech and mind is the supreme devotion.

22

THE WORLD OF DHAMMA

Itiha tena khaṇena tena muhuttena yāva brahmalokā saddo abbhuggacchi.
So indeed in that hour, at that moment,
the word traveled up to the realm of the highest divinities.

The message I'm trying to convey through this painting is a reminder that although the Universe—of matter or consciousness—can seem vast, to one who meditates or understands the nature of things, it can be known in its essence. Anything that has form can be classified in terms of the four elements: earth, water, air and fire. These elements are symbolized by the figures in the corner of the frame of this painting starting from earth in the top right and proceeding in a clockwise direction through water, air and fire. We have seen how these elements can be explained in general physical terms as size, shape, mobility and caloricity; or as psychological types. They also help to illustrate more specifically the human body for the purposes of meditation.

One of the meditations on the body equates flesh, bone and solid features with the earth; blood, sweat and other liquid features with water; breath and gases in the digestive system with the air element; and bodily heat with the fire element. Such a perceptual shift is conducive to a dispassionate experience of the body as not-self.

In the practice of meditation, this same analysis can be extended by translating mental states into one of these elemental states. This is not in order to deny or criticize them, but rather to see them in a more dispassionate light as views rather than facts, and is a skillful means in which mental phenomena come to be "known." So you can contemplate anger as "fire;" and that allows you to reflect upon it objectively rather than thinking: "I must not be angry, after all, I've no reason to be annoyed; I should be more peaceful!" To contemplate it as an element gives you a dispassionate perspective that allows the anger to pass or change into a more positive form such as vigor. This avoids suppressing feelings or creating guilt. If there is a reason to be annoyed, one can express the cause of the annoyance rather than blast out the result!

Visionary views—the "Air" element—are inherently abstract and can lead to a dogmatic idealism if blindly adhered to. Yet if one contemplates this quality of principles, it can be tempered by realism. The result is a malleable intelligence that guides the manifest world. Similarly, "Water" relates to the wavering quality of emotion and intuitions that break down definitions and blend everything together, and becomes a serene sensitivity if contemplated without attachment. We *feel* harmony and balance rather than form definitions of it. On the negative side, this faculty lacks discernment and confidence in making decisions or comparative judgements for conventional purposes. "Earth" represents the process of organizational thought. Earth is like a loyal secretary in the mind that works according to established systems. Thinking from the "Earth" position measures and gives definition, although the negative consequence is that it tends to categorize and emphasize the separative quality of phenomena. "Earth" inclines towards conservative attitudes that lack vision; some dispassion is needed to encourage it to respond to change and spontaneity.

This is the world that Tathagatas know. They have seen this world caused, arising, sustained and ceasing. Not knowing these elements as they are and how they manifest physically and mentally, as well as not learning the skill of responding to them wisely can get us into a lot of trouble. And there's no way out—if we don't act wisely with them, we act carelessly, or try to suppress them which causes more trouble. And for most of us, right up to the realm of the *brahmaloka,* there's the hope and the inclination that some aspect of these elements, some refined blend of body, emotion, energy or imagination—in either ourselves or in another—would be worth investing in. It seems that a sum total of changing elements is all there is and that is all we are. Even the Great Brahma did not know anything beyond the four elements. In his ethereal realm, the elements still remained, albeit in a refined mental form. And Brahma, like the *devata,* is not in the best position to know the elements as changeable and unsatisfactory and as selfless universal qualities. Brahmas are too refined and live too long to know about letting go.

To say that the word of the Dhamma traverses the *devaloka* signifies that this teaching is relevant to the most refined or coarse states of experience on a physical or mental plane. Every being on the Wheel of Becoming experiences the elements. To unenlightened beings, the elements appear in forms that are either delightful or repelling but always experienced as having some kind of personal quality. All of the devas and brahmas of refined form see things that way. So in essence, no world of form or formlessness, nor the deliverance from those worlds, are beyond what can be experienced through the human body and mind:

> *I do proclaim that in this fathom-long body, with its perceptions and consciousness, is the world, the world's arising, the world's cessation and the Path leading to the world's cessation.* (Anguttara Nikaya: [II], Fours, 45)

In this picture, the essential qualities from the realm of form, including the celestial realms, are being contemplated within the body and its perceptions. The body, which is much more calming and steadying than mental phenomena, is generally used as a tranquil and peaceful foundation for meditation. Sensual desire is cooled by reflection on the elements of the body; calm and tranquility is developed by attention to the breath — evaluating the breath and discerning its present quality. When these have been developed to some extent, brightness and expansiveness of heart is evoked by reflection on the "divine abodes" of kindness, compassion, sympathetic joy and equanimity. These are the elemental qualities of the happiness of the *devaloka*. Each of the concentric bands around the figure is colored according to the color that dominates the previous paintings of the *devaloka;* purple-violet and deep red refers to the *brahmakayika devaloka* and so on down to the ochre, golden yellows of the Bhumma deva which forms the innermost circle.

To unenlightened beings, the elements appear in forms that are either delightful or repelling but always experienced as having some kind of personal quality.

ayanca
dasasahassī lokadhātu
saṅkampi sampakampi sampavedhi

23

WHOLE LOTTA SHAKIN' GOING ON

Ayañca dasasahassī lokadhātu saṅkampi sampakampi sampavedhi.
And this ten-thousandfold world-system shook and rocked and quaked.

We've seen various ways in which the ten-thousandfold world-system can be experienced. In this painting, I return to the system of the five khandhas to portray it as something that can be known. Everything that can be sensed, perceived or conceived comes within the range of form, feeling, perception, mind formations and sense-consciousness. This summarizes the experience of the world in a way that makes it something to work on rather than as a measureless cosmos in which we feel lost.

This analysis of the khandhas is represented by five approximately concentric bands vibrating around the presence of the Buddha. The Four Noble Truths emanate out from his still center through that vibrating realm. The innermost band represents *rupa khandha,* physical form, which is relatively stable and clearly defined. Our most easily discernible aspect is our physical body. Subsequent khandhas (comprising the "nama" and "viññana" categories of experience) are of the mind and are more convoluted. These "mental" khandhas all arise together; although we talk about them as separate, actually they are four aspects of a whole. After *rupa* is *vedana*, feeling, of which there are three kinds: pleasant, neutral and unpleasant. The next is *sañña*, perception or associative recognition which occurs at that moment of knowing something. We feel it and then recognize what that feeling signifies: warmth for example. That's *sañña*. Then there is a mental formation: "My body is warm." A mental feeling (pleasant) arises, followed by various mental formations born of happiness, ease and so on. These "mental formations" comprise the fourth khandha, known as *sankhara*.

These "mental formations" include thoughts, emotions, visions and the like which occur within sense-consciousness, *viññana* — the fifth khandha. *Sañña* tends to produce *sankhara*. The mind begins to chatter about the perceptions that have arisen; then a further layer of feelings and perceptions arise, based upon which other *sankhara* are created. *Sankhara* are the formations that conscious self-views are founded upon. Our habit or attachment is towards establishing a reality out of perceptions — what we denote as agreeable, friendly, necessary, disgusting and so on. We build up a network of these through life, and our views and attitudes — the positions that our minds chatter, complain and feel excited from — are based on these. "I" am the apparent agent of all this, or the oppressed host to it all. This, generally, is how the self is created within sense-consciousness. The interweaving of the khandhas, most notably of perceptions and mind formations, is what gives rise to the sense of a person who is at first created by those forms, and then becomes the helpless victim of them.[*] So the movements of mind that operate within this system tend towards the inference of a very real self, although that self is constantly changing in dimension and expression. The effect is like that of a kaleidoscope in which the same fundamental phenomena get shifted around, but due to the internal mirror are always perceived as forming a single coherent unit. Our "internal mirror" is the mind. The mind is turned towards the world-system in a particular way that reflects a self. However, in that arrangement, the mind is only able to see one set of conditions arising at a time; each set producing a different self — a wise "me"; a hurt "me"; a tender "me"; a stern "me" etc. — so the picture that appears in time is a movie of many "selves" in precarious balance and frequent conflict.

This view is shaken by the teachings of the Buddha. If we have experienced the self-view as unsatisfying, we begin to watch its expressions more closely in order to understand why. The central core of this view originates with an assumption rooted in ignorance that there is a being or thing which is continuous or has some unchangeable aspects. Cultivation of watchfulness dispels the ignorance. With attention, we can notice that what makes up this view is an energy, a tendency, arising according to inclinations of which we are only vaguely aware. This energy, attachment or *upadana*, is the nuclear force that binds everything together and is dependent on ignorance. With knowing, the objects that attachment wants

The subtlest attachment, the view that there is something to attach to, is the most deeply-ingrained.

---

[*] The process outlined in the extract from the Madhupindika Sutta quoted in chapter 14.

to hold onto are seen as essentially impermanent, incapable of being held. And attachment itself is also changeable; we're not constantly experiencing attachment to any one thing. The subtlest attachment, the view that there *is* something to attach to, is the most deeply-ingrained. As one abides more in Truth, even this subtlest attachment fades.

Insight into the realm of the five khandhas that we take as reality reveals that what we experience is an artifact of feelings, perceptions and mental formations catalyzed by the presence (i.e., consciousness) of form. This is another way of expressing the co-dependency of "name-and-form" and "consciousness." These "mental formations" are based upon intention (will, volition)—direction towards or away from a feeling or perception; and attention—lingering and ruminating upon the same. They are the source of our "mental monologue" which describes and directs our experience of the world. However, when we no longer cling to our feelings and perceptions—when they are seen as ephemeral—the mind's intention and attention is no longer fixed upon them. There is the experience of cessation or emptiness described in the Kevaddha Sutta as "signless," "boundless," "all-luminous" consciousness. In brief, phenomena occur when there is both the arising of certain conditions and the mind holding them. "Dependent on Ignorance are *sankhara*, dependent on *sankhara* is consciousness, dependent on consciousness is name and form." But ... "with the cessation of ignorance ... is the cessation of name and form." For this reason, to the Awakened, no phenomena fundamentally "exist." Buddhas only hold to conventional reality out of compassion for beings.

The deepening practice of insight penetrates the very way that the apparent subject sees things. Everything that arises—be it an attachment, an impulse, good or bad—has the nature to pass away. That doesn't mean that we disapprove of them or want to get rid of them, it's just the way it is. This shakes the basis for the *belief* in attachment. It's not that we have yet to find the right object, and that we should attach to Buddha or to meditation or to the desire to attain Nibbana rather than go to a football game. It's not about becoming a good Buddhist meditator so that you can become enlightened. It's just the realization in the moment that one never can really get hold of anything—it is all ephemeral. It is finally impossible to become *anything:* there is only true being with all its potential. The whole appearance of becoming something at all has been an illusion fostered by the sleight-of-hand of the whirling khandhas. We can't really be born into anything. Our true nature is Deathless.

The insight into Dhamma shakes the view of a self. It is from that view that one needs to be liberated. The progressive experience of insight is one in which one's world does get rattled—for the better. Ideas about the kind of person one is, what one should be, or the way the world is or should be are all seen as impermanent and ephemeral. However, when the normal outlets for attachment and becoming no longer provide valid possibilities, the mind will produce fantasies, memories, sometimes peculiar visions and voices—anything to arouse desire, fear, anxiety or interest, and anchor it

The whole appearance of becoming something at all has been an illusion fostered by the sleight-of-hand of the whirling khandhas. We can't really be born into anything. Our true nature is Deathless.

... there is only one real alternative to spinning on the Wheel of Becoming. And that's to get to the heart of all this movement, and to abide in that which can know it all.

to the realm of self. It doesn't matter what it is—you can think the most ridiculous thoughts, and have the most bizarre cravings for things that you would never have dreamed of before you began to practice Dhamma. The self-view in the mind will come up with anxiety: "Maybe I'm going crazy, maybe I'm a really brutal person underneath it all, maybe the kamma from a past life as a dope-peddler is catching up with me." Then there are also mystical perceptions: "Maybe I am destined to be the new world-teacher. The Masters on the seventh level are communicating through me." Anything will do, no matter how corny, to reinforce the mind's view of self. As we begin to see how ruthless and creative the force of attachment is, we can more readily accept that the whole of this show is just movement of the khandhas. As such, there is only one real alternative to spinning on the Wheel of Becoming. And that's to get to the heart of all this movement, and to abide in that which can know it all.

We do this not by taking issue with the creations of the mind, but by investigating what they are all based upon. What do conditions depend on? What is the root of these *sankhara?* The root of it all is always ignorance, unknowing. That unknowing of Truth stimulates the outflows that imprint personal projections and biases onto the world we experience. So rather than create desires, hopes, aversions, and probabilities, we activate the principle of knowing. In iconographic terms, this means putting the Buddha at the center of the world-system as he is in this painting, with his hands in the *mudra* that Buddhas use to signify Suchness, unbiased attention.

Through cultivating Suchness, we can purify *sañña* and *sankhara.* We're not trying to destroy the khandhas. The purification is that the perceptions are no longer accumulated to create a personal habitual world. Instead of perceptions, there is the moment-by-moment act of perceiving. Pure recognition has a delightful quality to it—a radiant quality where all the accumulated perceptions are purified, and one sees things with greater clarity. This purification is also in terms of intention and attention—the primary sources of *sankhara.* With intention towards Truth, towards dispassionate seeing and attending to things as they are (rather than how we want things to be), the tendency to build perceptions out of wrong (self)-view can cease. Then clearer perceptions and selfless motivation can give rise to what is lovely in the world in terms of attitude, speech and action. And that is the theme of the next painting.

appamāno ca
ulāro obhāso loke pāturahosi
atikkammeva
devānaṃ devānubhāvaṃ

24

LIGHT IN THE WORLD

Appamāṇo ca ulāro obhāso loke pāturahosi atikkammeva devānaṁ devānubhāvaṁ.
And a great measureless radiance,
surpassing the very nature of the devas,
was displayed in the world.

One can take this to mean that, at that time, the Buddha produced a great light. There are said to be four such occasions: when a Buddha-to-be begins his last birth; when that Bodhisatta realizes complete enlightenment; when the Buddha first transmits the Dhamma; and when the Buddha passes from the mortal form. Such a light is said to be visible throughout the world-system — from Avici Hell to the *brahmaloka*. Impressive though this may be, to me such a light is measurable, or at least more measurable than the light of the Buddha's wisdom which extends through time also. The light of Truth certainly surpasses the glory of the devas.

> *Bhikkhus, there are these four radiances … The radiance of the moon; the radiance of the sun; the radiance of fire; the radiance of wisdom … Bhikkhus, among these four, the radiance of wisdom is indeed the most excellent.* (Anguttara Nikaya: [II], Fours, 142)

That is what Buddhas bring into the world, and it is boundless in that it can encompass the ten-thousandfold world-system—the *devaloka*, the hell worlds, the animal worlds; in fact, all the Six Realms of Existence. And it is brought into this world as a teaching for human beings.

When human beings incline towards Truth, they bring forth qualities that are lovely. Kindness, gentleness, patience, generosity are natural aspects of the abandonment of self-view through insight. They manifest in ways that are tangible in planetary life. This painting brings us back to earth which can be a very beautiful place when the light of Truth shines in it.

The painting depicts one way in which what is beautiful appears. It is a tribute to a practice of Dhamma that I have been fortunate enough to be a part of—that of going on alms round in the morning. Dawn in tropical countries is an exquisite time of day; the rest of the day one feels very hot and sticky, but the dawn is always fresh and evanescent. The scene of the painting is rather as I have imagined the alms round (*pindapada*) in India at the time of the Buddha. In fact, the rural districts of Thailand looked like this when I lived there as a monk. Some of the simple houses with their grass roofs were perched on stilts to prevent flooding during the rains. The village in the painting is very simple. Behind it is the river while in the background is perhaps Varanasi itself, near where the Buddha was teaching. And during the time when the Buddha gave these teachings, some of the Group of Five would go out collecting alms-food which they all shared.

In living as alms-mendicants, Buddhist monks and nuns relax their hold on the most fundamental requisite for existence. This is a great renunciation. It's not the food itself that is renounced but the hold on it. Monks and nuns have to live on what people offer, when it is offered. They don't store food past noon nor can they follow any preferences about food. Bhikkhus who had been strict vegetarian brahmins would train themselves to accept meat given by people of the Untouchable caste. That cuts through a lot. Even today, people still have strong views around food—protein, unsaturated fats, meat, vitamins—but to train yourself to live on what is given means that you eat generosity.

These mendicants are not even allowed to ask for food, but only to be present for those who wish to make an offering. It may sound phoney to you, but in the practice of walking for alms, any thought of where and whether any food is going to be found just causes suffering. Naturally, one is not inclined to emotionally pressurize anyone to give food; that would be difficult to live with. The result is that the only way to go for alms mindfully and without suffering, is to go without seeking but with the attitude: "May those who would be made happy by giving, offer what they please." Monks and nuns don't promise people long life or spiritual rewards, but in receiving in silence and composure, try to generate the kind of attention that will allow the donor to focus on the purity and joy of their own goodness. The act of receiving alms-food sets up the reflection to make oneself worthy of the generosity of others, and to share what one has received with fellow monks and nuns. For the spiritual life, such themes are the most precious form of nourishment.

When human beings incline towards Truth, they bring forth qualities that are lovely. Kindness, gentleness, patience, generosity are natural aspects of the abandonment of self-view through insight.

For the householders, the alms round helps to give the day a structure that reflects on spiritual themes and keeps them in touch with the example of renunciation—which is not always apparent in the world. The generosity that it entails is a fundamental aspect of the enlightened mind. The whole practice is based on a bringing forth from oneself; and it is nourished by the joy that comes when such giving of oneself is done without demand or expectation. When it is performed in a way that transcends any personal connections, people find it easier to focus on the quality of their own mind, and connect with their selflessness. Generosity is one example of the many illuminating experiences of the Way.

It is possible to live spiritually in the world if you don't hold it. There is no need to get rid of the body or not have contact with other people; the light of the Dhamma allows us to see the value of living according to spiritual conventions, standards and reflections rather than material values, ego-needs and social pressures. The Eightfold Path is the basis of a spiritual society in which householders and monastics can live. To sustain that relationship of mutual participation in Dhamma without personal holding is a very fine practice. The training in this area is what the Buddha called "Vinaya"—meaning "that which dispels (or leads out of)" delusion.

Vinaya is generally considered to be a monastic code of discipline, which is true in a way; but, more accurately, it is a very comprehensive practical exposition on the moral and ethical application of the Eightfold Path. There are books of Vinaya which describe the practice for the lifestyle of the *samana* disciple while some of the suttas, notably Sigolavada Sutta (*Digha Nikaya*) and Mahamangala Sutta (*Sutta Nipata*) address people living the family life. Thus the Vinaya trains us to live in ways that will be conducive to higher understanding and liberation. The frugality of a *samana's* material belongings, the code of polite and kindly behavior between monks, nuns and lay people, are all supportive of more composed and gentle mind states. And it is all a voluntary training that one takes on as a personal responsibility and living example of one's aspiration towards Truth. Yet it is concerned with mundane details of life such as monks not hassling nuns to wash their robes for them, avoiding currying favor with influential people, how to deal with disputes, and how to offer correction to someone in a non-threatening and kindly way. There is a lot of skill and little idealism in Vinaya. By using it, the mind comes to reflect upon the nature of ethics, realistically appraise material needs and learn about love without sentiment or fantasy.

This training has great beauty in it. It has a beauty on the conventional plane in that it provides the practical guidelines for non-attachment within the world of relationships, duties and possessions. No wonder that the Vinaya is described as the life-blood of the Buddhist life. Of course, you have to use Vinaya with Right View—with a mind that inclines towards understanding and working with the actualities of human nature; otherwise it can become a meaningless code of "do's and don'ts," with all the moralising righteousness or blind adherence to the letter of the law that

It is possible to live spiritually in the world if you don't hold it. There is no need to get rid of the body or not have contact with other people …

169

permeates immature humanity. So the complete teachings of the Buddha are a complementary pair: Dhamma-Vinaya. Vinaya keeps the Dhamma from becoming abstract and idealistic; Dhamma instills a non-dogmatic flexibility to Vinaya. Together, they keep the light of the Buddha's dispensation going—as it has for thousands of years, through many different countries and civilizations.

atha kho
Bhagavā
udānaṁ udānesi

Aññāsi
vata bho Kondañño
aññāsi vata bho kondañño'ti

iti'daṁ āyasmato Koṇḍaññassa
aññākoṇḍaññotveva nāmaṁ ahosī'ti

25

THE ONE WHO KNOWS

Athakho bhagavā udānam ... aññā koṇḍaññotveva nāmaṁ ahosīti.
Then the Blessed One uttered the great exclamation: "Truly, it is the good Koṇḍañña
who has understood, it is the good Koṇḍañña who has understood."
Thus it was that the name of Venerable Koṇḍañña became: Aññā-Koṇḍañña—
"Koṇḍañña who understands."

These are the concluding words of the Sutta. They remind us once again, after this long account, of the response to the turning of the Dhamma Wheel—the central significance of the teaching. The Buddha himself makes no comment on the delight of the devas or the effect of the teaching. He simply relishes the significance of that insight, "whatever has the nature to arise, all that has the nature to cease." When one person attains Right View, it means more in terms of transmission of the Dhamma than any other response, regardless how jubilant, where insight is lacking. Jubilation, after all, arises and passes away and the world in general remains none the wiser for it—as anyone who has witnessed the finals of a sporting event can testify.

This great utterance of the Buddha about Koṇḍañña's understanding is not meant to celebrate his teaching of the abstract doctrinal aspects of Dhamma but that of the Dhamma becoming a living experience through Right Understanding. Koṇḍañña heard the Buddha's words and his insight was a realization of the causal nature of existence. This is a true

When one person attains Right View, it means more in terms of transmission of the Dhamma than any other response, regardless how jubilant, where insight is lacking.

transmission, a personal realization expressed in his own terms, rather than a mimicking of the Teacher. No wonder the Buddha expresses his approval! And he does so with that difficult-to-translate word "bho," a term of address implying both friendship and respect. The first disciple has arisen. A way to the Truth which the Buddha felt would be difficult for people to understand has been communicated. There is hope for this world.

In this painting, I use the word "Aññasi"—"he has understood"—as the central feature with the serene and all-embracing sky as the background. Understanding is the subject, rather than Kondañña. More central to the theme than Kondañña as an identity is the non-personal quality of awareness. This quality of knowing, of insightful awareness, does not arise and pass away even though the mind consciousness that connects or looks into that state of knowing can be very impermanent. For most people, such moments of profound insight are very brief and rare at first. But they are never really forgotten, and there is the possibility of remembering. It becomes possible to let go, own up to timeless Truth and allow the mind consciousness to relax and move towards a more serene, timeless reflection. That which knows causality and the limitation of all causal conditions is not itself caused. So sometimes it is called the Uncaused, or the Unconditioned, or the Unborn. Because it does not arise, it does not pass away, so we also call it the Deathless.

Some people like to personalize that which knows and call it "The One Who Knows" or "Buddha-nature" or they give it a function such as "the Knowing." Of course, these are all terms, ideas that act as pointers but they too just arise and pass away. The cultivator of Dhamma contemplates this "Knowing" and sees that it does not belong to anyone—it has no personal characteristics, it is not bound or located in time or space. Hence arises the insight known as *anatta*, not-self (or non-self)—the complete freedom of the mind from any need to hold, identify or attain. Truth is no one's servant or possession, nor is it limited. It is like the sky of this painting. The sky above India in 500 B.C. may have been bluer and cleaner than that above the twentieth-century industrialized world, but its all-embracing quality has not changed. So Truth is void of all characteristics apart from boundlessness and the ability to contain all manner of phenomena. Here, it is painted blue—the color of peace and infinity, the coolest receding color. The focus of the painting is that sky—that all-embracing peace and infinity. It is accessible to all; that is the real encouragement. From our own insight, perhaps expressed in different words, we can all recognize Truth.

Truth, however, requires expression in ways that are not ultimate because language is not an ultimate reality. Language deals with appearances. Even the language of our own thoughts is based upon perceptions which we have seen are not ultimate truths. They mirror conventional reality. So when it comes down to the teaching and encapsulation of the Dhamma, conventional expressions are necessary because the Dhamma has to be realized by people living in the conventional world. There are many different means of describing the Path and the goal, and encouraging

... Truth is void of all characteristics apart from boundlessness and the ability to contain all manner of phenomena. ... It is accessible to all; that is the real encouragement.

the interest and right attitudes that will be conducive to practice. These paintings are of those means.

I use the elaborate arch that frames the sky to depict the conventions of the world. Conventional teachings can be elaborate or simple, beautiful or functional—it's a matter of taste. But there are plenty of them. Each teacher may add one or two more to the general stockpile. Some conventions get outdated or lose their appeal but for the most part they all have a beauty and a value, and when used skillfully, they encourage the realization of Ultimate Truth. In fact, most people would never realize Ultimate Truth without them. The Buddha left the teachings of Dhamma (which include the Four Noble Truths) and the Vinaya. These form the arch that improves our view of the Unconditioned sky and helps us to see it clearly. But if we get fascinated by the conventions, we miss the point too!

Another feature at the bottom of the painting is the bhikkhu giving a Dhamma talk. This could be Kondañña, or some other monk, giving a sermon to a few fellow monks and some lay people. It's true, Kondañña had insight but he was not mentioned as a great teacher. It is said that he spent most of his time practicing on his own, returning after twelve years to pay his respects to the Buddha. He did not become a chief disciple like Sariputta and Moggallana, nor a great teacher like Kaccayana, nor a bastion of the Sangha like Maha Kassapa, Upali and Ananda. Yet he did realize the Deathless.

Teaching Dhamma is not easy for everyone—some enlightened beings have no gift for words while some great speakers are far from enlightenment. Here, the speaker is meeting a rather unreceptive audience. One of the monks seems to be following what is being said. The others appear bored or even displeased. Similarly with the families below, only one couple seem to be interested. As for the rest of them, they're thinking, "Everything that arises passes away? So what!" The floor tells us why this message isn't well-received. The place where we are, where we walk, sit, live and die, is a place of strong movement this way and that. It is impermanent, true, but the movement whirls us away from the quiet reflection of wisdom. How many of the people in the painting are really listening? Does anyone notice the sky that looms behind?

Other teachers fare better. Some have a tool kit filled with skillful means such as clever arguments, meditation techniques or personal charisma which capture people's attention. Some great teachers have everything going for them; so do some great frauds. When one uses skillful means, and they are successful, it does not really matter who the teacher is. For this reason, much of Buddhist practice is described and conveyed in terms of skillful means. Techniques, practices or conventions are used as access points to the Dhamma. Skillful means are established but not each one is suitable for every personal taste. In order to survive through time, abstract concepts are needed. Myth, symbols, archetypes and even temples and shrines or living beings are commonly used vehicles by which conceptual and abstract terms can be conveyed. Within Buddhism, there is a rich

storehouse of skillful means as well as abstract concepts. It is so rich and varied, people actually quarrel over which is the right one! This is why the presence of a living teacher is invaluable to help us assess the suitability of skillful means or to properly interpret the language of the teaching. Such a person should be one who is well-trusted and who has contemplated the teachings in the light of his or her own experience. If this teaching can be communicated so that it is understood by just one person, then it can survive. The living, breathing individual experience of the Dhamma is an indispensable aspect of the teaching. It brings the teaching to a life that goes beyond the end of the discourse. Hence, the Buddha rejoices.

26

THE END
AND THE BEGINNING

Dhammacakkappavattanasuttaṁ niṭṭhitaṁ.
This concludes the Discourse on the Setting in Motion of the Wheel of Truth.

As we reach the end of the Sutta, let's keep the main point in mind—that is, it is not how interesting an exposition this has been, how well it has been chanted or, as in this case, whether or not we enjoyed the pictures and appreciated the commentary. These things are behind us and we are left to examine and question: "What is the aim of life, or is there any? What can we *know* without recourse to belief?" We all seem to experience our life passing from birth and youth towards age and death; and we are searching for … happiness? knowledge? purpose? salvation? There is a search for something.

When the mind searches, it looks into this present moment. Instead of imagining that there is somewhere else to be reached or being influenced by belief, speculation or denial—allow the mind to reflect. This is the Way to non-attachment, non-holding, non-gaining, non-losing. It is the Way, then, to the Permanent, the Absolute, to Ultimate Peace and Truth. Independent of what we may experience in the form of thought or feeling, a mind that is fully aware of things as they are is at peace. And it is from that peaceful mind that the understanding of how to respond to daily life arises.

This Path of Awakening advocated by the Buddha involves an investigation into life while it is being lived with the guidance of the Four Noble Truths. If that search increases discontent or unhappiness, it is because we are looking in the wrong way or the wrong place. Suffering arises from a wrong view that imposes our personal biases onto the Way Things Are. So the way to peace is also the way towards knowing Truth. This interdependent relationship is best and most fully known within one's own life and experience. It is our responsibility to discover it.

Life moves towards the three characters in the top of the panel—old age, sickness and death. But behind it all, there is the Law of Dhamma—all that arises passes away—and the Dhamma which is the Unconditioned Truth of our being. We can live this life following the Buddha-Dhamma of the Eightfold Path. In so doing, we will move towards the brightness of awareness like the figure at the bottom of the panel.

Those enormous footprints are Buddha footprints, quite commonly rendered in stone at religious places in the East. All the marks and symbols on them are auspicious signs. The footprints themselves represent those of previous Buddhas who lived in times when people were physically much larger; in other words, they represent the continuum of the Awakened from an age lost in the mists of time. Their size reminds us that, at a time when things were very different from the way they are now, Buddhas existed. So we can feel that the 2,500 years from the time of Gotama Buddha is not so far away. People were much the same then as they are now. Old age, sickness and death felt the same, though, at times, they may have arisen from different causes. And the practice and the possibilities for enlightenment are very much the same.

I copied these particular footprints from a set carved by Mike Champion as a gift to the Sangha at Chithurst Monastery. They had been set in the lawn next to the ordination precinct (*sima*). I had remembered them because at the time, I was on the *sima* quite often practicing my part in a forthcoming ordination. After the ordination, I was due to leave Chithurst to help Ajahn Sumedho establish the Amaravati (Deathless Realm) Buddhist Monastery. So things at Chithurst were fastening in my mind. And I realized that at Amaravati I would have no spare moments for painting. Things came to this natural departure point—end of painting, end of Chithurst, and moving to the Deathless. Later, Mike told me that he'd copied the footprints from some originals taken from an old pilgrimage site in India. It was also called Amaravati. So that is what those footprints mean for me—the Path to the Deathless. Follow these tracks; it's a Path you can walk on and it's been cleared by the serene Buddha. Don't settle for less.

In this painting, I tied things together. *Sutta* means "a thread" as well as "a discourse." In the end, I tried to arrange this thread to enclose some of the patterns that are common in Thai art. Suttas are conventions and Thai monasticism is a convention for which I am very grateful. The monks in the painting are following a Thai custom. In Thailand, when bhikkhus chant a blessing, they frequently hold a thread which links them all together and which can be given as a token to those who receive the blessing. This thread, as well as this Sutta that the monks in the painting have just chanted, is given as a blessing to all human beings. Please take it and use it well.